Analysing Discourse

'This is an important text which highlights not only why discourse analysis should be a central method within social science but, unusually, provides the resources necessary for putting this into practice. The book will be an inspiration for social scientists wishing to explore, in a sophisticated way, the importance of language and meaning making in social life.'

Annette Hastings, Department of Urban Studies, University of Glasgow, UK

'Covers a wide range of important contemporary concepts in social and political theory taken from many different sources and disciplines. I would certainly recommend it to other researchers in the field as a thought-provoking contribution to critical discourse analysis.'

Ulrike Meinhof, School of Modern Languages, University of Southampton, UK

Analysing Discourse is an accessible introduction to text and discourse analysis for all students and researchers working with real language data.

Students across disciplines rely on texts, conversations or interviews in their research. Many discover that they cannot get as much from this data as they would like, because they are unsure about exactly how to analyse their material. This book provides a step-by-step guide to using and investigating real language data, helping students and researchers to get the most out of their resources.

Drawing on a range of social theorists from Bourdieu to Habermas, as well as his own research, Fairclough's book presents a form of language analysis with a consistently social perspective. His approach is illustrated by and investigated through a range of real texts, from political speeches to management consultancy and broadcast news reports.

Offering accessible summaries, an appendix of examples and a glossary of terms and key theorists, *Analysing Discourse* is an essential resource for anyone using and investigating real language data.

Norman Fairclough is Professor of Language in Social Life at Lancaster University, UK. He has published seven books in the area of critical discourse analysis, including *New Labour, New Language?* (Routledge, 2000), *Critical Discourse Analysis* (1995) and *Language and Power* (second edition, 2001).

Analysing Discourse

Textual analysis for social research

Norman Fairclough

 Routledge
Taylor & Francis Group

LONDON AND NEW YORK

First published 2003
by Routledge
2 Park Square, Milton Park, Abingdon, Oxon, OX14 4RN

Simultaneously published in the USA and Canada
by Routledge
270 Madison Avenue, New York, NY 10016

Routledge is an imprint of the Taylor & Francis Group

Reprinted in 2004, 2005

Typeset in Perpetua by
Keystroke, Jacaranda Lodge, Wolverhampton
Printed and bound in Great Britain by
MPG Books Ltd, Bodmin

British Library Cataloguing in Publication Data
A catalogue record for this book is available from the British Library

Library of Congress Cataloging in Publication Data
A catalog record for this book has been requested

ISBN 0–415–25892–8 (hbk)
ISBN 0–415–25893–6 (pbk)

Contents

PART IV
Styles and identities 157

Acknowledgements

The publishers and editors would like to thank the following people and organizations for permission to reproduce copyright material:

BBC Radio 4 news broadcast 'Extradition of Two Libyans', 30 September 1993, reprinted by permission of BBC Radio 4; M. Barratt Brown and K. Coates, *The Blair Revelation* (Spokesman Books, 1996); Department for Education and Employment, *The Learning Age* (HMSO, 1998), pages 9–10; R. Iedema, 'Formalizing organizational meaning' *Discourse and Society* **10**(1), reprinted by permission of Sage Publications Ltd. Copyright © Sage Publications Ltd, 1999; Independent Television, Channel 3, 'Debate on the Future of the Monarchy', January 1997, reprinted by permission of Independent Television; Rosabeth Moss Kanter, *Evolve!* (Harvard Business School Press, 2001, reprinted by permission of Harvard Business School); P. Muntigl, G. Weiss and R. Wodak, *European Union Discourses on Un/employment* (John Benjamins, 2000), page 101; R. Sennett, *The Corrosion of Character* (W.W. Norton Inc., 1998); T.J. Watson, *In Search of Management: Culture, Chaos and Control in Managerial Work* (Routledge, 1994); World Economic Forum Annual Meeting, 'Globalization', January 2002, Davos, Switzerland.

While every effort has been made to contact copyright holders of material used in this volume, the publishers would be happy to hear from any we have been unable to contact, and we will make the necessary amendment at the earliest opportunity.

I am grateful to MA and Research students at Lancaster University and to members of the Language, Ideology and Power Research Group for responses to and comments on early versions of parts of the book. I am also grateful to Jim Gee, Annette Hastings and Bob Jessop for valuable comments on a draft of the whole manuscript which have been helpful in making revisions.

I want to thank Matthew and Simon for their long-suffering fortitude in the face of another of Daddy's interminable books. And Isabela, for meaning.

1 Introduction

This book is written with two main types of reader in mind: students and researchers in social science and humanities who have little if any background in language analysis (e.g. in Sociology, Political Science, Education, Geography, History, Social Administration, Media Studies, Cultural Studies, Women's Studies); and students and researchers specializing in language.

People working in various areas of social science are often confronted with questions about language, and are often working with language materials – written texts, or conversation, or research interviews. However, my experience in teaching discourse analysis (for instance in the Faculty of Social Science research training programme at Lancaster University) indicates that there is widespread uncertainty about how to analyse such language material. I find that research students in Social Sciences often see the need to say more detailed things about their language data than they feel equipped to do. The prospect of following courses or reading books in Linguistics is generally daunting to them – not least because much of contemporary Linguistics is quite unsuitable for their purposes (especially the 'formal linguistics' which is concerned with abstract properties of human language, and has little to offer in the analysis of what people say or write). This book aims to provide a useable framework for analysing spoken or written language for people in social sciences and humanities with little or no background in language study, presented in a way which suggests how language analysis may enhance research into a number of issues which concern social scientists.

The book can also be seen as an introduction to *social* analysis of spoken and written language for people who already have some background in language analysis. There have been significant moves towards analysing language socially within Linguistics in recent decades – sociolinguistics and discourse analysis are now well-established parts of the field. But there are two limitations in most of this work which in this book I hope to begin to correct. The first is that themes and issues which interest social researchers have been taken up only to a rather limited extent. The second is that it is difficult to think of a relatively detailed presentation of a framework for linguistic analysis in the existing literature which indicates how that framework might fruitfully be used to address a range of issues in social research. That is my aim in this book.

I envisage the book being used in a variety of ways. It is suitable for use as a coursebook for second or third year undergraduates, MA students and research students both in courses in research methods in social science departments, and in courses in analysis of language use in language departments. But it could also be used outside the context of a course by research students and academics in social science and humanities who are looking for a socially-oriented introduction to analysis of spoken and written language.

Given that readers are likely to vary considerably in their familiarity with the concepts and categories I draw from social research and discourse and text analysis, I have included glossaries of key terms and key people (pages 212–228), and references for them which in some cases extend the sources I have referred to in the main text of the book. Terms included in the glossaries are printed in **bold** at the point where they are first used.

Social analysis, discourse analysis, text analysis

I see this book as extending the work I have previously published in the area of discourse analysis in the direction of more detailed linguistic analysis of texts (Chouliaraki and Fairclough 1999, Fairclough 2001b, 1992, 1995a, 2000a). My approach to discourse analysis (a version of 'critical discourse analysis') is based upon the assumption that language is an irreducible part of social life, dialectically interconnected with other elements of social life, so that social analysis and research always has to take account of language. ('Dialectical' relations will be explained in chapter 2.) This means that one productive way of doing social research is through a focus on language, using some form of discourse analysis. This is not a matter of reducing social life to language, saying that everything is discourse – it isn't. Rather, it's one analytical strategy amongst many, and it often makes sense to use discourse analysis in conjunction with other forms of analysis, for instance ethnography or forms of institutional analysis.

There are many versions of discourse analysis (Van Dijk 1997). One major division is between approaches which include detailed analysis of texts (see below for the sense in which I am using this term), and approaches which don't. I have used the term 'textually oriented discourse analysis' to distinguish the former from the latter (Fairclough 1992). Discourse analysis in social sciences is often strongly influenced by the work of Foucault (Foucault 1972, Fairclough 1992). Social scientists working in this tradition generally pay little close attention to the linguistic features of texts. My own approach to discourse analysis has been to try to transcend the division between work inspired by social theory which tends not to analyse texts, and work which focuses upon the language of texts but tends not to engage with social theoretical issues. This is not, or should not be, an 'either/or'. On the one hand, any analysis of texts which aims to be significant in social scientific terms has to connect with theoretical questions about discourse (e.g. the socially 'constructive' effects of discourse). On the other hand, no real understanding of the social effects of discourse is possible without looking closely at what happens when people talk or write.

So, text analysis is an essential part of discourse analysis, but discourse analysis is not merely the linguistic analysis of texts. I see discourse analysis as 'oscillating' between a focus on specific texts and a focus on what I call the 'order of discourse', the relatively durable social structuring of language which is itself one element of the relatively durable structuring and networking of social practices. Critical discourse analysis is concerned with continuity and change at this more abstract, more structural, level, as well as with what happens in particular texts. The link between these two concerns is made through the way in which texts are analysed in critical discourse analysis. Text analysis is seen as not only linguistic analysis; it also includes what I have called 'interdiscursive analysis', that is, seeing texts in terms of the different discourses, genres and styles they draw upon and articulate together. I shall explain this more fully in chapter 2 (see Fairclough 2000a).

My focus in this book, however, is on the linguistic analysis of texts. But what I want to make clear is that this is not just another book on linguistic analysis of texts, it is part of a broader project of developing critical discourse analysis as a resource for social analysis and research. The book can be used without reference to that broader project, but I would like readers to be aware of it even if they do not subscribe to it. I include a brief 'manifesto' for the broader project at the end of the Conclusion. Some readers may wish to read this broader framing of the book (pages 202–11) at this point.

Terminology: text, discourse, language

I shall use the term text in a very broad sense. Written and printed texts such as shopping lists and newspaper articles are 'texts', but so also are transcripts of (spoken) conversations and interviews, as well as television programmes and web-pages. We might say that any actual instance of language in use is a 'text' – though even that is too limited, because texts such as television programmes involve not only language but also visual images and sound effects. The term 'language' will be used in its most usual sense to mean verbal language – words, sentences, etc. We can talk of 'language' in a general way, or of particular languages such as English or Swahili. The term **discourse** (in what is widely called 'discourse analysis') signals the particular view of language in use I have referred to above – as an element of social life which is closely interconnected with other elements. But, again, the term can be used in a particular as well as a general, abstract way – so I shall refer to particular 'discourses' such as the 'Third Way' political discourse of New Labour (Fairclough 2000b).

Language in new capitalism

The examples I use throughout the book to illustrate the approach will be particularly focused upon contemporary social change, and especially changes in contemporary capitalism and their impact on many areas of social life. The set of changes I am referring to are variously identified as 'globalization', post- or late-'modernity', 'information society', 'knowledge economy', 'new capitalism', 'consumer culture', and so forth (Held *et al.* 1999). I shall use the term **new capitalism**, meaning the most recent of a historical series of radical re-structurings through which capitalism has maintained its fundamental continuity (Jessop 2000). My reason for focusing on it is that a great deal of contemporary social research is concerned with the nature and consequences of these changes. And, quite simply, because no contemporary social research can ignore these changes, they are having a pervasive effect on our lives. A more specific reason for focusing on new capitalism is that this is now developing into a significant area of research for critical discourse analysts. There is a web-site devoted to it (http://www.cddc.vt.edu/host/lnc/) and the journal *Discourse and Society* has recently devoted a special issue to the theme (13 (2), 2002). I should add, however, that using the term 'new capitalism' does not imply an exclusive focus on economic issues: transformations in capitalism have ramifications throughout social life, and 'new capitalism' as a research theme should be inter-preted broadly as a concern with how these transformations impact on politics, education, artistic production, and many other areas of social life.

Capitalism has the capacity to overcome crises by radically transforming itself periodically, so that economic expansion can continue. Such a transformation towards new capitalism is taking place now in response to a crisis in the post-Second World War model (generally known as 'Fordism'). This transformation involves both 're-structuring' of relations between the economic, political and social domains (including the commodification and marketization of fields like education – it becomes subject to the economic logic of the market), and the 're-scaling' of relations between the different levels of social life – the global, the regional (e.g. the European Union), the national, and the local. Governments on different scales, social democratic as well as conservative, now take it as a mere fact of life (though a 'fact' produced in part by inter-governmental agreements) that all must bow to the emerging logic of a globalizing knowledge-driven economy, and have embraced or at least made adjustments to 'neo-liberalism'. Neo-liberalism is a political project for facilitating the re-structuring and re-scaling of social relations in accordance with the demands of an unrestrained global capitalism (Bourdieu 1998). It has been imposed on the post-socialist economies as the (allegedly) best means of rapid system transformation, economic renewal, and re-integration into the global economy. It has led to radical attacks on universal social welfare and the reduction of the protections against the effects of markets that welfare states provided for people. It has also led to an increasing division between rich and poor, increasing economic insecurity and stress even for the 'new middle' classes, and an intensification of the exploitation of labour. The unrestrained emphasis on growth also poses major threats to the environment. It has also produced a new imperialism, where international financial agencies under the tutelage of the USA and its rich allies indiscriminately impose restructuring on less fortunate countries, sometimes with disastrous consequences (e.g. Russia). It is not the impetus to increasing international economic integration that is the problem, but the particular form in which this is being imposed, and the particular consequences (e.g. in terms of unequal distribution of wealth) which inevitably follow. All this has resulted in the disorientation and disarming of economic, political and social forces committed to radical alternatives, and has contributed to a closure of public debate and a weakening of democracy (Boyer and Hollingsworth 1997, Brenner 1998, Crouch and Streek 1997, Jessop 2000).

Readers will find in the Appendix a set of texts which I have used for illustrative purposes throughout the book. In the main, I have selected these texts on the basis of their relevance to a number of research issues arising in a range of disciplines from the transformations of new capitalism. In some cases, I have taken examples from previous research to try to show how the approach adopted in this book might enhance existing methods of analysis.

The approach to text analysis

My main point of reference within existing literature on text analysis is Systemic Functional Linguistics (SFL), a linguistic theory and associated analytical methods particularly associated with Michael **Halliday** (Halliday 1978, 1994). In contrast with the more influential Chomskyan tradition within Linguistics, SFL is profoundly concerned with the relationship between language and other elements and aspects of social life, and its approach to the linguistic analysis of texts is always oriented to the social character of texts (particularly valuable sources include Halliday 1994, Halliday and Hasan 1976, 1989, Hasan 1996, Martin 1992, Van Leeuwen 1993, 1995, 1996). This makes it a valuable resource for critical discourse analysis, and indeed major contributions to critical discourse analysis have developed out of SFL (Fowler *et al.* 1979, Hodge and Kress 1988, 1993, Kress 1985, Kress and Van Leeuwen 2001, Lemke 1995, Thibault 1991).[1]

But the perspectives of critical discourse analysis and SFL do not precisely coincide, because of their different aims (for a critical dialogue between the two, see Chouliaraki and Fairclough 1999). There is a need to develop approaches to text analysis through a **transdisciplinary** dialogue with perspectives on language and discourse within social theory and research in order to develop our capacity to analyse texts as elements in social processes. A 'transdisciplinary' approach to theory or analytical method is a matter of working with the categories and 'logic' of for instance sociological theories in developing a theory of discourse and methods of analysing texts. This is inevitably a long-term project which is only begun in a modest way in this book, for instance in the discussion of 'genre chains' (chapter 2), 'dialogicality' (chapter 3), 'equivalence and difference' (chapter 5), and the representation of time and space (chapter 8). Van Leeuwen's work on representation (referred to above) can also be seen as developing text analysis in this transdisciplinary way. Another concern I have had is to try to make the analytical categories as transparent as possible for social analysis of discourse, moving away to an extent from the often forbidding technical terminology of Linguistics.

I should also briefly mention corpus analysis, though I shall not be dealing with it at all in this book (De Beaugrande 1997, McEnery and Wilson 2001, Stubbs 1996). The sort of detailed text analysis I introduce is a form of 'qualitative' social analysis. It is rather 'labour-intensive' and can be productively applied to samples of research material rather than large bodies of text. Though the amount of material that can be analysed depends on the level of detail: textual analysis can focus on just a selected few features of texts, or many features simultaneously. But this form of qualitative analysis can usefully be supplemented by the 'quantitative analysis' offered by corpus linguistics, as De Beaugrande (1997) and Stubbs (1996) argue. The packages available (such as Wordsmith, which I make some use of in Fairclough 2000b) allow one, for instance, to identify the 'keywords' in a corpus of texts, and to investigate distinctive patterns of co-occurrence or **collocation** between keywords and other words. Such findings are of value, though their value is limited, and they need to be complemented by more intensive and detailed qualitative textual analysis.

Critical discourse analysis can in fact draw upon a wide range of approaches to analysing text. I have chosen in this book to place the main emphasis on grammatical and semantic analysis because while this form of analysis can, I believe, be very productive in social research, it is often difficult for researchers without a background in Linguistics to access it. There are other approaches to analysis which are more familiar and more accessible (conversation analysis is a good example) which I have not dealt with in this book (for an overview, see Titscher *et al.* 2000). That does not mean that they cannot be drawn upon in critical discourse analysis – indeed I have made some use of them in earlier publications (Fairclough 1992, for example).

Social research themes

Each chapter of the book will address one or more social research themes, and I shall signal these at the beginning of the chapter. The aim will be to show how the particular aspects of text analysis dealt with in the chapter might productively be drawn upon in researching these themes. The themes include: the government or **governance** of new capitalist societies, **hybridity** or the blurring of social boundaries as a feature of what some social theorists call 'postmodernity', shifts in '**space–time**' (time and space) associated with '**globalization**', **hegemonic** struggles to give a '**universal**' status to particular discourses and representations, **ideologies**, citizenship and 'public space', social change and change in communication technologies, the **legitimation** of social action and social orders, the dominant **character** types of contemporary socities (including the manager and the therapist), **societal 'informalization'** and the shift away from overt hierarchies. (All the terms in bold are included in the glossary.)

From the perspective of a social scientist, the set of themes addressed and the social theorists and researchers I have drawn upon will no doubt seem rather disparate. Although I have selected themes and sources which I find generally helpful in addressing the theme of Language in New Capitalism, these should be seen as no more than illustrative with respect to my general aim: on the one hand, to consider how social research and theory might inform the approach to text analysis, and on the other hand, how text analysis might enhance social research. In a sense, the diversity of sources and themes is advantageous, because it may help to make the point that the relationship I am advocating between text analysis and social research is a general one which is not limited to particular theories, disciplines or research traditions in social science. Although I have chosen to focus on the research theme of Language in New Capitalism, this should not be taken to imply that textual analysis is *only* relevant to social research oriented to this theme. And of course a single book cannot possibly begin to show all the areas of social research which might be enhanced by text analysis.

I have drawn on the work of a number of social theorists. Again, this selection of sources should not be regarded as in any way exhaustive or exclusive – they are theorists with whom I have found it fruitful to conduct a dialogue when working within critical discourse analysis. They all, in one way or another, raise questions about language and discourse, though none of them use the resources for detailed analysis which, I am suggesting, can enhance such theoretical projects and associated research. See the glossary of the main social theorists to whom I refer.

A systematic discussion of the relationship between critical discourse analysis and social theory can be found in Chouliaraki and Fairclough (1999), which can be seen as complementary to this book. It includes extended discussion of the relationship of critical discourse analysis to the main social theories I refer to here, as well a detailed account of critical discourse analysis. Readers will find in Fairclough 2000b an extended application of critical discourse analysis to a particular case, the language of the 'New Labour' government in the UK.

Social effects of texts

Texts as elements of social events (see chapter 2) have causal effects – i.e. they bring about changes. Most immediately, texts can bring about changes in our knowledge (we can learn things from them), our beliefs, our attitudes, values and so forth. They also have longer-term causal effects – one might for instance argue that prolonged experience of advertising and other commercial texts contributes to shaping people's identities as 'consumers', or their gender identities. Texts can also start wars, or contribute to changes in education, or to changes in industrial relations, and so forth. Their effects can include changes in the material world, such as changes in urban design, or the architecture and design of particular types of building. In sum, texts have causal effects upon, and contribute to changes in, people (beliefs, attitudes, etc.), actions, social relations, and the material world. It would make little sense to focus on language in new capitalism if we didn't think that texts have causal effects of this sort, and effects on social change. Though as I shall argue below, these effects are mediated by meaning-making.

We need, however, to be clear what sort of causality this is. It is not a simple mechanical causality – we cannot for instance claim that particular features of texts automatically bring about particular changes in people's knowledge or behaviour or particular social or political effects. Nor is causality the same as regularity: there may be no regular cause–effect pattern associated with a particular type of text or particular features of texts, but that does not mean that there are no causal effects.[2] Texts can have causal effects without them necessarily being regular effects, because many other factors in the context determine whether particular texts actually have such effects, and can lead to a particular text having a variety of effects, for instance on different interpreters (Fairclough *et al.* 2002).

Contemporary social science has been widely influenced by 'social constructivism' – the claim that the (social) world is socially constructed. Many theories of social constructivism emphasize the role of texts (language, discourse) in the construction of the social world. These theories tend to be idealist rather than realist. A realist would argue that although aspects of the social world such as social institutions are ultimately socially constructed, once constructed they are realities which affect and limit the textual (or 'discursive') construction of the social. We need to distinguish 'construction' from 'construal', which social constructivists do not: we may textually construe (represent, imagine, etc.) the social world in particular ways, but whether our representations or construals have the effect of changing its construction depends upon various contextual factors – including the way social reality already is, who is construing it, and so forth. So we can accept a moderate version of the claim that the social world is textually constructed, but not an extreme version (Sayer 2000).

Ideologies

One of the causal effects of texts which has been of major concern for critical discourse analysis is ideological effects – the effects of texts in inculcating and sustaining or changing ideologies (Eagleton 1991, Larrain 1979, Thompson 1984, Van Dijk 1998). Ideologies are representations of aspects of the world which can be shown to contribute to establishing, maintaining and changing social relations of power, domination and exploitation. This 'critical' view of ideology, seeing it as a modality of power, contrasts with various 'descriptive' views of ideology as positions, attitudes, beliefs, perspectives, etc. of social groups without reference to relations of power and domination between such groups. Ideological representations can be identified in texts (Thompson 1984 glosses ideology as 'meaning in the service of power'), but in saying that ideologies are representations which can be shown to contribute to social relations of power and domination, I am suggesting that textual analysis needs to be framed in this respect in social analysis which can consider bodies of texts in terms of their effects on power relations. Moreover, if ideologies are primarily representations, they can nevertheless also be 'enacted' in ways of acting socially, and 'inculcated' in the identities of social agents. Ideologies can also have a durability and stability which transcends individual texts or bodies of texts – in terms of the distinctions I explain in chapter 2, they can be associated with discourses (as representations), with genres (as enactments), and with **styles** (as inculcations).

Let us take an example: the pervasive claim that in the new 'global' economy, countries must be highly competitive to survive. One can find this claim asserted or assumed in many contemporary texts. And one can see it (and the neo-liberal discourse with which it is associated) enacted in, for example, new, more 'business-like' ways of administering organizations like universities, and inculcated in new managerial styles which are also evident in many texts. We can only arrive at a judgement about whether this claim is ideological by looking at the causal effects it and related claims have in particular areas of social life (e.g. whether people come to believe that countries must be highly competitive to survive), and asking whether they and their enactments and inculcations contribute to sustaining or changing power relations (e.g. by making employees more amenable to the demands of managers). Notice that even if we did conclude that such a claim is ideological, that would not make it necessarily or simply untrue: we might for instance argue that contemporary economic relations do indeed impose greater competitiveness, though point out that this is not the inevitable 'law of nature' it is often represented as being, but the product of a particular economic order which could be changed. I return to the discussion of ideologies in chapter 3, with respect to ideological assumptions in particular, and in chapter 4, with respect to argumentation.

Text, meanings and interpretations

Part of what is implied in approaching texts as elements of social events is that we are not only concerned with texts as such, but also with interactive processes of meaning-making. In the case of a face-to-face conversation, the text is a transcript of what is said, and to a degree one can see meaning-making going on by looking at how participants respond to each other's conversational turns. Let us take a very simple example (from Cameron 2001):

1 *Customer*: Pint of Guiness, please.
2 *Bartender*: How old are you?
3 *Customer*: Twenty-two.
4 *Bartender*: OK, coming up.

In turns 2 and 3, the Bartender and the Customer are interactively establishing that the preconditions for ordering an alcoholic drink in a bar are met, i.e. that the Customer is (in the case of Britain) over the age of 18. The Customer in turn 3 shows his or her understanding that this legal constraint is at issue, and the Bartender's purpose of resolving the legal issue in asking the question, by collaboratively providing what may on the face of it seem irrelevant information in the context of ordering a drink. The Customer is able to recognize that the Bartender's question in 2 is relevant not only on the basis of his or her knowledge of the licensing laws, but also because of the position of the question – if a request (turn 1 in this case) is answered with a question, that tends to mean responding to the request is conditional upon the answer to the question.

This example suggests that there are three analytically separable elements in processes of meaning-making: the production of the text, the text itself, and the reception of the text. The production of the text puts the focus on producers, authors, speakers, writers; the reception of the text puts the focus on interpretation, interpreters, readers, listeners.[3] Each of these three elements has been given primacy at different points in the recent history of theories of meaning: first the intentions, identity etc. of the author, then the text itself, then more recently the interpretative work of the reader or listener. But it seems clear that meanings are made through the interplay between them: we must take account of the institutional position, interests, values, intentions, desires etc. of producers; the relations between elements at different levels in texts; and the institutional positions, knowledge, purposes, values etc. of receivers. It is very difficult to be precise about the processes involved in meaning-making for the obvious reason that they are mainly going on in people's heads, and there are no direct ways of accessing them. When we move from spoken dialogue to, for instance, published texts, the problems are compounded because we no longer have the ongoing negotiation of meaning within dialogue, which at least gives us some evidence of how things are being intended and interpreted. And a published text can figure in many different processes of meaning-making and contribute to diverse meanings, because it is open to diverse interpretations.

It is clear from the example above that meaning-making depends upon not only what is explicit in a text but also what is implicit – what is assumed. So we might say that the Bartender's question in turn 2 makes the assumption that alcoholic drinks can only be served if customers are over a certain age. What is 'said' in a text always rests upon 'unsaid' assumptions, so part of the analysis of texts is trying to identify what is assumed (see chapter 3).

Interpretation can be seen as a complex process with various different aspects. Partly it is a matter of understanding – understanding what words or sentences or longer stretches of text mean, understanding what speakers or writers mean (the latter involving problematic attributions of intentions). But it is also partly a matter of judgement and evaluation: for instance, judging whether someone is saying something sincerely or not, or seriously or not; judging whether the claims that are explicitly or implicitly made are true; judging whether people are speaking or writing in ways which accord with the social, institutional etc. relations within which the event takes place, or perhaps in ways which mystify those relations. Furthermore, there is an explanatory element to interpretation – we often try to understand why people are speaking or writing as they do, and even identify less immediate social causes. Having said this, it is clear that some texts receive a great deal more interpretative work than others: some texts are very transparent, others more or less opaque to particular interpreters; interpretation is sometimes unproblematic and effectively automatic, but sometimes highly reflexive, involving a great deal of conscious thought about what is meant, or why something has been said or written as it has.

The focus in this book is quite particular: it is on analysing texts, with a view to their social effects (discussed below). The social effects of texts depend upon processes of meaning-making – we might want to say that the social effects of texts are mediated by meaning-making, or indeed that it is meanings that have social effects rather than texts as such. But one resource that is necessary for any account of meaning-making is the capacity to analyse texts in order to clarify their contribution to processes of meaning-making, and my primary concern in this book is with providing that resource. So I shall not give a developed overall account of the process of meaning-making, though my approach does assume the need for such an account. However, I shall be looking at texts dynamically, in terms of how social agents make or 'texture' texts by setting up relations between their elements. This means that my approach to text-analysis will move further towards the production of texts than towards the reception and interpretation of texts. But what I have said above should hopefully make it clear that this does not imply any minimization of reception and interpretation.

Texts and authors

I shall refer to the 'author' of a text. Goffman (1981) differentiates the 'principal', the one whose position is put in the text, the 'author', the one who puts the words together and is responsible for the wording, and the 'animator', the person who makes the sounds or the marks on paper. In the simplest case, a single person simultaneously occupies all these positions, but in principle this may not be so – for instance, a spokesman may be simply the 'mouthpiece' for others in an organization (i.e. just the 'animator'), or a news report may be authored by a journalist while the principal may be some politician, for instance, whose position is being implicitly supported. There are various further possible complications: authorship can be collective without that necessarily being clear from a text (various hands for example may contribute to a news report). There are also objections to placing too much weight on authorship from a structuralist and post-structuralist point of view, but these are often linked to an excessive playing down of agency (see chapter 2 for my position on this question). When I refer to 'authors', I shall do so without getting too much into these complications, and I shall be primarily referring to whoever can be seen as having put the words together, and as taking on commitments to truth, obligations, necessity and values by virtue of choices in wording (see chapter 10).

Forms, meanings and effects

The analysis of texts is concerned with the linguistic forms of texts, and the distribution of different linguistic forms across different types of texts. One might attribute causal effects to particular linguistic forms (or more plausibly to a strong tendency to select one form in preference to other alternative forms in a significant body of texts), but again one has to be cautious and avoid any suggestion that such effects work mechanically or in a simple, regular way. They depend upon meaning and context. For example, a linguistic form which is heavily used in accounts or narratives about the 'global economy' is **nominalization** (which is discussed in chapter 8): instead of representing processes which are taking place in the world as processes (grammatically, in clauses or sentences with verbs), they are represented as entities (grammatically, through nominalization, i.e. transforming a clause into a nominal or noun-like entity). A simple example from a text of Tony Blair's: 'change' is a nominalization in 'The modern world is swept by change'. One common consequence of nominalization is that the agents of processes, people who initiate processes or act upon other people or objects, are absent from texts. For instance, a different way in which others might formulate the process Blair is referring to is: 'Multinational corporations in collaboration with governments are changing the world in a variety of ways'. In this case, agents ('multinational corporations', 'governments') are textualized.

However, it is not only nominalizations that elide agents, so too, for example, do passive verbs (e.g. 'can be made . . . and shipped') and what we might call passive adjectives ('mobile') as in this other sentence of Blair's: 'Capital is mobile, technology can migrate quickly, and goods can be made in low cost countries and shipped to developed markets'. Another relevant linguistic feature here is the intransitive verb 'migrate' where a transitive verb might have been used (e.g. 'corporations can move technology around quickly'), and the metaphor of 'migration'. It is also significant that one finds nominalizations like 'change' and inanimate nouns like 'capital' and 'technology' as the agents of verbs, rather than human agents. In thinking about the social effects of texts here, one might say that nominalization contributes to what is, I think, a widespread elision of human agency in and responsibility for processes in accounts of the 'new global economy', but it is clear that it is not nominalization alone that contributes to this effect but a configuration of different linguistic forms (Fowler *et al.* 1979).

Moreover, whether nominalization contributes to such effects depends upon meaning and context. One would not I think attribute such effects to the nominalizations 'house-cleaning' and 're-organization' in this sentence from a horoscope: 'It could even be a good time for house-cleaning and domestic re-organization'. As to context, it is only because this sort of account of the 'new global economy' is widespread in a particular type of text that we might ask whether nominalization contributes to the elision – and, to take it further, we might say thereby to the mystification and obfuscation – of agency and responsibility. These include very influential texts produced by international agencies such as the World Trade Organization and the World Bank, national governments, and so forth. We can measure the influence of such texts by looking at their wide international and national distribution, their extensive and diverse readership, and the extent to which they are 'intertextually' incorporated in other texts (e.g. in the media). We would also need to take account of how such texts are interpreted by people who read them and how they enter processes of meaning-making.

Summing up, we can attribute causal effects to linguistic forms, but only through a careful account of meaning and context.

Critical analysis and 'objectivity'

I see analysis of texts as part of social science, and I should say something about the view of social science which informs this book – the philosophy of social science. The position I take is a realist one, based on a realist ontology: both concrete social events and abstract social structures, as well as the rather less abstract 'social practices' which I discuss in chapter 2, are part of reality. We can make a distinction between the 'potential' and the 'actual' – what is possible because of the nature (constraints and allowances) of social structures and practices, as opposed to what actually happens. Both need to be distinguished from the 'empirical', what we know about reality. (These distinctions are a reformulation of those in **Bhaskar** 1979, see also Sayer 2000.) Reality (the potential, the actual) cannot be reduced to our knowledge of reality, which is contingent, shifting, and partial. This applies also to texts: we should not assume that the reality of texts is exhausted by our knowledge about texts. One consequence is that we should assume that no analysis of a text can tell us all there is to be said about it – there is no such thing as a complete and definitive analysis of a text. That does not mean they are unknowable – social scientific knowledge of them is possible and real enough, and hopefully increasing, but still inevitably partial. And it is extendable: the 'transdisciplinary' approach I argued for earlier aims to enhance our capacity to 'see' things in texts through 'operationalizing' (putting to work) social theoretical perspectives and insights in textual analysis.

Textual analysis is also inevitably selective: in any analysis, we choose to ask certain questions about social events and texts, and not other possible questions. For example, I might have focused in this book on a number of quantitative features of texts, comparing different types of text in terms of the average number of words per text, the average number of words per sentence, the relative frequencies of different parts of speech such as nouns, verbs, prepositions, etc. I might have perfectly good reasons for such a focus – perhaps because I am interested in texts from a pedagogical point of view, in the relative difficulty of texts for young children or people learning a foreign language. The general point is that there are always particular motivations for choosing to ask certain questions about texts and not others. My actual motivation for asking the sorts of questions I shall ask in this book is the belief that texts have social, political, cognitive, moral and material consequences and effects, and that it is vital to understand these consequences and effects if we are to raise moral and political questions about contemporary societies, and about the transformations of 'new capitalism' in particular.

Some readers may be concerned about the 'objectivity' of an approach to text analysis based upon these motivations. I don't see this as a problem. There is no such thing as an 'objective' analysis of a text, if by that we mean an analysis which simply describes what is 'there' in the text without being 'biased' by the 'subjectivity' of the analyst. As I have already indicated, our ability to know what is 'there' is inevitability limited and partial. And the questions we ask necessarily arise from particular motivations which go beyond what is 'there'. My approach belongs broadly within the tradition of 'critical social science' – social science which is motivated by the aim of providing a scientific basis for a critical questioning of social life in moral and political terms, e.g. in terms of social justice and power (Chouliaraki and Fairclough 1999, Morrow 1994). Conversely, much social research can be seen as motivated by aims of making existing forms of social life work more efficiently and effectively, without considering moral or political questions at all. Neither approach is 'objective' in a simple sense, both approaches are based in particular interests and perspectives, but that does not prevent either of them being perfectly good social science. Nor does it mean that the social import and effects of particular research are transparent: social research may have outcomes which are far from what was intended or expected.

Doing social scientific analysis of social events and texts entails shifting away from our ordinary experience of them. Human beings are reflexive about what they do in their practical social life – they have ways of talking about it, describing it, evaluating it, theorizing it. For example, we might describe what someone says as 'long-winded', or 'wordy', or say that someone is 'too fond of his (or her) own voice'. These are some of the categories we have for talking about texts. We also have categories when we do social scientific analysis of texts ('noun', 'sentence', 'genre', and so forth), but they are specialist categories which are different from the ones we use in our ordinary social interaction. These social scientific categories, unlike practical categories, allow particular texts to be seen in relation to elaborated general theories. But if we assume that our knowledge of texts is necessarily partial and incomplete as I have suggested, and if we assume that we are constantly seeking to extend and improve it, then we have to accept that our categories are always provisional and open to change.

The limits of textual analysis

Textual analysis is a resource for social research which can enhance it provided that it is used in conjunction with other methods of analysis. By itself, textual analysis is limited. I discussed above the involvement of texts in meaning-making, the causal effects of texts, and the specifically ideological effects of texts. None of these can be got at through textual analysis alone. To research meaning-making, one needs to look at interpretations of texts as well as texts themselves, and more generally at how texts practically figure in particular areas of social life, which suggests that textual analysis is best framed within ethnography. To assess the causal and ideological effects of texts, one would need to frame textual analysis within, for example, organizational analysis, and link the 'micro' analysis of texts to the 'macro' analysis of how power relations work across networks of practices and structures. Textual analysis is a valuable supplement to social research, not a replacement for other forms of social research and analysis.

There is a superficially plausible argument that we should produce descriptions of texts first, and only then social analysis and critique. For a version of this argument from the perspective of conversational analysis, see Schegloff (1997), and the replies in Wetherell (1998) and Chouliaraki and Fairclough (1999). This presupposes analytical categories and frameworks which are adequate for text description (and analysis of conversation) independently of particular research projects and problems. The objection to this position is that it precludes what I have referred to as a transdisciplinary process in which perspectives and categories from outside textual analysis or discourse analysis can be operationalized as ways of analysing texts which enhance insight into the textual aspect of the social practices, processes and relations which are the focus of the particular research project. An example is the discussion in chapter 8 of Example 1, Appendix (pages 229–30) in terms of the social research question of how people simultaneously inhabit different 'space–times' (e.g. 'global' and 'local' space–times) and routinely move between them. The description of how time and space are represented is an attempt to work textually with the social research question in a way which one would not arrive at by simply describing the text in terms of what grammars of English say about the representation of time and space.

Texual description and analysis should not be seen as prior to and independent of social analysis and critique – it should be seen as an open process which can be enhanced through dialogue across disciplines and theories, rather than a coding in the terms of an autonomous analytical framework or grammar. We can relate this to the distinction between 'actual' and 'empirical' which I drew above. We cannot assume that a text in its full actuality can be made transparent through applying the categories of a pre-existing analytical framework. What we are able to see of the actuality of a text depends upon the perspective from which we approach it, including the particular social issues in focus, and the social theory and discourse theory we draw upon.

The organization of the book

The book is organized into four Parts and an Introduction and a Conclusion, eleven chapters in all. Part 1 (chapters 2–3) provides a framing for the strictly 'internal' analysis of texts, locating text analysis in its relationship to discourse analysis and social analysis. This has partly been done in this introductory chapter, and will be developed in chapter 2, where I shall look at texts as elements of concrete **social events**, which are both shaped by and shape more abstract and durable **social structures** and **social practices**. Chapter 3 moves closer towards the text itself, but focuses on how the 'outside' of a text is brought into the text, as we might put it. This is partly a matter of **intertextuality** – how texts draw upon, incorporate, **recontextualize** and dialogue with other texts. It is also partly a matter of the **assumptions** and presuppositions people make when they speak or write. What is 'said' in a text is always said against the background of what is 'unsaid' – what is made explicit is always grounded in what is left implicit. In a sense, making assumptions is one way of being intertextual – linking this text to an ill-defined penumbra of other texts, what has been said or written or at least thought elsewhere.

The next three Parts are centred respectively on genres, discourses, and styles. Part II is concerned with **genres**, and with text as action. A genre is a way of acting and interacting linguistically – for example, interview, lecture and news report are all genres. Genres structure texts in specific ways – for instance, news reports have a characteristic generic structure of: headline + lead paragraph (summarizing the story) + 'satellite' paragraphs (adding detail). These are the concerns of chapter 4. The nature of the **semantic** and grammatical relations between sentences and **clauses** depends on genre (chapter 5), as do the type of '**exchange**' (e.g. giving information, eliciting action), **speech function** (e.g. statements, offers, demands) and the **grammatical mood** (declarative, interrogative, imperative), which are dealt with in chapter 6.

Part III's in concerned with **discourses**, and with text as representation. A discourse is a particular way of representing some part of the (physical, social, psychological) world – there are alternative and often competing discourses, associated with different groups of people in different social positions (chapter 7). Discourses differ in how social events are represented, what is excluded or included, how abstractly or concretely events are represented, and how more specifically the processes and relations, social actors, time and place of events are represented (chapter 8).

Part IV is concerned with styles, and with text as identification, i.e. texts in the process of constituting the social identities of the participants in the events of which they are a part (chapter 9). One aspect of identification is what people commit themselves to in what they say or write with respect to truth and with respect to obligation – matters of '**modality**'. Another is **evaluation** and the values to which people commit themselves. These are the focuses of chapter 10.

The aim in the Conclusion is twofold. First, synthesis – to pull together the various analytical concerns which have been discussed through the book and apply them to a single example, Example 7 (Appendix, pages 239–41). Second, to frame the focus on textual analysis in this book within the wider perspective of critical discourse analysis by offering a brief 'manifesto' for the latter as a resource which can contribute to social research and to social change in the direction of greater social justice.

Notes

1   Other work which I have found useful includes: Cameron (2001), De Beaugrande (1997), De Beaugrande and Dressler (1981), Gee (1999), Hoey (1983), (2001), Hunston and Thompson (2000), Lehtonen (2000), Stillar (1998), Stubbs (1996), Swales (1990), Titscher, Meyer, Wodak and Vetter (2000), Toolan (1998), Verschueren (1999).

2   The reduction of causality to regularity is only one view of causality – what is often referred to as Humean causality, the view of causality associated with the philosopher David Hume (Sayer 2000, Fairclough, Jessop and Sayer 2002).

3   Goffman (1981) has suggested that producer and receiver are both complex roles. In the case of producer, for instance, the person who actually puts the words together (author) may or may not be the same as the person whose words they are (principal).

Part I

Social analysis, discourse analysis, text analysis

2 Texts, social events and social practices

Text analysis issues

Main types of meaning: action, representation, identification
Genres, discourses, and styles
Genre chains and chains of texts
Genre mixing
Interdiscursive analysis

Social research issues

Structure and agency
Social structures, social practices, social events
Dialectics of discourse
Globalization and new capitalism
Mediation
Recontextualization
Governance
Hybridity and 'postmodernity'

Texts are seen in this book as parts of social events. One way in which people can act and interact in the course of social events is to speak or to write. It is not the only way. Some social events have a highly textual character, others don't. For example, while talk certainly has a part in a football match (e.g. a player calling for the ball), it is a relatively marginal element, and most of the action is non-linguistic. By contrast, most of the action in a lecture is linguistic – what the lecturer says, what is written on overheads and handouts, the notes taken by people listening to the lecture. But even a lecture is not just language – it is a bodily performance as well as a linguistic performance, and it is likely to involve physical action such as the lecturer operating an overhead projector.

In chapter 1, I discussed the causal effects of the textual elements of social events on social life. But events and texts themselves also have causes – factors which cause a particular text or type of text to have the features it has. We can broadly distinguish two causal 'powers' which shape texts: on the one hand, social structures and social practices; on the other hand, social agents, the people involved in social events (Archer 1995, Sayer 2000). The earlier cautionary note about causality applies also here: we are not talking about simple mechanical causality or implying predictable regularities.

In this chapter I shall focus on the relationship between texts, social events, social practices and social structures, after some preliminary comments on the agency of participants in events, a theme we shall return to, especially in the final chapter. A number of social research themes are relevant here, and I shall refer in particular to: the political economy of new capitalism (Jessop 2000), theorizing discourse within a 'critical realist' philosophy of science (Fairclough, Jessop and Sayer 2000), theories of **globalization** (Giddens 1991, Harvey 1990) and media/**mediation** (Silverstone 1999); research on shifts in government and '**governance**' in new capitalism (Bjerke 2000, Jessop 1998, forthcoming a); the concept of 'recontextualization' developed by **Bernstein** in his educational sociology (Bernstein 1990), and the work on the '**hybridity**' or blurring of boundaries which some social theorists associate with 'postmodernity' (e.g. Harvey 1990, Jameson 1991). I shall also discuss the concepts of 'genre' and 'discourse', both of which have received extensive attention in social research and theory ('genre' for instance in Media Studies, 'discourse' in the work of **Foucault** especially).

Texts and social agents

Social agents are not 'free' agents, they are socially constrained, but nor are their actions totally socially determined. Agents have their own 'causal powers' which are not reducible to the causal powers of social structures and practices (on this view of the relationship between **structure and agency**, see Archer 1995, 2000). Social agents texture texts, they set up relations between elements of texts. There are structural constraints on this process – for instance, the grammar of a language makes some combinations and orderings of grammatical forms possible but not others (e.g. 'but book the' is not an English sentence); and if the social event is an interview, there are genre conventions for how the talk should be organized. But this still leaves social agents with a great deal of freedom in texturing texts.

Take the following extract from Example 1 (see Appendix, pages 229–30) as an example, where a manager is talking about the 'culture' of people in his native city of Liverpool:

'They are totally suspicious of any change. They are totally suspicious of anybody trying to help them. They immediately look for the rip-off. They have also been educated to believe that it is actually clever to get "one over on them". So they are all at it. And the demarcation lines that the unions have been allowed to impose in those areas, because of this, makes it totally inflexible to the point where it is destructive. I know it. I can see it.'

'And how does this relate to what is happening here?'

'Well, I was going to say, how do you change this sort of negative culture?'

Notice in particular the semantic relation which is set up between 'negative culture' and being 'totally suspicious' of change, 'looking for the rip-off', trying to 'get one over on them', 'demarcation lines', 'inflexible' and 'destructive'. We can see this as the texturing of a semantic relation of 'meronymy', i.e. a relation between the whole ('negative culture') and its parts. No dictionary would identify such a semantic relation between these expressions – the relation is textured by the manager. We can attribute this meaning-making to the manager as a social agent. And notice what the making of meaning involves here: putting existing expressions into a new relation of equivalence as co-instances of 'negative culture'. The meaning does not have a pre-existing presence in these words and expressions, it is an effect of the relations that are set up between them (Merleau-Ponty 1964).

Social events, social practices, social structures

We shall come back to agency later, but I want to focus for the moment on the relationship between social events, social practices and social structures. The approach reflects recent work I have done in collaboration with sociological theorists on discourse within a 'critical realist' philosophy of science (Fairclough, Jessop and Sayer 2002).

Social structures are very abstract entities. One can think of a social structure (such as an economic structure, a social class or kinship system, or a language) as defining a potential, a set of possibilities. However, the relationship between what is structurally possible and what actually happens, between structures and events, is a very complex one. Events are not in any simple or direct way the effects of abstract social structures. Their relationship is mediated – there are intermediate organizational entities between structures and events. Let us call these 'social practices'. Examples would be practices of teaching and practices of management in educational institutions. Social practices can be thought of as ways of controlling the selection of certain structural possibilities and the exclusion of others, and the retention of these selections over time, in particular areas of social life. Social practices are networked together in particular and shifting ways – for instance, there has recently been a shift in the way in which practices of teaching and research are networked together with practices of management in institutions of higher education, a 'managerialization' (or more generally 'marketization', Fairclough 1993) of higher education.

Language (and more broadly 'semiosis', including for instance signification and communication through visual images) is an element of the social at all levels. Schematically:

Social structures: languages
Social practices: orders of discourse
Social events: texts

Languages can be regarded as amongst the abstract social structures to which I have just been referring. A language defines a certain potential, certain possibilities, and excludes others – certain ways of combining linguistic elements are possible, others are not (e.g. 'the book' is possible in English, 'book the' is not). But texts as elements of social events are not simply the effects of the potentials defined by languages. We need to recognize intermediate organizational entities of a specifically linguistic sort, the linguistic elements of networks of social practices. I shall call these **orders of discourse** (see Chouliaraki and Fairclough 1999, Fairclough 1992). An order of discourse is a network of social practices in its language aspect. The elements of orders of discourse are not things like nouns and sentences (elements of linguistic structures), but discourses, genres and styles (I shall differentiate them shortly). These elements select certain possibilities defined by languages and exclude others – they control linguistic variability for particular areas of social life. So orders of discourse can be seen as the social organization and control of linguistic variation.

There is a further point to make: as we move from abstract structures towards concrete events, it becomes increasingly difficult to separate language from other social elements. In the terminology of Althusser, language becomes increasingly 'overdetermined' by other social elements (Althusser and Balibar 1970). So at the level of abstract structures, we can talk more or less exclusively about language – more or less, because 'functional' theories of language see even the grammars of languages as socially shaped (Halliday 1978). The way I have defined orders of discourse makes it clear that at this intermediate level we are dealing with a much greater 'overdetermination' of language by other social elements – orders of discourse are the *social* organization and control of linguistic variation, and their elements (discourses, genres, styles) are correspondingly not purely linguistic categories but categories which cut across the division between language and 'non-language', the discoursal and the non-discoursal. When we come to texts as elements of social events, the 'overdetermination' of language by other social elements becomes massive: texts are not just effects of linguistic structures and orders of discourse, they are also effects of other social structures, and of social practices in all their aspects, so that it becomes difficult to separate out the factors shaping texts.

Social practices

Social practices can be seen as articulations of different types of social element which are associated with particular areas of social life – the social practice of classroom teaching in contemporary British education, for example. The important point about social practices from the perspective of this book is that they articulate discourse (hence language) together with other non-discoursal social elements. We might see any social practice as an articulation of these elements:

Action and interaction
Social relations
Persons (with beliefs, attitudes, histories etc.)
The material world
Discourse

So, for instance, classroom teaching articulates together particular ways of using language (on the part of both teachers and learners) with the social relations of the classroom, the structuring and use of the classroom as a physical space, and so forth. The relationship between these different elements of social practices is dialectical, as **Harvey** argues (Fairclough 2001a, Harvey 1996a): this is a way of putting the apparently paradoxical fact that although the discourse element of a social practice is not the same as for example its social relations, each in a sense contains or internalizes the other – social relations *are* partly discoursal in nature, discourse *is* partly social relations. Social events are causally shaped by (networks of) social practices – social practices define particular ways of acting, and although actual events may more or less diverge from these definitions and expectations (because they cut across different social practices, and because of the causal powers of social agents), they are still partly shaped by them.

Discourse as an element of social practices: genres, discourses and styles

We can say that discourse figures in three main ways in social practice. It figures as:

Genres (ways of acting)
Discourses (ways of representing)
Styles (ways of being)

One way of acting and interacting is through speaking or writing, so discourse figures first as 'part of the action'. We can distinguish different genres as different ways of (inter)acting discoursally – interviewing is a genre, for example. Secondly, discourse figures in the representations which are always a part of social practices – representations of the material world, of other social practices, reflexive self-representations of the practice in question. Representation is clearly a discoursal matter, and we can distinguish different discourses, which may represent the same area of the world from different perspectives or positions. Notice that 'discourse' is being used here in two senses: abstractly, as an abstract noun, meaning language and other types of semiosis as elements of social life; more concretely, as a count noun, meaning particular ways of representing part of the world. An example of a discourse in the latter sense would be the political discourse of New Labour, as opposed to the political discourse 'old' Labour, or the political discourse of 'Thatcherism' (Fairclough 2000b). Thirdly and finally, discourse figures alongside bodily behaviour in constituting particular ways of being, particular social or personal identities. I shall call the discoursal aspect of this a style. An example would be the style of a particular type of manager – his or her way of using language as a resource for self-identifying.

The concepts of 'discourse' and 'genre' in particular are used in a variety of disciplines and theories. The popularity of 'discourse' in social research owes a lot in particular to Foucault (1972). 'Genre' is used in cultural studies, media studies, film theory, and so forth (see for instance Fiske 1987, Silverstone 1999). These concepts cut across disciplines and theories, and can operate as 'bridges' between them – as focuses for a dialogue between them through which perspectives in the one can be drawn upon in the development of the other.

Text as action, representation, identification

'Functional' approaches to language have emphasized the 'multi-functionality' of texts. Systemic Functional Linguistics, for instance, claims that texts simultaneously have 'ideational', 'interpersonal' and 'textual' functions. That is, texts simultaneously represent aspects of the world (the physical world, the social world, the mental world); enact social relations between participants in social events and the attitudes, desires and values of participants; and coherently and cohesively connect parts of texts together, and connect texts with their situational contexts (Halliday 1978, 1994). Or rather, people do these things in the process of meaning-making in social events, which includes texturing, making texts.

I shall also view texts as multi-functional in this sort of sense, though in a rather different way, in accordance with the distinction between genres, discourses and styles as the three main ways in which discourse figures as a part of social practice – ways of acting, ways of representing, ways of being. Or to put it differently: the relationship of the text to the event, to the wider physical and social world, and to the persons involved in the event. However, I prefer to talk about three major **types of meaning**, rather than functions:

Major types of text meaning

Action

Representation

Identification.

Representation corresponds to Halliday's 'ideational' function; Action is closest to his 'interpersonal' function, though it puts more emphasis on text as a way of (inter)acting in social events, and it can be seen as incorporating Relation (enacting social relations); Halliday does not differentiate a separate function to do with identification – most of what I include in Identification is in his 'interpersonal' function. I do not distinguish a separate 'textual' function, rather I incorporate it within Action.

We can see Action, Representation and Identification simultaneously through whole texts and in small parts of texts. Take the first sentence of Example 1: 'The culture in successful businesses is different from in failing businesses'. What is represented here (Representation) is a relation between two entities – 'x is different from y'. The sentence is also (Action) an action, which implies a social relation: the manager is giving the interviewer information, telling him something, and that implies in broad terms a social relation between someone who knows and someone who doesn't – the social relations of this sort of interview are a specific variant of this, the relations between someone who has knowledge and opinions and someone who is eliciting them. Informing, advising, promising, warning and so forth are ways of acting. The sentence is also (Identification) an undertaking, a commitment, a judgement: in saying 'is different' rather than 'is perhaps different' or 'may be different', the manager is strongly committing himself. Focusing analysis of texts on the interplay of Action, Representation and Identification brings a social perspective into the heart and fine detail of the text.

There is, as I have indicated, a correspondence between Action and genres, Representation and discourses, Identification and styles. Genres, discourses and styles are respectively relatively stable and durable *ways* of acting, representing and identifying. They are identified as elements of orders of discourse at the level of social practices. When we analyse specific texts as part of specific events, we are doing two interconnected things: (a) looking at them in terms of the three aspects of meaning, Action, Representation and Identification, and how these are realized in the various features of texts (their vocabulary, their grammar, and so forth); (b) making a connection between the concrete social event and more abstract social practices by asking, which genres, discourses, and styles are drawn upon here, and how are the different genres, discourses and styles articulated together in the text?

Dialectical relations

I have so far written as if the three aspects of meaning (and genres, discourses and styles) were quite separate from one another, but the relation between them is a rather more subtle and complex one – a dialectical relation. Foucault (1994: 318) makes distinctions which are very similar to the three aspects of meaning, and he also suggests the dialectical character of the relationship between them (though he does not use the category of **dialectics**):

> These practical systems stem from three broad areas: relations of control over things, relations of action upon others, relations with oneself. This does not mean that each of these three areas is completely foreign to the others. It is well known that control over things is mediated by relations with others; and relations with others in turn always entails relations with oneself, and vice versa. But we have three axes whose specificity and whose interconnections have to be analyzed: the axis of knowledge, the axis of power, the axis of ethics . . . How are we constituted as subjects of our own knowledge? How are we constituted as subjects who exercise or submit to power relations? How are we constituted as moral subjects of our own actions?

There are several points here. First, Foucault's various formulations point to complexity within each of the three aspects of meaning (which correspond to Foucault's three 'axes'): Representation is to do with knowledge but also thereby 'control over things'; Action is to do generally with relations with others, but also 'action on others', and power. Identification is to do with relations with oneself, ethics, and the 'moral subject'. What these various formulations point to is the possibility of enriching our understanding of texts by connecting each of the three aspects of meaning with a variety of categories in social theories. Another example might be to see Identification as bringing what **Bourdieu** (Bourdieu and Wacquant 1992) calls the 'habitus' of the persons involved in the event into consideration in text analysis, i.e. their embodied dispositions to see and act in certain ways based upon socialization and experience, which is partly dispositions to talk and write in certain ways.

Secondly, although the three aspects of meaning need to be distinguished for analytical purposes and are in that sense different from one another, they are not *discrete*, not totally separate. I shall say, rather differently from Foucault, that they are dialectically related, i.e. there is a sense in which each 'internalizes' the others (Harvey 1996a). This is suggested in the three questions at the end of the quotation: all three can be seen in terms of a relation involving the persons in the event ('subjects') – their relation to knowledge, their relation with others (power relations), and their relation with themselves (as 'moral subjects'). Or we can say for instance that particular Representations (discourses) may be enacted in particular ways of Acting and Relating (genres), and inculcated in particular ways of Identifying (styles). Schematically:

Dialectics of discourse

Discourses (representational meanings) enacted in genres (actional meanings)
Discourses (representational meanings) inculcated in styles (identificational meanings)
Actions and identities (including genres and styles) represented in discourses
(representational meanings)

For instance, Example 14, from an 'appraisal training' session, can be seen as including a discourse of appraisal (i.e. a particular way of representing one aspect of the activities of university staff), but it also specifies how the discourse is to be enacted in an appraisal procedure which is made up of genres such as the appraisal interview, and it suggests associated ways of people identifying themselves within appraisal-associated styles. So we might say that the discourse of appraisal may be dialectically 'internalized' in genres and styles (Fairclough 2001a). Or, turning it around, we might say that such genres and styles presuppose particular representations, which draw upon particular discourses. These are complex issues, but the main point is that the distinction between the three aspects of meaning and between genres, discourses and styles, is a necessary analytical distinction which does not preclude them from 'flowing into' one another in various ways.

Mediation

The relationship between texts and social events is often m[ore complex than]
indicated so far. Many texts are 'mediated' by the 'mass [media]
which 'make use of copying technologies to disseminate co[mmunications' (Thompson]
2000). They involve media such as print, telephone, radio, [television etc.]
In some cases – most obviously the telephone – people ar[e not physically present but]
distant in space, and the interaction is one-to-one. These [are like ordinary]
conversation. Others are very different from ordinary conversation – for instance,
a printed book is written by one or a small number of authors but read by indefinitely
many people who may be widely dispersed in time and space. In this case, the text
connects different social events – the writing of a book on the one hand, and the
many and various social events which include reading (glancing at, referring to, etc.)
the book – a train journey, a class in a school, a visit to a bookshop, and so forth.

   Mediation according to Silverstone (1999) involves the 'movement of meaning'
– from one social practice to another, from one event to another, from one text to
another. As this implies, mediation does not just involve individual texts or types
of text, it is in many cases a complex process which involves what I shall call 'chains'
or 'networks' of texts. Think, for example, of a story in a newspaper. Journalists
write newspaper articles on the basis of a variety of sources – written documents,
speeches, interviews, and so forth – and the articles are read by those who buy the
newspaper and may be responded to in a variety of other texts – conversations about
the news, perhaps if the story is a particularly significant one further stories in other
newspapers or on television, and so on. The 'chain' or 'network' of texts in this
case thus includes quite a number of different types of text. There are fairly regular
and systematic relationship between some of them – for instance, journalists
produce articles on the basis of sources in fairly regular and predictable ways,
transforming the source materials according to quite well-established conventions
(e.g. for turning an interview into a report).

   Complex modern societies involve the networking together of different social
practices across different domains or fields of social life (e.g. the economy, education,
family life) and across different scales of social life (global, regional, national, local).
Texts are a crucial part of these networking relations – the orders of discourse
associated with networks of social practices specify particular chaining and networking relationships between types of text. The transformations of new capitalism
can be seen as transformations in the networking of social practices, which include
transformations in orders of discourse, and transformations in the chaining and
networking of texts, and in 'genre chains' (see below). For instance, the process of
'globalization' includes the enhanced capacity for some people to act upon and shape
the actions of others over considerable distances of space and time (Giddens 1991,
Harvey 1990). This partly depends upon more complex processes of textual

mediation of social events, and more complex chaining and networking relations between different types of text (facilitated through new communication technologies, notably the Internet). And the capacity to influence or control processes of mediation is an important aspect of power in contemporary societies.

'**Genre chains**' are of particular significance: these are different genres which are regularly linked together, involving systematic transformations from genre to genre. Genre chains contribute to the possibility of actions which transcend differences in space and time, linking together social events in different social practices, different countries, and different times, facilitating the enhanced capacity for 'action at a distance' which has been taken to be a defining feature of contemporary 'globalization', and therefore facilitating the exercise of power.

Genre chains

The extracts in Example 3 (taken from Iedema 1999) give some sense of a genre chain. The example relates to a project planning the renovation of a mental hospital. The extracts are from an interview with the 'architect-planner' responsible for drawing up a written report on the basis of consultation between 'stakeholders' in the project, from a meeting of 'stakeholders', and from the report. What is basically going on is that stakeholders are choosing amongst possible ways of carrying out the project, and finding compelling arguments for their choice to put in the report. The stakeholder meeting and the written report are elements of the genre chain in this case.

Iedema's analysis shows two things: first, that the language of the stakeholder meeting is 'translated' into the language of the report in quite systematic ways – a translation which reflects the difference in genre. Second, however, that this translation is anticipated in the meeting itself – different contributions at different stages (represented in the extracts) begin the process of translation, moving us towards the language of the report. Participants in the meeting build up to the well-argued, formal logic of the report – a characteristic of the official report genre.

In Extract 1 from the meeting, we see the informal decision-making characteristic of such meetings as the project manager elicits arguments in support of the favoured option. In Extract 2, the architect-planner begins to build up the logic of the report, though still in a conversational and personal way which interprets stakeholders' reasons for supporting the favoured option (e.g. 'I think we were happy that is why the solution that came out was staggered'). Extract 3 makes an important further move towards the report by transforming the arguments for the option into reported speech (e.g. 'what you're saying is *that option D is preferred because it's the most compact* . . .'). See chapter 3 on reported speech. Finally, the extract from the report itself shows an impersonal logic in which the logical connectors (e.g. 'This means', 'The solution', 'In this way') are foregrounded by being located initially in sentences and clauses ('thematized' in a terminology I shall introduce later). These comments on the logic of the argument illustrate how moving along a genre chain entails transforming the language in particular ways.

We can also see Example 1 as part of a genre chain. It is an extract from an ethnographic interview between an academic researcher and a business manager. The example is taken from a book whose main genre is academic analysis. More- over, there is an Appendix to the book containing 'A Scheme of Management Competencies' produced for the company by the author on the basis of his research, a management education genre. We can thus see the ethnographic interview as part of a chain of genres. More specifically, it can be seen as a generic device for accessing the language of practical management, part of a chain of genres which transform it into the language of academic analysis, and transform that in turn into the language of management education – a language which enters into the governance of business organizations. This way of describing it brings out the significance of genre chains in the networking of social practices (in this case, business and academic research) and in action across different networks of social practices.

Genres and governance

Genres are important in sustaining the institutional structure of contemporary society – structural relations between (local) government, business, universities, the media, etc. We can think of such institutions as interlocking elements in the governance of society (Bjerke 2000), and of such genres as genres of governance. I am using 'governance' here in a very broad sense for any activity within an institution or organization directed at regulating or managing some other (network of) social practice(s). The increasing popularity of the term 'governance' is associated with a search for ways of managing social life (often referred to as 'networks', 'partnerships' etc.) which avoid both the chaotic effects of markets and the top- down hierarchies of states. Though, as **Jessop** points out, contemporary governance can be seen as combining all of these forms – markets, hierarchies, networks (Jessop 1998). We can contrast genres of governance with 'practical genres' – roughly, genres which figure in doing things rather than governing the way things are done. It may seem on the face of it rather surprising to see the ethnographic interview of Example 1 as a genre of governance, but the case for claiming this becomes clearer when we locate the ethnographic interview as above in a chain of genres. This shows in a relatively concrete way what is often discussed more abstractly – the extensive incorporation of academic research into networks and processes of governance.

The genres of governance are characterized by specific properties of recon- textualization – the appropriation of elements of one social practice within another, placing the former within the context of the latter, and transforming it in particular ways in the process (Bernstein 1990, Chouliaraki and Fairclough 1999).

'Recontextualization' is a concept developed in the sociology of education (Bernstein 1990) which can be fruitfully operationalized, put to work, within discourse and text analysis. In the case of Example 1, the practices (and language) of managing are recontextualized (and so transformed) within academic practices (and language), which are in turn recontextualized within the business organization in the form of management education. For example, the conclusion to the manager's argument in the interview ('any business has got to keep faith with all those it deals with if it is going to deserve to survive') is recontextualized in the academic analysis as evidence that managers appreciate the need for 'trust and reciprocity', which it is suggested may be enacted in 'a form of practice in which there is a mutual recognition of one another as interdependent subjects'. One guideline in the Scheme of Management Competencies formulates such an enactment as follows: 'Good mangers are sensitive to the attitudes and feelings of all those they work with; they treat others and their ideas with respect; they listen carefully to the ideas and viewpoints of others, working actively to elicit positive contributions from them.' Of course the guideline is presumably based on what many managers have said, not just this one claim in this extract. But we might represent this as a movement of appropriation, transformation, and colonization – a terminology which brings into focus the social relations of power in governance of which these recontextualizations are a part.

Genres of governance include promotional genres, genres which have the purpose of 'selling' commodities, brands, organizations, or individuals. One aspect of new capitalism is an immense proliferation of promotional genres (see Wernick 1991) which constitutes a part of the colonization of new areas of social life by markets. Example 2 illustrates this: within new capitalism, individual towns and cities need to promote themselves to attract investment (see 'Genre mixing' below for discussion of this example).

Another point to note about Example 1 is that the movement from manager talk in the ethnographic interview to 'A Scheme for Management Competencies' is a move from the local towards the global. We can see so-called 'globalization' as actually a matter of changes in the *relationships* between different scales of social life and social organization (Jessop 2000). So this is a move in 'scale', in the sense that research in a specific business organization leads to precepts (e.g. 'Good managers seek and create opportunities, initiate actions and want to be "ahead of the game"') which might apply to any business organization anywhere in the world. And indeed the resources for management education produced by academics do have an international circulation. Genres of governance more generally have this property of linking different scales – connecting the local and particular to the national/ regional/global and general. What this indicates is that genres are important in sustaining not only the structural relations between, for example, the academy and business, but also scalar relations between the local, the national, the regional (e.g. the European Union) and the 'global'. So changes in genres are germane to both the restructuring and the rescaling of social life in new capitalism.

Example 3 is a further illustration: the stakeholder meeting is a local event, yet one effect of the recontextualization of that into the report is a shift towards a global scale – such reports filter out what is specific to local events and situations in their move to an impersonal logic which can accommodate endless specific local events and cases. Reports of this sort can circulate nationally, regionally (e.g. within the EU) and globally, and in that way link local and global scales. Part of the 'filtering' effect as we move along genre chains is on discourses: discourses which are drawn upon in one genre (e.g. meetings) may be 'filtered out' in the movement to another (e.g. report), so that the genre chain works as a regulative device for selecting and privileging some discourses and excluding others.

Much action and interaction in modern societies is 'mediated', as I pointed out above. Mediated (inter)action is 'action at a distance', action involving participants who are distant from one another in space and/or time, which depends upon some communication technology (print, television, the Internet etc.). The genres of governance are essentially mediated genres specialized for 'action at a distance' – both of the examples above involve mediation through print, an academic book and a written report. What are usually referred to as 'the mass media' are, one might argue, a part of the apparatus of governance – a media genre such as television news recontextualizes and transforms other social practices, such as politics and government, and is in turn recontextualized in the texts and interactions of different practices, including, crucially, everyday life, where it contributes to the shaping of how we live, and the meanings we give to our lives (Silverstone 1999).

Genre mixing

The relationship between texts and genres is a potentially complex one: a text may not be 'in' a single genre, it may 'mix' or hybridize genres. Example 2, a promotional feature from the English-language *Budapest Sun* for the Hungarian town of Békéscsaba, is an example of **genre mixing**. As I said above, one aspect of the transformations associated with new capitalism is that individual towns and cities (rather than just national governments) now need to actively promote and 'sell' themselves, as in this case. This change in the relationship between cities and business corporations involves the chaining of genres – a chain linking the genres of local government to business genres, in which texts like Example 2 are a crucial mediating link. The change manifests itself partly in the emergence of a new genre within the genre chain, through the mixing of existing genres. We can see the genre in this case is a mixture of a journalistic feature article, corporate advertising (extended to local government), and tourist brochure. This hybridity is immediately evident in the layout and organization of the page: the headline ('Festival town flourishes') and the quotation from the City Mayor in bold at the bottom are characteristics of newspaper articles; the three photographs at the top of the page might be found in a tourist brochure; but the style of the photograph of the Mayor at the bottom of the page is that of corporate advertising. Other features of the three genres combined here include: alternation between report and quotation or indirect representation of the words of significant sources such as the Mayor (characteristic of newspaper articles); the predominance of self-promotion in positive self evaluations (e.g. 'A capable workforce, improving infrastructure and flexible labour is readily available') in the quotations (characteristic of corporate advertising); a description of Békéscsaba in the report which is thematically organized according to the conventions of tourist literature (buildings, squares etc. of architectural or historical interest, geographical location, cultural life, etc.).

A genre within a chain characteristically enters both 'retrospective' and 'prospective' relations with the genres 'preceding' and 'following' it in the chain, which may progressively lead to hybridization of the genre through a sort of assimilation to these preceding and following genres. In this case, the incorporation of corporate advertising into a local authority genre can be seen as a form of prospective **interdiscursivity** – the local authority anticipating the practices of business within which it hopes its publicity will be taken up. Another widespread example is the 'conversationalization' of various genres such as radio talks or broadcast news – they take on certain features of the conversational language within the (anticipated) contexts in which they are listened to or watched (typically in the home). (See Scannell 1991 on this aspect of the history of broadcast talk.)

A number of social researchers and theorists have drawn attention to ways in which social boundaries are blurred in contemporary social life, and to the forms of 'hybridity' or mixing of social practices which results. This is widely seen for instance as a feature of 'postmodernity', which writers such as Jameson (1991) and Harvey (1990) view as the cultural facet of what I am calling new capitalism. One area of social life where hybridity has received particularly intense attention is media – the texts of mass media can be seen as instantiating the blurring of boundaries of various sorts: fact and fiction, news and entertainment, drama and documentary, and so forth (McLuhan 1964, Silverstone 1999). The analysis of interdiscursive hybridity in texts provides a potentially valuable resource for enhancing research based upon these perspectives, offering a level of detailed analysis which is not achievable within other methods.

Relational approach to text analysis

I shall adopt a relational view of texts, and a relational approach to text analysis. We are concerned with several 'levels' of analysis, and relations between these 'levels':

Social structures

Social practices

Social events
    Actions and their social relations
    Identification of persons
    Representations of the world

Discourse (genres, discourses, styles)

Semantics

Grammar and vocabulary

Phonology/graphology

We can distinguish the 'external' relations of texts and the 'internal' relations of texts. Analysis of the 'external' relations of texts is analysis of their relations with other elements of social events and, more abstractly, social practices and social structures. Analysis of relations of texts to other elements of social events includes analysis of how they figure in Actions, Identifications, and Representations (the basis for differentiating the three major aspects of text meaning). There is another dimension to 'external' relations which will be the concern of chapter 3: relations between a text and other ('external') texts, how elements of other texts are 'intertextually' incorporated and, since these may be 'other people's' texts, how the voices of others are incorporated; how other texts are alluded to, assumed, dialogued with, and so forth.

Analysis of the 'internal relations' of texts includes analysis of:

● **Semantic relations**

Meaning relations between words and longer expressions, between elements of clauses, between clauses and between sentences, and over larger stretches of text (Allan 2001, Lyons 1997).

● **Grammatical relations**

The relationship between 'morphemes' in words (e.g. 'sick' and 'ness' in 'sickness'), between words in phrases (e.g. between definite article ('the'), adjective ('old') and noun ('house') in 'the old house'), between phrases within clauses (see chapters 6 and 8), and between clauses in sentences (e.g. clauses may be **paratactically** or **hypotactically** related (see chapter 5) – i.e. have equal grammatical status, or be in a superordinate/subordinate relationship) (Eggins 1994, Halliday 1994, Quirk *et al.* 1995).

● *Vocabulary (or 'lexical') relations*

Relations of collocation, i.e. patterns of co-occurrence between items of vocabulary (words or expressions). For example, 'work' collocates with 'into' and 'back to' more than with 'out of' in the texts of Blair's 'New Labour' party in the UK, whereas in earlier Labour texts the pattern was reversed – 'into work', 'back to work', 'out of work' (Fairclough 2000b, Firth 1957, Sinclair 1991, Stubbs 1996).

● *Phonological relations*

Relations in spoken language, including prosodic patterns of intonation and rhythm; graphological relations in written language – eg relations between different fonts or type sizes in a written text. I do not deal with phonological or graphological relations in this book.

Internal relations are both, in a classical terminology, 'relations *in praesentia*' and relations '*in absentia*' – syntagmatic relations, and paradigmatic relations. The examples I have just given are examples of syntagmatic relations, relations between elements which are actually present in a text. Paradigmatic relations are relations of choice, and they draw attention to relations between what is actually present and what might have been present but is not – 'significant absences'. This applies on different levels – the text includes certain grammatical structures and a certain vocabulary and certain semantic relations and certain discourses or genres; it might have included others, which were available and possible, but not selected.

The level of discourse is the level at which relations between genres, discourses and styles are analysed – 'interdiscursive' relations as I call them. The level of discourse is an intermediate level, a mediating level between the text *per se* and its social context (social events, social practices, social structures). Discourses, genres and styles are both elements of texts, and social elements. In texts they are organized together in interdiscursive relations, relations in which different genres, discourses and styles may be 'mixed', articulated and textured together in particular ways. As social elements, they are articulated together in particular ways in orders of discourse – the language aspects of social practices in which language variation is socially controlled. They make the link between the text and other elements of the social, between the internal relations of the text and its external relations.

The relations between the discourse, semantic, and grammatical and vocabulary levels are relations of 'realization' (Halliday 1994). That is, interdiscursive relations between genres, discourses and styles are realized, or instantiated, as semantic relations, which are realized as ('formal') grammatical and vocabulary relations.

Summary

We have seen that texts are parts of social events which are shaped by the causal powers of social structures (including languages) and social practices (including orders of discourse) on the one hand, and social agents on the other. There are three main aspects of meaning in texts, Action and Social Relation, Representation, and Identification, which correspond to the categories of Genres, Discourses and Styles at the level of social practices. These aspects of meaning and categories are analytically separate without being discrete – they are dialectically related.

The central sections of the chapter have shown us that:

1   The forms of action and interaction in social events are defined by its social practices and the ways in which they are networked together.
2   The social transformations of 'new capitalism' can be seen as changes in the networking of social practices, and so change in the forms of action and interaction, which includes change in genres. Genre change is an important part of the transformations of new capitalism.
3   Some genres are relatively 'local' in scale, associated with relatively delimited networks of social practices (e.g. within an organization such as a business). Others are specialized for relatively 'global' (inter)action across networks, and for governance.
4   Change in genres is change in how different genres are combined together, and how new genres develop through combination of existing genres.
5   A chain of events may involve a chain or network of different, interconnected texts which manifest a 'chain' of different genres. Genre chains are significant for relations of recontextualization.
6   A particular text or interaction is not 'in' a particular genre – it is likely to involve a combination of different genres, genre hybridity.

Finally, we have considered a relational view of texts and text analysis, in which the 'internal' (semantic, grammatical, lexical (vocabulary)) relations of texts are connected with their 'external' relations (to other elements of social events, and to social practices and social structures) through the mediation of an 'interdiscursive' analysis of the genres, discourses and styles which they draw upon and articulate together.

3 Intertextuality and assumptions

Text analysis issues

Intertextuality and reported speech
Assumptions and implicit meaning
Dialogicality

Social research issues

Social difference
Hegemony, the universal and the particular
Ideology
The public sphere

At the end of chapter 2, I drew a distinction between the 'external' and 'internal' relations of a text, and briefly referred to the aspect of the 'external' relations of texts which is the focus of this chapter: relations between one text and other texts which are 'external' to it, outside it, yet in some way brought into it. The 'intertextual' relations of a text. I shall take a very broad view of intertextuality. In its most obvious sense, intertextuality is the presence of actual elements of other texts within a text – quotations. But there are various less obvious ways of incorporating elements of other texts. If we think, for instance, of reported speech, writing or thought, it is possible not only to quote what has been said or written elsewhere, it is possible to summarize it. This is the difference between what is conventionally called 'direct speech' (which may quote writing and purported thoughts as well as speech – e.g. 'She said, "I'll be late"') and forms of 'indirect speech' (e.g. 'She said she'd be late'). The former claims to reproduce the actual words used, the latter does not; a summary may reword what was actually said or written. Reported speech, writing or thought attributes what is quoted or summarized to the persons who said or wrote or thought it. But elements of other texts may also be incorporated without attribution. So intertextuality covers a range of possibilities (see Fairclough 1992, Ivanic 1998).

But I am also going to link assumptions to intertextuality. I use the general term 'assumptions' to include types of implicitness which are generally distinguished in the literature of linguistic pragmatics (Blakemore 1992, Levinson 1983, Verschueren 1999) as presuppositions, logical implications or entailments, and implicatures. My main concern is with presuppositions, but I shall briefly discuss these distinctions at the end of this chapter. Texts inevitably make assumptions. What is 'said' in a text is 'said' against a background of what is 'unsaid', but taken as given. As with intertextuality, assumptions connect one text to other texts, to the 'world of texts' as one might put it. The difference between assumptions and intertextuality is that the former are not generally attributed or attributable to specific texts. It is a matter rather of a relation between this text and what has been said or written or thought elsewhere, with the 'elsewhere' left vague. If, for example, I had begun this book with 'The intertextual relations of a text are a significant part of it', I would be assuming that texts have intertextual relations, committing myself to this as something which has been said or written elsewhere, and to the belief that readers have heard or read it elsewhere. I am not alluding to any specific text or set of texts, but I am nevertheless alluding to the world of texts.

Both intertextuality and assumption can be seen in terms of claims on the part of the 'author' – the claim that what is reported was actually said, that what is assumed has indeed been said or written elsewhere, that one's interlocutors have indeed heard it or read it elsewhere. Such claims may or may not be substantiated. People may mistakenly, or dishonestly, or manipulatively make such implicit claims – assertions may for instance be manipulatively passed off as assumptions, statements may mistakenly or dishonestly be attributed to others.

This chapter will address in particular three themes in social research. The first is 'difference'. One important aspect of recent transformations in social life is that **social difference**, the salience of particular social identities (be it those of women, of lesbians, of ethnic groups, and so forth), has become more pronounced (Benhabib 1996, Butler 1998, Fraser 1998). For instance the 'universal' class-based politics of an earlier period has largely given way to political struggles based around the interests and identities of such particular groups. I shall suggest a broad framework for dealing with different orientations to difference in texts which may be used as a resource for researching ways in which difference is accentuated, negotiated, bracketed or suppressed. (I shall refer particularly to the question of the '**public sphere**'.) The second, connected, theme is: the universal and the particular (Butler, Laclau and Zizek 2000). The issue here is how particulars come to be represented as universals – how particular identities, interests, representations come under certain conditions to be claimed as universal. This issue can be framed within questions of hegemony – of the establishment, maintenance and contestation of the social dominance of particular social groups: achieving hegemony entails achieving a measure of success in projecting certain particulars as universals. But this is in part a textual achievement, and textual analysis can again enhance research on these issues. The third theme, also connected to the other two, is ideology, which I have already discussed in chapter 1: in particular, the ideological significance of assumptions in texts.

Difference and dialogicality

An important contrast between intertextuality and assumption is that the former broadly opens up difference by bringing other 'voices' into a text, whereas the latter broadly reduces difference by assuming common ground. Or to put it differently, the former accentuates the dialogicality of a text, the dialogue between the voice of the author of a text and other voices, the latter diminishes it. The term 'voice' is in part similar to the way I use the term 'style' (meaning ways of being or identities in their linguistic and more broadly semiotic aspects), but it is useful in also allowing us to focus on the co-presence in texts of the 'voices' of particular individuals (Bakhtin 1981, Ivanic 1998, Wertsch 1991). People differ in all sorts of ways, and orientation to difference is fundamental to social interaction. **Giddens** suggested in one of his earlier books that 'the production of interaction has three fundamental elements: its constitution as "meaningful"; its constitution as a moral order; and its constitution as the operation of relations of power' (1993:104). Orientation to difference is central to the account of these three elements which he went on to give. The production of interaction as meaningful entails active and continual 'negotiation' of differences of meaning; the 'norms' of interaction as a moral order are oriented to and interpreted differently by different social actors, and these differences are negotiated. Power in its most general sense of 'the transformative capacity of human action', the capacity to 'intervene in a series of events so as to alter their course', depends upon 'resources or facilities' which are differentially available to social actors; and power in the 'relational' sense of 'the capability to secure outcomes where the realization of these outcomes depends upon the agency of others' is also differentially available to different social actors.

But social events and interaction vary in the nature of their orientation to difference, as do texts as elements of social events. We can schematically differentiate five scenarios at a very general level:

(a) an openness to, acceptance of, recognition of difference; an exploration of difference, as in 'dialogue' in the richest sense of the term;

(b)   an accentuation of difference, conflict, polemic, a struggle over meaning, norms, power;

(c)   an attempt to resolve or overcome difference;

(d)   a bracketing of difference, a focus on commonality, solidarity;

(e)   consensus, a normalization and acceptance of differences of power which brackets or suppresses differences of meaning and norms

This is not a typology of actual social events and interactions; social events, and texts, may combine these scenarios in various ways.

Kress suggested a number of years ago that it is productive to see texts in terms of orientation to difference: 'difference is the motor that produces texts' (1985). However, Kress's view of difference is rather limited, focusing in particular on scenario (c) above, the resolution of differences. As Kress points out, difference is most immediately accessible in actual dialogue, text which is co-produced by two or more people, and the five scenarios above provide a basis of comparison between dialogues in terms of how difference is oriented to. But difference is no less central in 'monological' texts, including written texts – most obviously because all texts are addressed, have particular addressees and readers in view, and assume and anticipate differences between 'author' and addressees. On one level, orientation to difference can be understood as a matter of the dynamics of the interaction itself. But differences are not only or even mainly occasioned, local effects of specific encounters. This is clear from Kress's focus upon differences between people as differences between discourses. Discourses are durable entities which take us to the more abstract level of social practices, and we must clearly include the question of how longer-term orientations to difference at this level are instantiated in particular social events – and interactionally worked upon, for, as I have already stressed, events (and hence texts) are shaped by the agency of participants as well as social structures and social practices.

Orientation to difference brings into focus degrees and forms of **dialogicality** in texts. What I am referring to here is an aspect of **Bakhktin**'s 'dialogical' theory of language: 'a word, discourse, language or culture undergoes "dialogization" when it becomes relativized, de-privileged, aware of competing definitions for the same things. Undialogized language is authoritative or absolute' (Holquist 1981: 427). Texts are inevitably and unavoidably dialogical in the sense that 'any utterance is a link in a very complexly organized chain of other utterances' with which it 'enters into one kind of relation or another' (Bakhtin 1986a: 69). But as the Holquist quotation suggests, texts differ in their orientation to difference, i.e. in respect of 'dialogization'. Bakhtin points to such differences in noting that the relation of an utterance to others may be a matter of 'building on' them, 'polemicizing with' them, or simply 'presuming that they are already known to the listener' (1986a: 69). And as Holquist suggests, one option is 'undialogized language', corresponding to scenario (e) above: excluding dialogicality and difference.

Let us look at some examples. Example 1 (see Appendix, pages 229–30) is from an ethnographic interview, a form of dialogue. The orientation to difference in the dialogue itself can be seen a particular version of scenario (d): any differences between interviewer and interviewee are bracketed, for the interviewer is concerned only to elicit the views of the interviewee. But the interviewee, the manager, does show some openness to difference (scenario (a)) in the intertextuality of his talk. He quotes 'an operator', and 'the union people' (though the latter is what they might say rather than what they have said). He also accentuates difference (scenario (b)), setting the summarized voice of the managers (himself included) who 'preach this flexibility, this personal and business development' against the quoted voice of the operator. But the main polemic is directed against the senior management – notice that their voice is not represented in the text. But while relations between senior management, middle management (represented by the interviewee himself) and workers are dialogized, other issues are not. For example it is assumed that a business is (can be seen as) a 'culture', and it is assumed that the unions have taken power away from the managers and the workforce – that both of them once had power (an assumption which is triggered by 'give it *back*'). The latter in particular is scenario (e) – an assumed consensus which suppresses actual difference. We have a situation which is common in texts: some things are dialogized, others are not; there is an orientation to difference in some respects but not in others.

Example 4 (see Appendix, page 236) is different. This is a paragraph from a policy paper produced by the European Union Competitiveness Advisory Group, a committee with representatives of employers and trade unions as well as some politicians and bureaucrats. The text is the final version of a paragraph which went through a number of earlier drafts. It is a negotiated text, the outcome of a process of negotiation about which voices should be included in the text and in what relation. For instance, sentences 5–7 were missing from the initial draft. They represent the voice of the trade unions, an emphasis on social cohesion and implicitly on the risk to the social welfare state, seen not as a burden but as a source of efficiency (the example is taken from Wodak 2000, where there is a detailed analysis). Yet this is not a dialogical text: the process of producing a policy paper is a process of moving 'from conflict to consensus' (the title of Wodak's paper), to a text where there is no intertextualizing of different voices. What we have is categorical assertions (statements of fact and, in sentence 9, a prediction) about globalization and the 'adjustments' which it 'imposes', and about social cohesion which are grounded in a set of assumptions. The assertions are 'categorical' in the sense that they are not modalized (see chapter 10) – for instance in sentence 4 we have 'it imposes', not 'it may impose', in sentence 5 we have 'social cohesion is threatened', not 'social cohesion is perhaps threatened'. The assumptions about 'globalization' (pronominalized as 'it' in the first sentence) are that it exists, it is a reality, that it is a 'process' (sentence 1), that it constitutes 'economic progress' (sentence 2 – to make a coherent link in meaning between the first and second sentences, one must assume that globalization *is* economic progress). It is also assumed that 'social cohesion' is a reality, though under threat. All of these assumptions are contentious: there are those who would say that globalization is a myth to cover up a new imperialism, that the economic changes it registers are not things that are just happening (a 'process') and therefore inevitable but strategic decisions by powerful agents, and that the consequences for large parts of the world are economic regress rather than 'progress', and that it is a myth that 'social cohesion' has existed in the social welfare state. Yet the divergent voices of employers and trade unions are smoothed into an apparent consensus in the coexistence of these assumptions. One might see this as scenarios (c) and (d), attempting to resolve difference and focus on commonality, yet one can also see such texts in terms of scenario (e), as suppressing difference. Compare this with Example 3, which was discussed in chapter 2, where again one can see the process of producing an apparently consensual text.

The public sphere

Example 8 is taken from a TV 'debate' (this is how the programme was represented) on the future of the monarchy in Britain. One can see Extract 1 of Example 8 as basically scenario (b), a polemical accentuation of the differences between members of the panel. TV 'debate' often takes this form (Fairclough 1995b, Livingstone and Lunt 1994). Speakers are selected to represent different 'views', and the 'debate' is orchestrated by the journalist (Roger Cook) to set these 'views' against each other.

One might consider this way of dealing with difference in terms of the 'public sphere' (Arendt 1958, Calhoun 1992, Fairclough 1999, Habermas 1989). The public sphere is in **Habermas**'s terms (1984) a zone of connection between social systems and the 'lifeworld', the domain of everyday living, in which people can deliberate on matters of social and political concern as citizens, and in principle influence policy decisions. The contemporary status of the public sphere has attracted a great deal of debate, much of it about the 'crisis' of the public sphere, its problematic character in contemporary societies in which it tends to get 'squeezed out', especially by the mass media. One limitation of 'debates' like that in Example 8 from this perspective is that they don't go beyond confrontation and polemic. One might see effective public sphere debate or dialogue as reasonably including an element of polemic, but also incorporating elements of scenarios (a) and (c), and exploration of differences, and a move towards resolving them so as to reach agreement and form alliances. Without that element it is difficult to see how 'debates' can influence the formation of policy. The same might be said of Extract 2, where a journalist gathers 'views' from the audience but in a way which separates and fragments them, leaving no possibility of dialogue between them. This is one illustration of how analysis of the treatment of difference in texts can contribute to issues in social research. I shall discuss Example 8 more fully in relation to the public sphere in chapter 4.

Hegemony, universal and particular

The concept of 'hegemony' is central to the version of Marxism associated with Antonio Gramsci (Gramsci 1971). In a Gramscian view, politics is seen as a struggle for hegemony, a particular way of conceptualizing power which amongst other things emphasizes how power depends upon achieving consent or at least acquiescence rather than just having the resources to use force, and the importance of ideology in sustaining relations of power. The concept of 'hegemony' has recently been approached in terms of a version of discourse theory in the 'post-Marxist' political theory of Ernesto **Laclau** (Laclau and Mouffe 1985). The hegemonic struggle between political forces can be seen as partly a contention over the claims of their particular visions and representations of the world to having a universal status (Butler *et al.* 2000).

Representations of 'globalization' and especially of global economic change are a good example. Let us go back to Example 4, the European Union text. It is similar to many other contemporary texts in representing global economic change as a process without human agents, in which change is nominalized ('globalization', see chapter 8) and so represented as itself an entity which can act as an agent (it 'imposes deep and rapid adjustments'), a process in a general and ill-defined present and without a history (it is just what 'is') which is universal (or, precisely, 'global') in terms of place, and an inevitable process which must be responded to in particular ways – an 'is' which imposes an 'ought', or rather a 'must' (Fairclough 2000c). One can see the hegemonic aspirations of neo-liberalism as partly a matter of seeking universal status for this particular representation and vision of economic change. Of course it is indeed particular and contentious. There are other representations in which 'globalization' is a result of human agency and strategy (e.g. the progressive removal of barriers to the free movement of goods and finance through inter-governmental agreements dominated by the USA and other powerful states), with a particular history, which excludes large areas of the world (e.g. much of Africa), is in no sense inevitable, and need not therefore close down the political space by making certain policies also inevitable.

Such representations of 'globalization' vary in the extent to which they are asserted or assumed, in the balance between assertion and assumption. The European Union text is relatively assertive – there are, as I have pointed out, certain grounding assumptions, but much of this vision of global economic change is explicit, asserted. In many texts however one finds the whole vision as part of an assumed and taken-for-granted background. Take, for instance, the following short extract from a leaflet produced by the British government Department for Education and Employment on changes in the post-16 curriculum. The leaflet is identified as a 'guide to parents'.

> Many European students take a broader study package and have a more demanding study schedule – typically 30 hours of teaching a week, compared to 18 in the UK. These are the students with whom our young people must compete for jobs and university places in a global marketplace.

The only reference in the leaflet to the global economy is in the second sentence, which assumes that there is a global marketplace, and that our young people must compete for jobs and university places within it (what is asserted is with whom – these 'European students'). A measure of the successful universalization of such a particular representation is the extent to which it figures in this way as a background assumption (and one might say as an ideology – see below) in a wide variety of texts.

I suggested in chapter 2, discussing genres of governance, that Example 1 can be seen as positioned in a genre chain which facilitates a move from the local to the global – general precepts for managers which might apply anywhere are produced (in the 'scheme of management competencies' in the Appendix to Watson's book) on the basis of the local experience of managers in a specific company. But this can simultaneously be seen in terms of hegemony as a universalization of a particular – universal claims are made for one view of management amongst others.

Coming back to representations of globalization in Example 4, we can refine the claim I made earlier that intertextuality opens up difference, whereas assumptions reduce difference. The most dialogical option would be to explicitly attribute representations to sources, to 'voices', and to include much of the range of voices that actually exists. A less dialogical option is one I briefly alluded to above: modalized assertion (see chapter 10). If for example sentence 4 in the European Union text were to be worded as, 'It may impose deep and rapid adjustments', i.e. if the statement of fact were to be reworded as a statement of possibility, that would at least be dialogically open to other possibilities. An even less dialogical option is the categorical, non-modalized assertions which we actually have in the text, which leave no room for other possibilities. And the least dialogical option is assumption, simply taking this vision of the global economy for granted, as in the extract from the Department of Education and Employment leaflet which I quoted above (see also White 2001). Schematically:

```
ʻtribute, quote
ʻalized assertion
    ᴴnodalized assertion
    ᴺtion
```

ʻ ᴺt for any particular text or type of text, there is a set of
. of voices which are potentially relevant, and potentially
.ₒ the text. It may not be possible to identify these sets with great
.ₐ.₁, and they may be rather extensive and complex. But it is analytically useful
ᴸₒ begin with some rough idea of them, for a significant initial question is: which
texts and voices are included, which are excluded, and what significant absences are
there? I noted above, for instance, that in the case of Example 1, the ethnographic
interview, the manager does not incorporate the voice of the senior management
even though he is mainly talking about the senior management: he represents
what senior management do, but not what they say, whereas the voices of a worker
and of trade-unionists are incorporated (though the latter in terms of what they
'would' say).

Where other texts are intertextually incorporated in a text, they may or may
not be attributed. For instance, Example 5, an extract from Tony Blair's speech
following the attack on the World Trade Centre in September 2001, includes quite
a lot of non-attributed intertextuality, and this is true of the speech as a whole. One
example is:

> In the world of the Internet, information technology and TV, there will be
> globalization. And in trade, the problem is not that there's too much of it; on
> the contrary there's too little of it. The issue is not how to stop globalization.
> The issue is how we use the power of the community to combine it with justice.

There is a repeated pattern here of denial followed by assertion – negative clause
followed by positive clause. Denials imply the assertion 'elsewhere' of what is being
denied – in this case, that someone has asserted that there is too much globalization
in trade, and that the issue is how to stop globalization. In the context from
which this extract comes, Blair has been referring to people who 'protest against
globalization'. What he is implying is that these people do assert or have asserted
these things, but he is not actually attributing these assertions to them. In fact, many
who 'protest against globalization' are not claiming that there is 'too much' of it in

trade or that it should be 'stopped', but rather that there is a need to redress imbalances of power in the *way* in which international trade in increasing.

When intertextuality is attributed, it may be specifically attributed to particular people, or non-specifically (vaguely) attributed. Elsewhere in the same speech, for instance, Blair says:

> Don't overreact some say. We aren't. We haven't lashed out. No missiles on the first night just for effect.
>
> Don't kill innocent people. We are not the ones who waged war on the innocent. We seek the guilty.
>
> Look for a diplomatic solution. There is no diplomacy with Bin Laden or the Taliban regime.
>
> State an ultimatum and get their response. We stated the ultimatum, they haven't responded.
>
> Understand the causes of terror. Yes, we should try, but let there be no moral ambiguity about this: nothing could ever justify the events of 11 September, and it is to turn justice on its head to pretend it could.

This is a simulated dialogue in which Blair does not so much represent a critical voice as dramatically enact a dialogue with such a voice, which appears as a series of injunctions (grammatically, imperative sentences, see chapter 6). Yet he does attribute the words of his imaginary interlocutor, though vaguely, to 'some'. One can see this vagueness as giving Blair a licence to represent what critics of the war were saying in a way which a more specific attribution would make it easier to challenge. The final sentence is the significant one in this regard. It begins with a qualified acceptance of the injunction to 'understand the causes of terror' (we should 'try'), but this is followed by an objection which rests upon the implication that those who call for an understanding of causes are thereby seeking to justify the events of September 11. Notice that, as with the previous example, there is a denial ('nothing could ever justify the events of September 11') which implies the assertion 'elsewhere' that 'terror' may be justified by its 'causes'. Of course, calling for a better understanding of why people resort to terrorism does not imply, and did not imply for critics of the policies of Bush and Blair at the time, that terrorism is justified so long as the causes are sufficiently compelling.

When the speech or writing or thought of another is reported, two different texts, two different voices, are brought into dialogue, and potentially two different perspectives, objectives, interests and so forth (Volosinov 1973). There is always likely to be a tension between what is going on in the reporting text, including the work which the reporting of other texts is doing within that text, and what was going on in the reported text. I earlier suggested a broad contrast between intertextuality and assumption in terms of the openness of the former, but not the latter, to difference and dialogicality. The form of intertextuality I particularly had in mind is direct reporting, quoted speech or writing (see below). But as soon as we get into the detail of how the speech and writing and thought of others can be reported, the diverse possible forms that it can take, it becomes clear that the picture is more complicated – that reporting, as a form of intertextuality, itself subsumes much of the range of orientations to difference which I summed up in the five scenarios above.

One important contrast in reporting is between reports which are relatively 'faithful' to what is reported, quoting it, claiming to reproduce what was actually said or written, and those which are not. Or, to put it differently, reports which keep a relatively strong and clear boundary between the speech or writing or thought that is reported and the text in which they are reported, and those which do not (Fairclough 1988, Volosinov 1973). This is the difference between 'direct' and 'indirect' reporting. We can differentiate four ways of reporting (see Leech and Short 1981 for a fuller account):

- *Direct reporting*

  Quotation, purportedly the actual words used, in quotation marks, with a reporting clause (e.g. She said: 'He'll be there by now').

- *Indirect reporting*

  Summary, the content of what was said or written, not the actual words used, no quotation marks, with a reporting clause (e.g. She said he'd be there by then). Shifts in the tense ('he'll' becomes 'he'd') and deixis ('now' becomes 'then') of direct reports.

- *Free indirect reporting*

  Intermediate between direct and indirect – it has some of the tense and deixis shifts typical of indirect speech, but without a reporting clause. It is mainly significant in literary language (e.g. Mary gazed out of the window. *He would be there by now*. She smiled to herself.).

- *Narrative report of speech act*

  Reports the sort of speech act without reporting its content (e.g. She made a prediction).

In Example 2 ('Festival Town Flourishes'), two voices are included, both local official ones, representing respectively local government and business – the Mayor, and the Managing Director of the local entrepreneurs' centre. Other voices (e.g. representing the cultural community, or inhabitants of the town giving their experience of what it's like to live there) might have been included but are not. It would seem that the feature has been written on the basis of interviews with the two officials. Some information about the town is included in the author's account, some is attributed to the officials, sometimes as direct report (quotation), sometimes as indirect report (summary). Since it is likely that most of the information came from the interviews, one might wonder what dictates its distribution between authorial account, direct report, and indirect report. The answer would seem to be: genre. This text is 'mixed' in terms of genre, as I pointed out in chapter 2, but its intertextuality is typical of press reports. The pattern is an alternation between authorial accounts and indirect reports, backed up or substantiated with direct quotations. Even if, as seems likely in this case, all the information about the town emanates from other voices, the genre of press report favours this distribution of information between the authorial voice and attributed voices.

The relationship between authorial account and attributed speech is rather straightforward in this case, showing none of the tension I alluded to above, or the associated issues of orientation to difference. These issues do arise however in the following extract from the British New Labour government's Green Paper on Welfare Reform (1998):

> There will be a full, independent evaluation of the first phase of the New Deal for Lone Parents, available in autumn 1999. Early indications are encouraging. *Lone parent organisations, employers, and lone parents themselves have all welcomed this New Deal,* and *the staff responsible for delivering the service have been particularly enthusiastic. The staff have welcomed the opportunity to become involved in providing practical help and advice.* The first phase of this New Deal has aroused considerable interest: *lone parents in other parts of the country are asking if they can join in.*

This document is remarkable overall for its lack of dialogicality, one indication of which is that there are very few instances in the whole document of reported speech or writing. Other voices hardly appear. This extract is one of the few exceptions. I have italicized those parts which I take to be representing other voices (lone parents, staff, etc.). There is only one instance here which is obviously reported speech, the indirect report ('lone parents in other parts of the country are asking if they can join in') at the end. The other instances imply things that have been said or written without actually reporting them – if lone parents' organizations and so forth 'have welcomed this New Deal', then presumably they have said or written positive things about it, but all that is represented here are generalized attitudes (welcoming, being enthusiastic) which abstract away from specific statements or evaluations. It is representation of thought (and, specifically, attitude) rather than of speech or writing, but it can only be based upon speech or writing. Other voices are brought into the document at this point, but in a way which abstracts away from what must surely be the diverse things that have actually been said or written, and which reduces difference. One might ask what these generalized representations of attitude are based upon. There is no indication of this, but the most obvious answer is some form of opinion survey. Of course, if the results of such surveys had been explicitly given, it would have been in the form of percentages, but that would undermine the impression of consensus (cf. scenario (d)). The strategic and rhetorical motivation for the form of reporting in this extract is clear enough, and one can locate it broadly within the functioning of 'public opinion' in contemporary politics and governance (see further in Fairclough 2000a, 2000b).

Both of the last two examples show that intertextuality is a matter of recontextualization (a concept introduced in chapter 2) – a movement from one context to another, entailing particular transformations consequent upon how the material that is moved, recontextualized, figures within that new context. So in the case of reported speech, writing or thought, there are two interconnected issues to address:

(a) the relationship between the report and the original (the event that is reported);
(b) the relationship between the report and the rest of the text in which it occurs – how the report figures in the text, what work the reporting does in the text.

The interconnection of the two is clear from the examples: one function of reports in the 'Festival Town Flourishes' text is to substantiate authorial claims, which makes sense of the emphasis on quoting and the implicit claim to faithfulness to the original. By contrast, the reports in the Green Paper contribute to legitimizing policy, and the emphasis is correspondingly on producing an impression of consensus through generalizing away from specific evaluations or statements in a way which reduces difference.

Example 6[1] is a report from a radio news broadcast (*Today*, BBC Radio 4, 30 September 1993) on the extradition of two Libyans accused of responsibility for the Lockerbie bombing in 1988, when an aircraft exploded near the town of Lockerbie in Scotland killing all those on board (see Fairclough 1995b).

'Headlines': *Newsreader*:   Libya has now told the United Nations that it is willing to see the two men accused of the Lockerbie bombing stand trial in Scotland, but it cannot meet the deadline to hand them over.

Newsreader: Libya has told the United Nations that it's willing to let the two men accused of the Lockerbie bombing come to Scotland to stand trial. The position was spelt out in New York last night by the Foreign Minister, OM, when he emerged from a meeting with the Secretary-General, Dr Boutros-Ghali.

OM: The answers we have received from the UK and the US though the Secretary-General are very acceptable to us and we see them as a positive e: answer and enough guarantees to secure a fair . trial for these two suspects once they submit themselves to e: such jurisdiction.

Newsreader: Libyan officials at the UN, faced by the threat of more sanctions, said they wanted more time to sort out the details of the handover. Relatives of the 270 people who died on Flight 103 in December 1988 are treating the statement with caution. From the UN, our correspondent John Nian.

Correspondent: Western diplomats still believe Libya is playing for time. However on the face of it Libya does appear to be inching closer to handing over the two suspects. If this initiative is only a delaying tactic, its aim would be to persuade the waverers on the Security Council not to vote for the new sanctions, in what is likely to be a close vote. However the UN Secretary-General is reported to have been taking a tough line with Libya, demanding that it specify exactly when the two suspects would be handed over. The Libyan Foreign Minister has promised a reply on that point later today, but he's asked for more time to arrange the handover. Meanwhile the West has maintained the pressure on Libya. The Foreign Secretary Douglas Hurd, and the American Secretary of State Warren Christopher, have both reiterated the threat of sanctions. Western diplomats say that unless the two suspects are handed over immediately, a new resolution will be tabled tomorrow.

The main voices represented here are: the Libyan government (Libyan officials, the Libyan Foreign Minister, OM), western governments, politicians and diplomats (the UK, the US, western diplomats, the UK Foreign Minister, the US Secretary of State), the UN Secretary-General, and relatives of the people who died. There are also the journalistic voices of the Newsreader and the Correspondent. Apart from the recorded statement by the Libyan Foreign Minister, reported speech and thought are indirect. A superficial measure of 'balance' might appear quite positive: the voice of the Libyan government is as prominent as the voice of western governments. Yet if we look at the text in terms of recontextualization, and in particular in terms of how the different voices are textured together in the text, the report seems more problematic, and less favourable to the Libyan government.

One issue is 'framing': when the voice of another is incorporated into a text, there are always choices about how to 'frame' it, how to contextualize it, in terms of other parts of the text – about relations between report and authorial account. For example, the report that the Libyans 'said they wanted more time to sort out the details of the handover' is framed with 'faced by the threat of more sanctions', and one might see this framing as conducive to a rather negative interpretation of what the Libyan officials are reported to have said as, for instance, 'stalling' – indeed the Correspondent does later hypothesize about 'a delaying tactic'. Another example: 'the UN Secretary-General is reported to have been taking a tough line with Libya, demanding that it specify exactly when the two suspects would be handed over'. Part of the framing here is the choice of 'demand' as the reporting verb – it is highly improbable that the Secretary-General said 'I demand that . . .', so 'demand' rather than, for example, 'ask' would seem to be a framing conducive to an interpretation which casts the Libyans in an unfavourable light: if the supposedly impartial UN is getting tough with Libya, they must be in the wrong. One report is in this case also framed by another – the 'demand' is framed by the report that the Secretary-General 'has been taking a tough line with Libya'. So there is a build-up of framing which is heavily conducive to an interpretation unfavourable to Libya.

Framing also brings in questions about the ordering of voices in relation to each other in a text. But to address that issue here, we also need to consider one aspect of the reports being predominantly indirect. It is the question of how the process of extradition (or, more neutrally, the movement of the accused from Libya to Scotland to stand trial) is represented. In the recorded statement of the Libyan Foreign Minister, it is represented as the men 'submitting themselves' to jurisdiction. In the Newsreader's opening account which precedes that statement, it is represented as the men 'coming to Scotland to stand trial'. Otherwise, it is represented, six times, as the men being 'handed over' (or 'the handover'). This representation casts both the accused and the Libyan government in a different and more negative light: a country 'hands over' for instance a fugitive or a prisoner rather than its citizens, and one 'hands over' people or objects under duress rather than, for instance, in fulfilment of one's legal obligations. Yet this representation appears in the indirect reports of not only what western diplomats have said but also of what the Libyans and the UN Secretary-General have said, as well as in the account of (and the voice of) the Correspondent. Given that this is the representation generally adopted through the report, the representation which one imagines others may have been 'translated' into, whose representation is it? It is difficult to be sure, but it is clearly a 'western' representation rather than a Libyan one.

Returning to framing with this in mind, notice that this representation occurs in the salient position of the headline (headlines in this type of news report are all read at the beginning of the broadcast), as well as in the also salient position of what is sometimes called the 'wrap-up' (the final part of the report which brings us back to the present, initiated here by 'meanwhile'). Moreover, if we look at the way in which voices are ordered in relation to each other in the Correspondent's report, there seems to be a covert 'antagonist–protagonist' structuring which effectively sets the 'good guys' (western diplomats and politicians) against the 'bad guys' (the Libyans). Libyan voices are more prominent in the earlier part of the report, whereas in the second half of the report, from the BBC UN correspondent, the voices of 'the West' and the UN – both portrayed as critical of the Libyan position – are dominant. The last three sentences, from 'meanwhile', wrap up the report with western voices, with the last sentence summarizing what is implicitly a western dismissal of the Libyan overture, and containing a threat. Sentence connectors ('however', 'meanwhile') and a conjunction ('but') are markers of the ordering of voices in the BBC UN correspondent's report. The first and second sentences are linked with 'however'. This sets up a contrast between what western diplomats believe Libya is doing and what Libya appears to be doing. The second and third sentences are interesting. The second sentence is the correspondent's voice, not a representation of another voice. Reporters' statements are generally authoritative, but this one is doubly hedged ('on the face of it', 'appear to be'), so there is little conviction expressed that Libya is actually moving towards a 'handover'. Sentences 2 and 3 are also in a contrastive relationship though there is no marker of it, in that there is an implicit shift in sentence 3 back to the voice of the western diplomats in the formulation of Libya's 'aim' ('to persuade the waverers on the Security Council not to vote for new sanctions'). 'However' in sentence 4 sets the 'tough' voice of the UN Secretary-General against the hypothetical manipulative 'aim' of Libya. Sentence 5 is the only one in the Correspondent's report that represents a Libyan voice, though the 'but' in the sentence implicitly contrasts positive and negative sides of the Libyan Foreign Minister's response to the UN Secretary-General – his 'promise' and his request for more time. Finally 'meanwhile' draws a line between these diplomatic moves and what 'the West' is doing, using the latter to frame and to minimize the former.

The representation of the movement of the accused from Libya to Scotland to stand trial as 'handing over' is a matter of selecting a particular discourse which I have made some comments on above. There are two points to make here. First, that the difference between different voices reported in a text may include the fact that that different voices draw upon different discourses. Second, that voices can be represented more or less concretely or abstractly, ranging from the direct reporting of what was actually said or written within some particular concrete event, to an indirect summary of what was said or written within a particular event, to the sort of generalized representation in the Blair speech discussed above of what a group of people typically say (or are purported to typically say) which is detached from particular events, to the evocation of a voice simply through drawing upon a discourse which is recognisably associated with that voice. An example of the latter is in the extract from the Department of Education and Employment leaflet which I discussed earlier: 'These are the students with whom our young people must compete for jobs and university places in a global marketplace.' I said earlier that it is assumed that there is a global marketplace. But there is more to it than that: the expression 'global marketplace' belongs to the dominant neo-liberal economic and political discourse which is associated with the nationally and internationally dominant voices in the economic and political fields, voices which are evoked through the fragmentary presence of this discourse in the text.

Let me finally point out that intertextuality is inevitably selective with respect to what is included and what is excluded from the events and texts represented. Take for instance this sentence from the radio news report: 'The position was spelt out in New York last night by the Foreign Minister, OM, when he emerged from a meeting with the Secretary General, Dr Boutros-Ghali.' This includes the place of the event, the time of the event, and its positioning in relation to another event (the meeting with the UN Secretary General). None of the other reports in the text includes so much detail. One explanation is that such detail becomes important for potentially politically significant statements by important people. But selectivity relates to genre. How something was said is much more likely to be specified in a representation of speech in a novel (for example, 'Go on up and see for yourself,' I said, trying to keep the agony out of my voice. Raymond Chandler, *Farewell my Lovely*) than in a news report, where the focus is likely to be more exclusively on the representational meaning, or content, of what people say.

Assumptions

Implicitness is a pervasive property of texts, and a property of considerable social importance. All forms of fellowship, community and solidarity depend upon meanings which are shared and can be taken as given, and no form of social communication or interaction is conceivable without some such 'common ground'. On the other hand, the capacity to exercise social power, domination and hegemony includes the capacity to shape to some significant degree the nature and content of this 'common ground', which makes implicitness and assumptions an important issue with respect to ideology.

We can distinguish three main types of assumptions:

Existential assumptions: assumptions about what exists
Propositional assumptions: assumptions about what is or can be or will be the case
Value assumptions: assumptions about what is good or desirable

---

Each of these may be marked or 'triggered' (Levinson 1983) by linguistic features of a text, though not all assumptions are 'triggered'. For example, existential assumptions are triggered by markers of definite reference such as definite articles and demonstratives (the, this, that, these, those). Factual assumptions are triggered by certain verbs ('factive verbs') – for instance 'I *realized* (*forgot, remembered*) that managers have to be flexible' assumes that managers have to be flexible. Value assumptions can also be triggered by certain verbs – for instance, 'help' (e.g. 'a good training programme can *help* develop flexibility') assumes that developing flexibility is desirable.

Let us go back to Example 4, the extract from a European Union policy paper, to illustrate these types of assumption.

1   But (globalization) is also a demanding process, and often a painful one.
2   Economic progress has always been accompanied by destruction of obsolete activities and creation of new ones.
3   The pace has become swifter and the game has taken on planetary dimensions.
4   It imposes deep and rapid adjustments on all countries – including European countries, where industrial civilization was born.
5   Social cohesion is threatened by a widespread sense of unease, inequality and polarization.
6   There is a risk of a disjunct between the hopes and aspirations of people and the demands of a global economy.
7   And yet social cohesion is not only a worthwhile social and political goal; it is also a source of efficiency and adaptability in a knowledge-based economy that increasingly depends on human quality and the ability to work as a team.
8   It is more than ever the duty of governments, trade-unions and employers to work together
    •   to describe the stakes and refute a number of mistakes;
    •   to stress that our countries should have high ambitions and they can be realized; and
    •   to implement the necessary reforms consistently and without delay.
9   Failure to move quickly and decisively will result in loss of resources, both human and capital, which will leave for more promising parts of the world if Europe provides less attractive opportunities.

Existential assumptions include the assumption that there are such things as globalization (pronominalized as 'it' in sentence 1) and as social cohesion (sentence 5);

that there is a widespread sense of unease, inequality and polarization (sentence 5); that there is a global economy (sentence 6) and a knowledge-based economy (sentence 7). Propositional assumptions include the assumption that globalization is a process (in sentence 1 – what is asserted is the *sort* of process that it is, i.e. 'demanding'); that globalization is or constitutes economic progress (sentences 1 and 2); that people have hopes and aspirations and that the global economy makes demands (sentence 6); that social cohesion is a worthwhile social and political goal and that the knowledge-based economy does increasingly depend on human quality and the ability to work as a team (sentence 7); that reforms are necessary (sentence 8). The assumption that globalization constitutes economic progress is an example of the relationship between assumptions and coherence of meaning: we can talk about 'bridging assumptions', assumptions which are necessary to create a coherent link or 'bridge' between parts of a text, so that a text 'makes sense'. In this case, it is a bridging assumption which allows a coherent semantic connection to be made between sentences 1 and 2. There is also a propositional assumption associated with 'obsolete activities' in sentence 2: that (economic) activities can become obsolete.

Texts may include explicit evaluation ('That's wonderful/excellent!'), but most evaluation in texts is assumed (see chapter 10 for a fuller discussion of evaluation). Value assumptions are triggered by 'threatened' in sentence 5 and by 'risk' in sentence 6. If X threatens (is a threat to) Y, there is an assumption that 'X' is undesirable and 'Y' is desirable; similarly if there is a risk that X, there is assumption that 'X' is undesirable. In this case, social cohesion is assumed to be desirable, a widespread sense of unease, inequality and polarization to be undesirable; and a disjunct between hopes and demands to be undesirable. But value assumptions are not necessarily triggered. There is no need for a trigger such as 'threaten' for 'a sense of unease, inequality and polarization' to be implicitly undesirable, one can interpret it as such on the basis of one's knowledge and recognition of the value system which underlies the text. In sentence 7, it is clear that within the value system of the text social cohesion is being represented as desirable – as is anything which enhances 'efficiency and adaptability'. Notice that one can as a reader recognize the value system and therefore the assumed meaning without accepting or agreeing with it – critics of the new 'global economy' do not accept that efficiency and adaptability are unconditional goods, but they are still likely to be able to recognize that assumption. The corollary is that one's interpretation of texts in terms of values depends upon one's knowledge and recognition of such value systems.

Questions of implicitness and assumptions take us into territory which is conventionally seen as that of linguistic pragmatics (Blakemore 1992, Levinson 1983, Mey 1993, Verschueren 1999). Linguistic pragmatics is the study of 'language in relation to its users' (Mey 1993). It focuses on meaning, but the making of meaning in actual communication, as opposed to what is often seen as the concern of linguistic semantics with semantic relations which can be attributed to a language as such, in abstraction from actual communication. Linguistic pragmatics has produced valuable insights about assumptions (presuppositions, implicatures), speech acts, and so forth which have been drawn upon in critical discourse analysis (e.g. Fairclough 1992), but it is also (at least in its Anglo-American as opposed to continental European versions) sometimes problematic in overstating social agency and tending to work with isolated (often invented) utterances (Fairclough 2001b).

Ideologies and assumptions

Value systems and associated assumptions can be regarded as belonging to particular discourses – a neo-liberal economic and political discourse in the case of the assumption that anything which enhances 'efficiency and adaptability' is desirable. Existential and propositional assumptions may also be discourse-specific – a particular discourse includes assumptions about what there is, what is the case, what is possible, what is necessary, what will be the case, and so forth. In some instances, one might argue that such assumptions, and indeed the discourses they are associated with, are ideological. Assumed meanings are of particular ideological significance – one can argue that relations of power are best served by meanings which are widely taken as given. The ideological work of texts is connected to what I said earlier about hegemony and universalization. Seeking hegemony is a matter of seeking to universalize particular meanings in the service of achieving and maintaining dominance, and this is ideological work. So for instance texts can be seen as doing ideological work in assuming, taking as an unquestioned and unavoidable reality, the factuality of a global economy (e.g. assuming the existence of a 'global marketplace' in the sentence referred to in the discussion of hegemony: 'These are the students with whom our young people must compete for jobs and university places in a global marketplace'). Similarly in the European Union text, both the assumption that globalization is a reality and the assumption that globalization is economic progress might be seen as doing ideological work.

To make such claims, however, one needs to go beyond textual analysis. Let us take a very different example, an extract from a horoscope (*Lancaster Guardian*, 23 November 2001).

Virgo

Spiritual growth will be more important to you than outer ambition for a few weeks. Rather inward looking, you would like to feel more in touch with your soul. If you can push heavier chores at work to one side for a few weeks it will help. Though it may not be easy since you will be fizzing at points. Think about anger as blocked assertion and you can see why it is better to constantly put forward what you need and don't need. If you don't assert yourself in small ways, the resentment builds up, and then suddenly you let fly.

A number of propositional assumptions can be identified here. First, there is a the 'dualist' and religious assumption that the 'spirit' stands in contrast with the body, the inner self with the 'outer' self. Second, it is assumed that focusing on 'spiritual growth' means being 'inward looking' and 'feeling in touch with your soul', a bridging assumption which is necessary for a coherent semantic relation between the first two sentences. There is also an existential assumption that there are such things as 'souls' – or that people have souls. Third, there is an assumption that if one is 'fizzing', it is difficult to 'push heavier chores to one side'. Fourth, that thinking about things in certain ways allows one to understand things, that it's better to constantly put forward what you need and don't need, that you need some things and you don't need others. Fifth, that when resentment builds up, people are liable to suddenly let fly.

One might argue that the 'dualist' and religious assumption of a contrast between an inner, spiritual self and an outer self is ideological. This is the classic argument about religion as ideology, as the 'opiate of the masses' in Marx's famous phrase. But to claim that it is an ideological assumption, one would need a plausible argument that it is indeed effective, along with other related propositions and beliefs, in sustaining relations of power. This would need to be based upon a complex social scientific analysis of the relationship between religious beliefs and power relations, and of course such a claim would be controversial. The analysis would have to go beyond texts, though a textual analysis showing that such religious dualism is pervasively assumed, taken for granted, could be seen as a significant part of the analysis. Certainly one cannot simply look at a text, identify assumptions, and decide on textual evidence alone which of them are ideological.

Other types of assumptions

What I have been calling 'assumptions' are one of the types of implicitness generally distinguished in linguistic **pragmatics** – presuppositions. Verschueren (1999) differentiates four (I have changed his terminology somewhat):

Presuppositions (what I am calling 'assumptions')
Logical implications

> Standard conversational implicatures
>
> Non-standard conversational implicatures

Logical implications are implicit meanings which can be logically inferred from features of language – for example, 'I have been married for twenty years' implies that I am (still) married (because of the perfect aspect, 'have been'), or 'he is poor but honest' implies that poor people can be expected to be dishonest (because of the contrastive meaning of 'but'). Standard conversational implicatures are implicit meanings which can conventionally be inferred on the basis of our normal assumption that people are adhering to what Grice (1975) called conversational 'maxims'. The four maxims are:

> Quantity: Give as much information, and no more information than is required in
>   the context;
>
> Quality: Try to speak the truth;
>
> Relevance: Be relevant;
>
> Manner: Be clear.

For example, if I ask 'Is there anything to see in Lancaster?', you can infer on the basis of the second of these maxims (the maxim of Quality) that I don't know much about Lancaster.

The most interesting type apart from presuppositions is the fourth, non-standard conversational implicatures. The basic contrast between presuppositions and such implicatures is that the former take as given what is assumed to be known or believed, whereas the latter are fundamentally about the strategic avoidance of explicitness. However, this contrast is made less simple by the possibility of strategically purporting to assume that something is known or believed when one has reason to believe it isn't – for instance, passing off something contentious as if it were uncontentious (e.g. saying 'I didn't realize that Fred was paid by the CIA' as a way of getting one's interlocutor to accept that he is paid by the CIA). While implicatures are inherently strategic, assumptions may be strategic.

This type of implicature arises from what Grice called the 'flouting' of a maxim – apparently breaking a maxim, but adhering to it on an implicit level of meaning. To take a classic example, if I write in a reference for an academic post only that the candidate is 'well-dressed and punctual', this appears to break the maxims of Quantity (it doesn't provide enough information) and Relevance (what information it does provide is not relevant). But if a person reading the reference assumes that

I am being co-operative rather than perverse, s/he may infer that the candidate does not have the qualifications or qualities needed for the post, which is both informative enough (if curt) and relevant.

Summary

We began by distinguishing five orientations to difference in social interaction, and in texts as parts of social interaction, and we used this as a basis for assessing the relative degree of 'dialogicality' of a text, and discussed what sort of orientation to difference would characterize an effective 'public sphere'. Following Laclau, we can see hegemony as the attempted universalization of particulars (e.g. particular representations of economic change), which entails a reduction of dialogicality. We considered a scale of dialogicality, in which the most dialogical option is the inclusion of other voices and the attribution to them of quotations (a form of intertextuality), and the least dialogical option is assumption, taking things as given. The two categories of intertextuality and assumption take up the rest of the chapter. Discussion of intertextuality begins with the question of which relevant 'external' texts and voices are included in a text, and which are (significantly) excluded; and, where texts are included, whether or not they are attributed, and how specifically. We distinguished several types of report, and especially direct reporting which claims some faithfulness to what was originally said or written, and indirect reporting, which does not. I suggested that there are two main issues with reports: their relationship to the reported original, and how reported texts and voices are recontextualized within the reporting text – positioned and framed in relation to each other and in relation to the authorial voice. We distinguished three types of assumptions (existential, propositional, value), suggesting that assumptions may or may not be textually 'triggered', that assumptions are relative to discourses, and that assumptions are of particular significance in terms of the ideological work of texts. Finally, we distinguished assumptions from other types of implicit meaning.

Note

1   See Appendix, page 229, for note about transcription conventions.

Part II

Genres and action

4 Genres and generic structure

Text analysis issues

Genres and linguistic features of texts
Pre-genres, disembedded genres, situated genres
Formats
Genre analysis: activity, social relations, communication technology
Generic structure
Dialogue
Argument
Narrative

Social research issues

Globalization and disembedding
Communicative and strategic action
Societal informalization
The public sphere
Social change and technological change
Ideology
News

Genres are the specifically discoursal aspect of ways of acting and interacting in the course of social events: we might say that (inter)acting is never just discourse, but it is often mainly discourse. So when we analyse a text or interaction in terms of genre, we are asking how it figures within and contributes to social action and interaction in social events – especially, given the orientation of this book, within the transformations associated with new capitalism. I have already discussed certain aspects of genres in chapter 2. Let me repeat the summary of that discussion:

1   The forms of action and interaction in social events are defined by its social practices and the ways in which they are networked together.

2   The social transformations of new capitalism can be seen as changes in the networking of social practices, and so change in the forms of action and interaction, which includes change in genres. Genre change is an important part of the transformations of new capitalism.

3   Some genres are relatively 'local' in scale, associated with relatively delimited networks of social practices (e.g. within an organization such as a business). Others are specialized for relatively 'global' (inter)action across networks (genres of 'governance').

4   Change in genres is change in how different genres are combined together. New genres develop through combination of existing genres.

5   A chain of events may involve a chain or network of different, interconnected texts which manifest a 'chain' of different genres.

6   A particular text or interaction is not 'in' a particular genre – it is likely to involve a combination of different genres.

We can conclude from points 5 and 6 that genre analysis proceeds as follows:

(a)   analysis of 'genre chains';
(b)   analysis of genre mixtures in a particular text;
(c)   analysis of individual genres in a particular text.

The focus in this chapter is on the latter. On genres see: Bakhtin (1986a), Bazerman (1988), Chouliaraki and Fairclough 1999, Eggins and Martin (1997), Martin (1992), Swales (1990).

Let me make two preliminary points about genre. First, genres vary quite considerably in terms of their degree of stabilization, fixity and homogenization. Some genres, for instance the genre of the research paper in certain areas of science (Swales 1990), are well-defined almost to the point of being ritualized. Others, for example, advertisements for academic posts, are quite variable and in flux. In this period of rapid and profound social transformation, there is a tension between pressures towards stabilization, part of the consolidation of the new social order (for example, the new genres of telemarketing – see below), and pressures towards flux and change.

Second, there is no established terminology for genres. Some genres have fairly well-established names within the social practices in which they are used, others do not. Even where there are well-established names, we should treat them with caution, because the classification schemes upon which they are based may give a misleading picture of what actually goes on. For instance, the term 'seminar' as used now not only in education but in business covers a variety of activities and genres.

Genres and texts

The general approach I am adopting in the book is to see the interdiscursive character of a text (the particular mix of genres, discourses and styles) as realized in semantic, grammatical and lexical (vocabulary) features of the text at various levels of text organization. Genres are realized in actional meanings and forms of a text, discourses in representational meanings and forms, and styles in identificational meanings and forms (see chapter 2 for these three main types of meaning and form in texts). This means that particular semantic relations or grammatical categories and relations will be seen as primarily associated with either genres, or discourses, or styles. 'Primarily', because there is not a simple one-to-one relation – so for instance modality will be seen as primarily associated with styles, but also germane to genres and discourses (see chapter 10). Recall the discussion in chapter 2 of the dialectical nature of the relations between the three aspects of meaning, and genres, discourses and styles.

There are various aspects of text organization and various features of texts at different levels which are primarily shaped by and dependent upon genre. We can summarize these as follows. I have indicated which chapters deal with which issues.

The overall ('generic') structure or organization of a text (chapter 4)

Semantic (logical, temporal etc.) relations between clauses and sentences, and over larger stretches of text (chapter 5)

Formal, including grammatical, relations between sentences and clauses (chapter 5)

At the level of the clause (simple sentence), types of exchange, speech function, mood (chapter 6)

The mode of intertextuality of a text, the way in which other texts and voices are incorporated (chapter 4)

This chapter will connect analysis of genres to a number of themes in social research. The first theme is Giddens' analysis (1991) of globalization as involving the **disembedding** of social material from particular social contexts and practices, so that it becomes available across different fields and scales as what one might call 'social technologies'. Genres can be, I suggest, disembedded in this sense. Secondly, Habermas's distinction (1984) between **communicative and strategic action**, is, I shall suggest, relevant to the commonly assumed relationship between genres and social purposes or goals. Third, societal informalization (Misztal 2000) and the move away from overt hierarchies, can be textually researched in terms of the 'conversationalization' of public discourse (Fairclough 1992). The fourth theme is the question of the public sphere (Arendt 1958, Habermas 1989 and Fairclough 1999) and dialogue – approaching research questions about the state of the public sphere, the sphere in which people act as citizens, in terms of analysis of dialogical features of texts, an issue I have touched upon already in chapter 3. Fifth, is the relationship between social change and technological change – new communication technologies are associated, I shall suggest, with the emergence of new genres. Sixth, is a further discussion of ideology (see chapters 1 and 3) with respect particularly to argumentation and argument as a class of genres. And finally, the seventh theme, is a discussion of news narratives.

I shall first outline a general framework for analysis of genres, and then look specifically at three types of genre (each of which can be seen as 'families' of many different specific genres – see the discussion of levels of abstraction immediately below): dialogue, argument, and narrative. I shall discuss these with particular attention to, respectively, the social research issues of public space and citizenship, ideologies, and news.

Pre-genres, disembedded genres, and situated genres

One of the difficulties with the concept of genre is that genres can be defined on different levels of abstraction. For example, one might say that Narrative is a genre, but then so, too, is Report in the sense of a factual narrative about actual events, and so, too, is a Television News Report, i.e. the particular form of report characteristic of television news. If Narrative, Argument, Description, and Conversation are genres, they are genres on a high level of abstraction. They are categories which transcend particular networks of social practices, and there are for instance many different types of Narrative genres (e.g. conversational narratives, the endless 'stories' in the press and on television, the 'stories' that clients tell counsellors in therapy, etc.) which are more specifically situated in terms of social practices. If we say that a genre is tied to a particular social practice or network of social practices, then we should call Narrative, etc. something different. Swales (1990) suggest the term 'pre-genre', which I shall use.

However, this does not entirely resolve the problem, because there are other categories such as Interview or Report which are less abstract than Narrative or Argument, yet clearly do transcend particular networks of practices. We should note that there is a socio-historical process involved here – what Giddens (1991) has called 'disembedding'. That is, genres being, so to speak, lifted out of, 'disem- bedded' from, particular networks of social practices where they initially developed, and becoming available as a sort of 'social technology' which transcends both differences between networks of practices and differences of scale. Interview, for instance, encompasses many different types which are specialized for particular social practices (job interview, celebrity interview on television, political interview etc.), and even quite specific forms such as political interview transcend differences of scale to become internationally used forms. The disembedding of genres is a part of the restructuring and rescaling of capitalism. For instance, the self-publicizing genre used by towns and cities to attract investment (see Example 2 in the Appendix, pages 231–3) involves the disembedding of the genre of corporate advertising from business practices (as local government has become more like a business; but this specialized self-publicizing genre itself transcends differences of scale (exemplified by the fact that it has only recently been adopted in ex-socialist countries such as Hungary, where the example comes from – the example also points to the significance of the 'global' spread of English in the scalar disembedding of genres).

I think it is useful to elaborate the terminology here in order to avoid confusion between different levels of abstraction. I shall use 'pre-genre' as suggested above for the most abstract categories like Narrative, 'disembedded genre' for somewhat less abstract categories like Interview, 'situated genre' for genres which are specific to particular networks of practices such as 'ethnographic interview' (see Example 1, pages 229–30).

An added complication, which I discussed in chapter 2, is that particular texts may be innovative in terms of genre – they may mix different genres in novel ways. So one cannot assume any simple correspondence between situated genres and actual texts and interactions – which like any form of social activity are open to the creativity and indeed transgression of individual agents. For this reason, I do not agree with Swales when he defines a genre as 'a class of communicative events' (Swales 1990): actual events (texts, interactions) are not 'in' a particular genre, they do not instantiate a particular genre – rather they draw upon the socially available resource of genres in potentially quite complex and creative ways. The genres associated with a particular network of social practices constitute a *potential* which is variably drawn upon in *actual* texts and interactions. It is true however that some classes of text are less generically complex than others – so Swales' view of genre may perhaps make sense, for example, in the case of journal articles in certain natural sciences, but not as a general view of the relationship between text and genre.

In addition to the sort of genre mixing discussed in chapter 2, the mixing of genres in texts takes the form of what we can call the emergence of 'formats', texts which are effectively assemblies of different texts involving different genres. Websites are a good example of formats. For example, Reclaim the Streets is anti-globalization network which specializes is forms of political action directed at 'reclaiming' the public space of the street, which global capitalism is seen as having taken away from the people. The website offers the following menu: What's up, Archive, Propaganda, How to, Where, Images, Ideas. A variety of different things are being done in these different parts of the site, bringing together a variety of different genres. For instance, 'Propaganda' is an expository argument in favour of the political strategy of Reclaim the Streets, whereas 'How to' (e.g. 'How to sort a street party') is a 10-point 'recipe' for organizing an action. See Hawisher and Selfe (2000).

There is another way in which genres can be mixed in texts: there may be several genres which are hierarchically related. In Example 1 for instance we can say that the main genre is ethnographic interview, but other genres are drawn upon in the manager's responses. In the manager's first turn at the beginning of the extract, there is a narrative about the history of Liverpool; and the manager is developing an argument in the course of the extract. We can identify, then, a main genre and what we can call 'sub-genres'.

Analysing individual genres

The individual genres of a text or interaction (e.g. the main and sub-genres of Example 1, ethnographic interview, expository argument, conversational narrative) can be analysed in terms of: Activity, Social Relations, and Communication Technology – what are people doing, what are the social relations between them, and what communication technology (if any) does their activity depend on?

Activity

The question, 'what are people doing?', here means specifically, 'what are people doing discoursally?' When we think of social events, we are concerned with activities overall, in their non-discoursal as well as discoursal aspect. Here the focus is on the discourse. But a distinction needs to be drawn between cases where the social activity is primarily discoursal (a lecture, for example), and cases where discourse has an ancillary role (e.g. fixing the engine of a car, or playing football). In the case of a lecture, there is a specifically discoursal activity with its own organizational properties, which can be analysed separately from relatively secondary non-discoursal elements of the overall activity such as the use of an overhead projector or power-point. In the case of a game of football, it would be difficult to argue that there is a specifically discoursal activity distinct from the overall activity. Whether discourse is primary or ancillary is a matter of degree.

It is common for genre to be defined in terms of the purposes of the activity. For instance, according to Swales (1990) a genre 'comprises a class of communicative events, the members of which share some set of communicative purposes'. A particular genre may have a number of purposes. For instance, one might see

Example 2 as having the primary purpose of attracting investment to Békéscsaba, but it would also seem to have other purposes such as convincing people that it is a good place to live in, and that it has a dynamic and perhaps 'enterprising' local authority (and mayor in particular). And, as this indicates, purposes can be hierarchically ordered: one might see the main overall purpose as to attract investment, and the other purposes are means to doing that. Purposes may be relatively explicit or implicit.

Example 1 can be seen as having a hierarchy of purposes: a relatively explicit purpose of finding out how managers see themselves and what they do, but also 'higher' implicit purposes, one tied to academic practices ('to bring out the theoretical thinking which lies beneath the surface of the practical activity of managerial work'), another to business practices (to produce a statement of management competencies). This example shows that looking at hierarchies of purposes is one way in which to see how a text or interaction figures within networks of practices. The explicit purpose of finding out how managers see things is the purpose associated with the practice of social research and the genre of ethnographic interview, the other purposes can be seen as anticipating transformations across the network of social practices (ethnographic research, academic writing, business) and the chain of genres (interview, expository argument, checklist) which the interviewer will certainly 'have in mind' though the manager may not.

However, there are problems in privileging purpose too much in one's definition of genre. While it is true that many genres are clearly purposive, clearly tied to broadly recognized social purposes, this is not true of all genres. What are the purposes of having a chat with a friend, for example? Of course, it is perfectly possible to identify purposes even in a friendly chat, but it seems quite misleading to see it as purpose-driven in the sense that an interview is. We can see the source of the problem of over-privileging purpose in terms of Habermas's distinction between 'communicative' and 'strategic' action (1984) – interaction oriented to arriving at understanding, as opposed to interaction oriented to getting results. The modernization of social life involves the emergence of increasingly complex social systems whose rationality is 'instrumental' (rather than communicative), in which interaction is predominantly strategic – which are, in short, oriented to efficiently producing results. Purpose-driven genres characterized by determinate structure are a significant part of these instrumental social systems. But, in Habermas's terms, the 'lifeworld' (while under threat from these systems) has a predominantly communicative rationality and predominantly communicative interaction, and correspondingly genres which do not have such determinate structure. The problem is confusing the modernizing tendency towards purpose-driven genres with genre as such. We might even see this as ideological, in the sense it legitimizes what Habermas diagnoses as the 'pathological' over-extension of systems and instrumental rationality – the 'colonization' of the lifeworld by them.

The distinction between strategic and communicative is not as neat as this suggests. They sometimes occur in combination, in various ways. For example, a widespread strategy in strategic interaction is the simulation of communicative interaction – the apparent informal chattiness of much communication between employees in service industries (e.g. in hotels or shops) and customers or clients is at least in part strategically motivated by the instrumental purposes of business organizations. We can see this in terms of higher-level, implicit purposes. Conversely, even a friendly chat does not necessarily preclude purpose-driven strategies – the point is rather that it cannot be reduced to them.

The conclusion from these reservations about the over-privileging of purpose is not that we should no longer see purpose as relevant to genre, but that we should avoid centring our view of genre on purpose. Rather, we can say in less loaded terms that genres vary in terms of the nature of the activity they constitute or are a part of, and that some activities but not others are strategic and purpose-driven. Or rather, since it is a matter of degree, that some activities are more strategic (and less communicative in Habermas's sense) than others.

Generic structure

The privileging of purpose goes along with a view of genre analysis as primarily concerned with 'staging', differentiating genres in terms of their **generic structure**. Analysis of generic structure is of value for more strategic, purpose-driven genres. But it follows from what I have said above about genre mixing that it will not always be possible or indeed helpful to identify a clear staging or generic structure in an actual text or interaction. The more ritualized an activity is, the more relevant such an analysis is. For example, mundane market transactions described by Mitchell in Morocco or Hasan in Australia (Halliday and Hasan 1989, Mitchell 1957) seem to be quite highly ritualized, with predictable elements occurring in a predictable order, so analysis of their generic structure would seem to be relevant. But even in this case, there are complications – certain elements always occur (e.g. the customer asking for goods, the salesperson giving the customer the goods, the customer paying, etc.) whereas others only sometimes occur (e.g. the salesperson initiating the sale by asking for instance 'What can I get you?'); the sequence in which some elements occur is rigid, whereas for other elements it can be varied (e.g. there may be an exchange of greetings before or after the salesperson initiates the sale).

My conclusion is that we need to look for staging in analysing texts and inter-actions, but not expect to always find that they are organized in terms of a clear generic structure, and link analysis in these terms to the question of ritualization (Connerton 1989). A point of tension in the social transformations of new capitalism is between pressures towards instability, variability, flexibility etc., and pressure towards social control, stabilization and ritualization. Even in a period of fast social change where 'flexibility' is one of the buzz-words, organizations have an interest is establishing and maintaining control through ritualization. This is widely effected through training. A good example in the area of market transactions is the training of workers in 'call centres' who either initiate telephone sales or deal with customer service inquiries. Cameron (2000) cites the following memorandum to staff in a financial services centre:

Standard Call Speech

You should all know by now that we intend to introduce a standard telephone speech. There are a number of reasons for standardising the speech and improving call techniques. The most important of which is Meeting and Exceeding Customer Expectations. If we don't, someone else will.
Some more reasons are:

- Creating a professional image
- Improves quality of processing
- Allows you to manage the call sequence and pace

Every operator must use the speech, no exceptions!

Cameron found call centres that 'provided employees with a script covering more or less any interactional move that could occur in the course of a transaction, imposed detailed style rules regarding how they could speak, and monitored compliance assiduously'. This implies not only a rigid staging of telephone conversations, but also control over how operators speak (answering the phone with a smile, sounding energetic, etc.). Call centres are as Cameron says 'communication factories' in which communication is commodified and industrialized. This is linked to the overwhelming focus on 'skills' in education and training, including the sort of 'communication skills' which are demanded for this sort of work.

Let us look at one or two examples of generic structure and organization. The first is an accident report from a local newspaper.

Firemen Tackle Blaze

Night shift workers on a coating line at Nairn Coated Products, St George's Quay, Lancaster had to be evacuated when fire broke out in an oven on Wednesday evening.

> Four fire engines attended the incident and firemen wearing breathing
> apparatus tackled the flames which had started when a break off in an oven
> caught fire under the infra red element.
> The fire caused severe damage to 20 metres of metal trunking, and to the
> interior of a coating machine and the coating room was smoke logged.
> But the department was running again by Thursday morning.
>
> *Lancaster Guardian*, 7 October 1986

Such reports have a rather predictable and well-defined generic structure which we
can summarize as: headline + lead paragraph (the opening paragraph of the story)
+ satellites (paragraphs 2 and 3) + wrap-up (paragraph 4). The headline and lead
give summaries of the story – the gist of the story. The satellites add detail – typically
the ordering of satellites is flexible, one can more or less freely change the ordering
without affecting the story. The wrap-up gives the outcome of the events reported
(the accident and the action taken in response to it), often as in this case how things
came back to normal. One can relate this typical generic structure to the way in
which news not only reports disturbances of normality, but also their rectification.

The next example is taken from Hasan's discussion of shopping transactions
referred to above (Halliday and Hasan 1989):

> C: Can I have ten oranges and a kilo of bananas please?
> V: Yes, anything else?
> C: No, thanks.
> V: That'll be dollar forty.
> C: Two dollars.
> V: Sixty, eighty, two dollars. Thank you.

Here again, there is a relatively clear and predictable generic structure. The
Customer begins with a Sale Request, the Vendor responds with a Sale Compliance
(which will actually consist primarily of non-linguistic action, getting the goods
and wrapping them up, as well as optionally a linguistic element – 'Yes' in this case)
plus a Bid for a further Sale. In this case the Customer rejects the Bid, then the
Vendor makes a Payment Request to which the Customer responds with a Payment
Compliance (again, primarily non-linguistic, giving the Vendor some money, though
accompanied with a linguistic element). The Vendor Gives Change (and verbally
counts it out in this case), followed by Thanks. (I have capitalized the stages in the
generic structure.)

Even where there is a relatively clear and predictable generic structure, as in these cases, we find quite a lot of variation in actual texts. There is a limit to how far we can really talk about structure in a tight sense, i.e. obligatory elements in an obligatory order. Some stages may for instance be missing (e.g. not all accident reports have wrap-ups, not all buying transactions include a vendor bidding for a further sale). But for many texts, it seems pointless to talk about an overall 'structure' at all. Consider for instance Example 2 ('Festival Town Flourishes'). We can see the text as made up of generically different parts: main 'report', 'basic facts' inset, photographs with captions, 'leader' photo + highlighted quote. The main report consists of a headline + series of factual statements (descriptions) interspersed with reported speech. The sequence of elements in the body of the text is topically controlled. The text begins with the sort of topical development one expects in tourist literature, starting from the region and working towards the town itself and its notable features. The topical choice then for most of the text would seem to be determined by a sense of what makes a town attractive to investors. There is a degree of organization here, but it's not obvious that we can call it structure.

I shall return to the question of generic structure below in discussing the analysis of dialogues, narrative, and argument.

Social relations

Genres as forms of interaction constitute particular sorts of social relations between interactants. Social relations are relations between social agents, which can be of different types: organizations (e.g. local government, a business organization), groups (e.g. a campaigning group such as Reclaim the Streets), or individuals. Communication can be between organizations or groups or individuals, or combine different types of social agents. An influential sociolinguistic study by Brown and Gilman (1960) suggests that social relations vary in two dimensions, 'power' and 'solidarity', or social hierarchy and social distance. An issue of particular contemporary interest is the relationship between what a social analysis of networks of practices, institutions etc. might suggest about social hierarchy and distance, and how social hierarchy and distance are construed in genres.

Consider for instance communication between organizations and individuals, which is pervasive in contemporary social life, in advertising, government, and so forth. We might say, sociologically speaking, that communication between organizations and individuals is high in both social hierarchy (organizations tend to exercise power over individuals) and social distance (organizations operate on national, regional or global scales whereas individuals occupy specific locales). Indeed, new capitalism is characterized by the increasing power of organizations operating at increasingly global scales over individuals. But this entails potentially risky problems of legitimacy and alienation, as one can see from the sometimes virulent reactions of local communities to the impact upon them of policies imposed by organizations such as the International Monetary Fund. And it is noteworthy that contemporary genres for 'action at a distance', genres of governance (see chapter 2), through which organizations communicate with individuals, are pervasively characterized by simulated social relations which, we might argue, tend to mystify social hierarchy and social distance.

Example 7 (Appendix, pages 239–41) illustrates this at the level of format. The World Economic Forum, alarmed perhaps at the mounting critiques of the neo-liberal globalization it has advocated and its own influence as a non-democratic organization, set up an interactive web-site which invites individuals to contribute to its debates by sending email messages which are (selectively) published on the web-site. The web-site therefore combines the voice of the organization (the summary of the debate, in the example) with the voices of individuals from all over the world, in the form of extracts from emails they have sent (not included in the example). The key question, however, is whether this constitutes a substantive change in social relations between this powerful international organization and individuals and the local communities they belong to.

Example 5 (Appendix, pages 237–8) is an extract from a speech by the British Prime Minister Tony Blair which is immediately addressed to a Labour Party conference, but inevitably also addressed, anticipating reports in the media, to the wider public. Again, a social analysis of British politics and government would suggest that there is substantial inequality of power and social distance between the government (the organization Blair speaks for) and individuals hearing or reading reports of the speech in the media. Yet it is now a commonplace of political communication that political leaders appear to speak for themselves rather than just on behalf of governments (e.g. 'I realise why people protest against globalization'), which we might see as communication between an organization and individuals simulating person-to-person communication ('conversationalization' of public discourse as I have called it, Fairclough 1992 – see also literature on social 'informalization' and the shift away from explicit hiearchies, e.g. Misztal 2000). Example 11 (Appendix, pages 246–7), an extract from a government consultation paper, begins with an inclusive 'we' which reduces hierarchy and distance by implying that all of 'us' are in the same boat, and uses expressions ('ways of doing things', 'the types of jobs we do') which evoke everyday experience and language.

Similar points might even be made about Example 1. A positive view of ethnographic interview might see it as a worthy resource for reducing the distance between the practical lives of people being researched, and the academy. Alternatively, if we see academic research as part of the apparatus of governance as suggested in chapter 2, we might see it as mystifying social hierarchy and distance. Perhaps more reasonably, we might see a certain ambivalence.

Communication technologies

Discourse can be differentiated with respect to communication technologies in terms of two distinctions (compare Martin 1992): two-way versus one-way communication, and mediated versus non-mediated communication. This gives us, schematically, four possibilities:

Two-way non-mediated: face-to-face conversation
Two-way mediated: telephone, email, video conferencing
One-way non-mediated: lecture, etc.
One-way mediated: print, radio, television, Internet, film

The increasing complexity of the networking of social practices in contemporary societies is linked to new communication technologies – telegraph, telephone, radio, television, and more recently electronic information technology (e.g. the Internet) – which have significantly enhanced both one-way and two-way mediated communication. One way in which genres differ from one another is in the communication technologies they are specialized for, and one factor in changing genres is developments in communication technologies: the development of new communication technologies goes along with the development of new genres.

An example is the development of 'formats' on the web, which I have already referred to. Example 7 is taken from a web-site which combines different genres, including expository arguments providing summaries of the debates at the World Economic Forum annual meeting (as in the extract included in the example), email messages sent in from people around the world in response to the debates (both forms of written language), and excerpts from the debate (spoken language) – it is a 'format' in the sense I discussed above. The format brings together genres which are taken from other technologies (e.g. print in the case of the expository argument of the example) and genres which have developed as part of technological change (e.g. email). The novelty of the format is partly to do with its particular form of 'multimodality' (Kress and Van Leeuwen 2001) – it combines different semiotic modalities, including photographs, visual imagery (including the logo of the World Economic Forum), video (it is possible to view extracts from the debates), as well as language. A general issue that arises in analysing genre is which semiotic modalities are drawn upon and how they are combined. The format is also non-sequential:

one is offered a range of choices which allow one to take many different paths through the web-site. And it is consequently interactive, in the sense that a visitor to the web-site can decide what to look at and what not to look at, in what order; but also in the sense that the debates at Davos were 'opened' to visitors, who had the option of contributing through emails which were then selectively included in the site. However, one should not overstate 'interactive': the design of the web-site is constraining as well as enabling, i.e. it offers options, but also strongly limits them.

The transformations of new capitalism, the restructuring and re-scaling of network relations between social practices, both depend upon new technologies (see Castells 1996 for one account). Genre analysis has a significant contribution to make to research on the relationship between technological change, mediation (Silverstone 1999), economic change, and wider social change – both in terms of how the integration of new technologies into economic, political, social and cultural processes is instantiated through new genres, and in terms of how genre chains (chapter 2) are woven into the fabric of the 'information society'. Another issue is the restructuring of relations between the different forms of communication associated with different technologies. For instance, email has displaced print (memos, etc.) and probably to some extent face-to-face communication (conversation) in communication within organizations, though all three coexist in particular relations with each other. Or again, conversation in everyday life increasingly intersects with, draws upon, and is shaped by, various forms of mediated communication such as television.

Dialogue and the public sphere

Let us begin with conversation, 'chat' (on the analysis of conversational dialogue, see Cameron 2001). Informal conversation can be characterized in terms of an unconstrained alternation of speaker turns. Participants are equal in their right to take turns, in the sort of turns they can take (e.g. being able to ask questions as well as answer them), in their right to expect to be able to speak without interruption, and so forth. Much informal conversation has something approximating these features, but one must immediately add that even informal conversation shows inequalities which can be attributed to social relations between participants. For instance, research on language and gender (Talbot 1996) has suggested that there is an unequal distribution of turns in conversation between women and men in, for example, intimate relationships (that women tend to be interrupted more than men, that men give less conversational indications of active listening than women, and so forth).

One approach to analysing dialogue is to set actual dialogues against a co-operative and egalitarian template which is approximated only in some dialogues. Such a template can be specified as participants being equal with respect to the 'right' to, for instance (Fairclough 1999):

1	take turns
2	use turns to act in various ways – asking questions, making requests, complaining, etc.
3	speak without interruption
4	select and change topics
5	offer interpretations or summaries of what has been said

Dialogue in various institutional contexts often involves unequal restrictions on such conversational 'rights'. For instance, in interviews turns are likely to be assigned to an interviewee by an interviewer rather than taken by the interviewee, only interviewers have the right to ask questions while interviewees have the obligation to answer them, interviewers are more likely to interrupt interviewees than vice-versa, interviewers have greater control over topics and are more likely to offer interpretations or summaries of what has been said, and to 'repair' what interviewees say. However, this characterizes perhaps a certain type of job interview more closely than for instance the ethnographic interview of Example 1, where although there is, for instance, this unequal distribution of questions and answers, the interviewee is able to speak at length without interruption, to select and change topics, and so forth.

Questions about dialogue are of considerable contemporary importance with respect to effects of new capitalism on democracy and the 'public sphere', which I briefly discussed in chapter 3. The worry is that the restructuring of capitalism is eroding democracy and the public sphere. This is a partly a matter of its effects upon nation-states and their political systems: given the increasing consensus within the political mainstream that neo-liberal globalization is a mere fact of life which nation-states have to compete to succeed in, the space for political debate on issues of substance becomes more limited. This is evident in the relative marginalization of national parliaments in favour of specialist committees, in the limited effect of the European Parliament on policy-formation, as well as in a perceived decline in substantive public debate in public meetings, the media, and so forth.

What does this have to do with dialogue? There is a great deal of talk about 'dialogue', 'deliberation', 'consultation' and so forth in contemporary politics, not to mention the widespread advocacy of 'partnerships' of various sorts, all of which implies a strong commitment to democracy which the considerations mentioned above make somewhat suspect (Fairclough 2000b). An effective public sphere can be defined in terms of the quality of the dialogue which takes place within it, as theorists of the public sphere (e.g. Habermas 1989, Arendt 1958) have implied. This suggests that the quality and limits of contemporary democratic forms can be fruitfully assessed by looking at the properties and qualities of what passes as political or social 'dialogue'. For instance, there is quite a lot of experimentation in progress towards developing effective forms of public deliberation and consultation – focus groups, citizens' panels, and so forth. How might we evaluate these as public sphere dialogue?

I used the approach of setting actual dialogue against a normative template with particular reference to the public sphere in an earlier paper (Fairclough 1999), and reformulated this as a set of specifications for 'real dialogue' in Fairclough (2000b). This is a normative characterization of features which dialogue needs to have in order to be effective public sphere dialogue:

(a) People decide to enter dialogue, and can continue the dialogue on other occasions;

(b) Access is open to anyone who wants to join in, and people have equal opportunities to contribute to the dialogue;

(c) People are free to disagree, and differences between them are recognized;

(d) There is space for consensus to be reached, alliances to be formed;

(e) It is talk that makes a difference – it can lead to action (e.g. policy change).

Consider Example 8 (Appendix, pages 241–4), an extract from a British television 'debate' on the future of the monarchy, on which I commented in Chapter 3 with respect to difference. The introduction to the programme depicts it in terms of the audience casting their votes in the telephone 'referendum' after rationally weighing up the evidence and arguments provided in the programme – though this was in fact impossible, because votes had to be cast *during* the programme. There was also a highly questionable implication that the referendum may actually affect the future of the monarchy. Thus the programme seems to claim to be constituting a public sphere drawing citizens into speech and action. Yet the sort of 'dialogue' we have here is problematic as public sphere dialogue which can involve people as citizens on a number of counts. First, participation was by invitation only, whereas public sphere dialogue should be accessible to anyone with an interest. Second, this was a one-off event with tight regulation of time, so there was no room for a process of properly voicing differences and perhaps moving beyond differences to form consensus or alliances, which effective public sphere dialogue would entail. Third, this is not dialogue between equals: the 'dialogue' was regulated by the journalists in terms of who took turns in what order and at what length, selection and change of topic, etc. (In fact the panel of 'experts' in the programme did become a more open dialogue, but only because its members sometimes ignored the chairman's attempts to regulate them.) Aspirations of television towards constituting a public sphere are always limited by commercial pressures to making what journalists perceive as 'good television' – which implies tight regulation of the conduct of dialogue. See Fairclough 1999.

Another problematic area in terms of citizenship and the public sphere is processes of 'consultation' over contentious issues such as the disposal of nuclear waste and the siting of trials of genetically-modified crops (see Example 15). While there is some official provision for 'consultation' with the public on such matters, there is little chance for the development of effective public sphere dialogue or for people to act as citizens on such issues (though they may do so in other forums organized by campaigning groups such as Friends of the Earth). Public meetings tend to be officially viewed as 'consultation' only in the highly reduced sense of officials giving information and answering questions – hardly 'consultation' in any meaningful sense. In so far as real dialogue does emerge on such occasions, it does so through members of the public stretching or by-passing or contesting the 'rules' of the genre. I shall discuss Example 15 in Chapter 10 with respect to citizenship and expertise.

Argument, assumptions and ideologies

A general view of the generic structure of an argument (based on Toulmin 1958) is that it combines three primary moves: Grounds, Warrants, Claim (Gieve 2000, Van Eemeren *et al.* 1997). The Grounds are the premises of the argument, the Warrant is what justifies the inference from the Grounds to the Claim. We can also distinguish Backing, which gives support for Warrants. Let us look at Example 7 (Appendix, pages 239–41). There seem to be two main arguments here which are somewhat confusingly intermingled. The first can be summed up as follows: globalization is often not delivering the goods in the South (Grounds); globalization will deliver the goods if changes are made in national and global governance (Warrant); globalization can deliver the goods (Backing); changes should be made in global and national governance (Claim). The second: globalization is often perceived in the South in terms of social challenges rather than economic opportunities (Grounds); perceptions can be changed through organizational change (change in governance) (Warrant); changes should be made in national and global governance (Claim). The mixture of these two arguments leads to an ambivalence: is this an argument about how to make globalization work for the South, or about how to make it seem to work ('seem more humane')?

Notice also that the Backing for the first argument is assumed rather than explicitly asserted – indeed the title presupposes that globalization can deliver the goods. A general difficulty in analysing arguments is that elements of arguments may be implicit, taken for granted, assumed (recall the discussion of assumptions in chapter 3). But notice also that the assumption that globalization *can* deliver the goods (in 'the South') is a highly contentious assumption, and an assumption which is associated with a particular, neo-liberal, economic discourse, as are other claims and assumptions here (that growth will come if certain structural and policy changes are made, that the benefits of growth 'should' reach all, that 'transparency' reduces inequality). Warrants and Backing for arguments are often specific to particular discourses, and often assumed rather than made explicit (Gieve 2000). Where this is so, one might consider the ideological work that a text is doing, i.e. the work of making contentious, positioned and interested representations a matter of general 'common sense'. From a different point of view, one might see arguing on the basis of a contentious and questionable assumption as flawed argument.

This analysis is very abstract, however – it represents the logical structure of the main arguments but not the texturing of the arguments, not the way they are developed in the text, which also contains a number of what we might call 'sub-arguments' as well as the main arguments. So it is useful to supplement such an abstract formulation of arguments with analysis of their textual elaboration. One complication here is 'voice': is this text reporting (the arguments within) a debate (as it purports to be – that is implied in 'a view from the South' in the heading), developing an argument 'of its own', or both? I think the answer is, both, which means it is ambivalent in terms of its main genre – is it a report, or an exposition?

Let's look more closely at the second half of paragraph 4, from 'Cultural homogenization'. Two arguments are reported on the theme of cultural homogenization, one attributed to 'many', the other to 'others'. The former is identified as a 'fear'. The latter is developed over three sentences, only the first of which contains an attribution ('others disagree'). Notice in particular the third of these sentences ('In a world with close contact . . .'), which formulates the Claim ('governors must be careful not to steer diversity down the destructive paths of the past'). Whose Claim is this? There is a similar ambivalence in the following argument about rich and poor, which consists only of Claims without Grounds (or Warrants). The first of its two sentences vaguely attributes a Claim by identifying it as 'concern' (somebody is concerned – but who?), whereas the two Claims of the second sentence ('the benefits of overall growth should reach all', 'economies that are more transparent tend to have less income inequalities') are not attributed. Again, whose Claims are these?

Arguments can take a dialogical form, i.e. the form of two or more people arguing. But it is also useful to analyse 'monological' arguments such as this one in a dialogical way. Some arguments have a more or less explicit or implicit 'protagonist–antagonist' organization. This is arguably the case here, though the identity of the protagonist in particular is not that clear. The 'fear' and 'concern' of antagonists are answered by the counter-arguments of a protagonist. The title ('a view from the South') would seem to suggest that the antagonist is (someone speaking for) the South, representing the view and the arguments of the South. Yet here and elsewhere, the text seems to be organized in terms of some unidentified protagonist (someone speaking for the executive of the World Economic Forum, perhaps?) arguing against views from the South. So I am left wondering whether this is a summary of views from the South, or an argument against these views.

The argument around the case of Ghana in paragraph 5 shows a similar ambivalence. The second sentence of the paragraph (beginning 'Ghana') formulates the Grounds. The following sentences again set up an antagonist–protagonist opposition over Claims, opposing the 'common' claim that globalization is to blame with what 'some say', with an unattributed elaboration of the Claim in the final sentence ('the fundamental structures of a market economy . . . must first be in place'). The mantra of neo-liberalism is implicit in the (again unidentified) protagonist's argument: countries must compete for investment and growth, and follow the prescriptions of organizations like the IMF to succeed. In the final paragraph, the Claim 'leaders will make things easier by striving for good governance', which is also reformulated in the following sentence, seems to be addressed to 'the South', though it's not clear by whom, who the protagonist is – are we perhaps to take it as what some people from 'the South' say about others? It isn't clear. 'Leaders' are the antagonists in this case, though we are not given their arguments (maybe to the effect that there are problems in increasing 'transparency', etc.). These two final paragraphs contain the clearest formulations of the Claims of main arguments 1 and 2 respectively, so we can see the text as a whole as building up to these key Claims.

The points can be related to the discussion of difference in chapter 3: there is an obfuscation of difference here, perhaps a covert polemic in which the identities of the two 'sides' are left unclear.

Narrative

Bal (1997) approaches the analysis of narratives in terms of an analytical distinction between: fabula, story (this distinction originates in Russian formalism), and narrative text (see also Ochs 1997, Toolan 1998). The fabula is the 'material or content that is worked into a story', a 'series of logically and chronologically related events'. The story is a fabula that is 'presented in a certain manner' – this involves for instance the arrangement of events in a sequence which can be different from their actual chronological order, providing the social agents of actual events with 'distinct traits' which transform them into 'characters', and 'focalizing' the story in terms of a particular 'point of view'. The same story can appear in a range of narrative texts, texts in which a narrator relates the story in a particular medium – for instance a story in conversation, a radio news story, a television news story, a documentary, or a film.

I shall use this general framework to discuss specifically the stories one finds in news. Let us go back first to the short newspaper story I discussed above:

> *Firemen Tackle Blaze*
>
> Night shift workers on a coating line at Nairn Coated Products, St George's Quay, Lancaster had to be evacuated when fire broke out in an oven on Wednesday evening.
>
> Four fire engines attended the incident and firemen wearing breathing apparatus tackled the flames which had started when a break off in an oven caught fire under the infra red element.
>
> The fire caused severe damage to 20 metres of metal trunking, and to the interior of a coating machine and the coating room was smoke logged.
>
> But the department was running again by Thursday morning.
>
> *Lancaster Guardian*, 7 October 1986

The fabula can be summed up in terms of the events in their actual chronological order (which can be more or less deduced from the story): a fire broke out (a break off in an oven caught fire; the coating room was smoke logged; metal trunking and a coating machine were damaged), workers were evacuated, firefighters tackled the flames, the department was running again the next morning. The story places events in a sequence which differs from their chronological order. In the headline, the action by the firefighters is in focus (the fire is represented in a nominalization ('blaze') which is grammatically the object of 'tackle'). The lead paragraph, the representation of the evacuation of workers precedes the representation of the fire (the latter is in a subordinate clause). In the following paragraph, representation of the action of the firefighters precedes representation of the fire (again the latter is in a subordinate clause). The sequence is then: the damage caused by the fire, the department getting back to normal. These sequential features focalize the story in terms of the response to the fire (evacuation, firefighters tackling the fire) rather than the fire itself. This is not just a matter of sequence: the genre of news (accident) report provides positions of salience which are germane to this focalization. It is there in the headine and the lead-paragraph, and one might see the positioning of 'resumption of work as normal' in the wrap-up as giving it a salience which is also part of the focalization: the journalistic point of focalizes reponses to the accident and the restoration of normality. The narrative text is a written report, and the narrator is of course a journalist.

News is making stories out of series of logically and chronologically related events. One way of seeing news is as a form of social regulation, even a form of violence: news reduces complex series of events whose relationship may not be terribly clear to stories, imposing narrative order upon them. And it is not simply the relationship between an actual series of events in a particular order, and the story about them. Producing news stories is more fundamentally a matter of construing what may be fragmentary and ill-defined happenings as distinct and separate events, including certain happenings and excluding others, as well setting these constructed events into particular relations with each other. Making news is a heavily interpretative and constructive process, not simply a report of 'the facts'. This does not mean that news narratives are just the same as fictional narratives: news narratives, like historical narratives (Callinicos 1995), have a 'referential intention' which makes them open to questions about the relationship between story and actual events, questions of truth. They also have, one might say, an 'explanatory intention' which we can liken to 'focalization': to make sense of events by drawing them into a relation which incorporates a particular point of view. If we see news as part of the apparatus of governance (see chapter 2), this highlights the sense in which news stories are oriented to regulating and controlling events, and the ways in which people respond to events (Allan 1999).

I discussed Example 6 in chapter 3 from the perspective of intertextuality, the representation of voices and of speech. This is a story whose fabula is made up of events which are primarily speech events, as is often the case in news stories. The issue of selectivity necessarily arises: journalists are in the business of including some things which were said and excluding others (which often means excluding certain voices), selecting particular parts of what was said, and generally ordering what is often a cacophony of speech and writing into separate speech events. My comments on the example in chapter 3 point to the way in which the sequencing of events in the story, as well as the framing of events, contribute to a particular focalization which sets up a covert protagonist–antagonist relation between the West and Libya.

Let me briefly comment on this example in terms of Activity, Social Relations, and Communication Technologies. Radio news stories have a relatively well-defined generic structure which is similar to the generic structure of stories in newspapers (in having a headline and a lead, for example) but differs in ways which are linked to medium and communication technology – such as the movement between a main narrator (the newsreader) and a subsidiary narrator (the correspondent) and the inclusion of recorded extracts (in this case, from a statement by the Libyan Foreign Minister). The question of purpose is a complex and controversial one. On the most obvious level, news stories have the purpose of telling people what of significance has happened in the world, but if we think in terms of hierarchies of purpose, and of the relationship between the fields of news media, politics, business and so forth, we are faced with questions about news media as part of an apparatus of governance – in this case, for instance, can we reasonably attribute to such stories higher-level purposes which connect them to international politics? The same issues arise with respect to social relations: are the social relations of news simply the social relations between journalists and audiences (relations of information giving, which give rise to questions about the authoritativeness of journalists, and so forth)? Or are the social relations of news stories covertly social relations between rulers and ruled – between government, business and so forth and the people? We might ask: whose focalization, whose point of view, is this? Finally, shifts in communication technologies have had a significant effect on news. This is clearer if we think of television news, where the whole balance between verbal story and visual and filmic image has shifted, to the point where it seems that the availability or unavailability of good film footage can be decisive in determining whether there is a story or not. At this point, we perhaps need to wonder whether the distinction between news narratives and fictional narratives is really clearcut: the aesthetics of news stories seems to become an increasingly salient issue, sometimes at the expense of their answerability to real events and questions of truth, at the same time as 'wall-to-wall news' assumes the social psychological role (once held by religion) of 'inoculating us from dread, from the numbing anxieties of a high-risk world' (Silverstone 1999).

Summary

We have seen that genre analysis proceeds from genre chains, to genre mixture, to properties of individual genres. Genres can be identified at different levels of abstraction: pre-genres, disembedded genres (which are significant within the 'disembedding' which is a feature of 'globalization'), and situated genres. Texts can combine different genres in various ways – mixing or hybridizing them, combining them in 'formats', or hierarchizing them into main genres and sub-genres. Individual genres can be differentiated in terms of Activity, Social Relations, and Communication Technology (what are people doing, what are the social relations between them, and what communication technology (if any) does their activity depend on?). With respect to Activity, only certain genres are well-defined in terms of purpose and generic structure (organization into well-defined stages), and these tend to be specialized within social systems for 'strategic' (rather than 'communicative') action. Some genres can be seen as mystifying Social Relations through 'conversationalization', simulation of conversational exchange in public contexts, which is an aspect of societal 'informalization'. Change in genres (including genre chains) is a significant aspect of technological change and the new information technologies. We discussed three specific (pre-)genres: dialogue, specifically in relation to the question of what constitutes adequate or effective public sphere dialogue, argument, in terms of the ideological significance of implicit assumptions in argument, and narrative, especially in relation to news.

5 Meaning relations between sentences and clauses

Text analysis issues

Semantic relations between sentences and clauses: causal, conditional, temporal, additive, elaborative, contrastive
Grammatical relations between clauses: paratactic and hypotactic relations

Social research issues

Legitimation
Hegemony, equivalence and difference
Appearance and reality

The focus in this chapter is on meaning relations, semantic relations, between sentences, and between clauses (or 'simple sentences') within sentences. We shall be looking for instance at causal or logical relations between sentences and clauses (for instance relations of purpose, e.g. 'You will be weighed *so that* your subsequent weight gain can be assessed', from an ante-natal text which I discuss below), or contrastive relations (e.g. 'You look at a set of elements, the same ones that everyone else sees, *but* then reassemble those floating bits and pieces into an enticing new possibility', from Example 9, a management 'guru' text also discussed later). We shall also look at how these semantic relations are 'realized' in various grammatical structures. The connection between this chapter and chapter 4 is that the type of semantic relations between sentences and clauses that one finds in a text depends on genre.

A number of social research issues can be elucidated by focusing on these semantic relations. One of these is the issue of legitimation (Habermas 1976, Van Leeuwen (undated), Van Leeuwen and Wodak 1999). According to Weber (1964), 'every system of authority attempts to establish and to cultivate the belief in its legitimacy', and according to Berger and Luckmann (1966) 'legitimation provides the 'explanations' and justifications of the salient elements of the institutional tradition'. One issue in research on the transformations of new capitalism is changes in legitimation, changes in how the new order is explained and justified. People are constantly concerned in social life, and in what they say or write, with claiming or questioning the legitimacy of actions which are taken, procedures which exist in organizations, and so forth. This means that textual analysis is a significant resource for researching legitimation.

The second issue is **equivalence and difference** – what Laclau and Mouffe (1985) identify, with respect to political hegemony, as the simultaneous operation of a 'logic of difference' and a 'logic of equivalence'. These are respectively tendencies towards creating and proliferating differences between objects, entities, groups of people, etc. and collapsing or 'subverting' differences by representing objects, entities, groups of people, etc. as equivalent to each other. This may seem to be a rather abstract theoretical point, but it is an aspect of the continuous social process of **classification**. Classification has crucial effects such as whether political processes and relations are predominantly represented, understood and acted upon in terms of a division between 'left' and 'right', or how diverse economic and social phenomena and changes are subsumed under 'globalization' as equivalent instances or aspects of it. Thus classification and categorization shape how people think and act as social agents. Equivalence and difference are in part textual relations, and it is fruitful to 'operationalize' this rather abstract theoretical point in text analysis, looking at how entities of various sorts (people, objects, organizations, and so forth) are differentiated in texts, and how differences between them are collapsed by 'texturing' relations of equivalence between them. With respect to semantic relations between clauses and sentences, the former involves contrastive relations (which may be formally marked by conjunctions 'but', 'instead of', and sentence adverbials like 'however'), the latter involves additive and elaborative relations, for example making entities equivalent by including them in lists. One can put the point in different terms: the 'work' of classification is constantly going on in texts, with entities being either differentiated from one another, put in opposition to one another, or being set up as equivalent to one another.

A third issue might be contentiously formulated as: appearances and reality. A classical form of critique within the Marxist tradition is directed at social (economic, political) analysis which does not go beyond 'surface' appearances to 'underlying' realities, takes things at face value rather than considering them as the causal effects of structures. I have taken a position on this issue in chapter 2, arguing that events be seen as the effects of the causal powers of both social structures and practices, and of the agency of their participants. In the context of new capitalism, this issue is of some relevance to when one looks for instance at representations of the economic and social changes which are going on, for example in policy documents of various types. I shall contrast an 'explanatory logic' and a 'logic of appearances' – these representations often do not go any 'deeper' than listing appearances which evidence change, rather than offering explanatory accounts of change in terms of causal relations.

I shall proceed by briefly setting out the analytical categories and distinctions, and then use them in a discussion of the social research issues.

Semantic relations

Below is a summary of the main semantic relations between sentences and clauses. I have given examples in brackets, italicizing conjunctions (e.g. 'because', 'and', 'but') which mark these relations. Notice that there is no conjunction in the case of Elaboration – these semantic relations are not always explicitly marked. I have distinguished a relatively small number of main semantic relations – further distinctions are certainly possible. (These distinctions draw upon similar accounts in Halliday 1994, Martin 1992.)

Causal
  Reason (We were late *because* the train was delayed)
  Consequence (The train was delayed, *so* we were late)
  Purpose (We left early *in order to* catch the first train)

Conditional (*If* the train is delayed, we shall be late))

Temporal (We were worried *when* the train was delayed)

Additive (What a day! The train was delayed, *and* the dog was sick)

Elaboration (including Exemplification, Rewording) (The train was delayed – it was due at 7.30 and arrived at 9.00)

Contrastive/concessive (The train was delayed, *but* we were still in time)

The following short examples illustrate a number of these semantic relations – I have identified the relations in capitals between the sentences or clauses which are related, and underlined connectors which mark the relations where they occur (in some cases they don't).

Firemen Tackle Blaze

Night shift workers on a coating line at Nairn Coated Products, St George's Quay, Lancaster had to be evacuated TEMPORAL <u>when</u> fire broke out in an oven on Wednesday evening.

Four fire engines attended the incident ELABORATION <u>and</u> firemen wearing breathing apparatus tackled the flames ADDITIVE <u>which</u> had started TEMPORAL <u>when</u> a break off in an oven caught fire under the infra red element.

ADDITIVE The fire caused severe damage to 20 metres of metal trunking, and to the interior of a coating machine ADDITIVE <u>and</u> the coating room was smoke logged.

CONTRASTIVE <u>But</u> the department was running again by Thursday morning.

Lancaster Guardian, 7 October 1986

Examination

You will be weighed PURPOSE <u>so that</u> your subsequent weight gain can be assessed. ADDITIVE Your height will be measured, REASON <u>since</u> small women on the whole have a slightly smaller pelvis than tall women – ELABORATION <u>which</u> is not surprising. TEMPORAL A complete physical examination will <u>then</u> be carried out ELABORATION <u>which</u> will include checking your breasts, heart, lungs, blood pressure, abdomen and pelvis. PURPOSE <u>The purpose of this</u> is to identify any abnormalities which might be present, CONTRASTIVE <u>but</u> which so far have not caused you any problems. ADDITIVE A vaginal examination will enable the pelvis to be assessed PURPOSE <u>in order to</u> check the condition of the uterus, cervix and the vagina. ADDITIVE A cervical smear is <u>also</u> often taken at this time PURPOSE <u>to</u> exclude any early pre-cancerous change which rarely may be present.

(Morris 1986)

We can begin to see even from these short examples the relationship between semantic relations and genre. The first example is a report from a local newspaper – more specifically, an accident report. I discussed its generic structure in chapter 4. News reports are a type of narrative, so one would expect temporal relations between events to be specified ('this happened, then that happened'). Additive and elaborative relations are also predictable – reports accumulate details about events.

A rough test of whether clauses or sentences are in additive or elaborative relations is to see whether the order in which they come can be reversed. For instance, the third paragraph ('The fire caused . . .' – notice that these paragraphs consist of only one sentence) could have preceded the second paragraph, and the second clause of the third paragraph ('the coating room . . .') could have preceded the first. These are additive relations – one thing is simply added to another, there is no implication of any further relationship between them. By contrast, the first two clauses of the second paragraph are in an elaborative relationship: the second clause ('firemen wearing breathing apparatus . . .') specifies and fills out the information given in the first, and their order could not really be reversed. The contrastive semantic relation at the end is also predictable in this genre – it realizes what I called the 'wrap-up' in chapter 4, they way in which such reports tend to conclude with how things got back to 'normal'.

The second example, an extract from a booklet given out in ante-natal clinics, can also be seen as a sort of narrative in the broad sense that it represents events in temporal sequence. But rather than recounting actual events, it describes a procedure (see Martin 1992 for this distinction). Temporal, additive and elaborative relations are still salient, but what is striking is the prominence of a relation which does not occur in the other example – purpose. There are four purpose relations even in this short extract. Why? Because texts of this sort foreground legitimation. To put the point in a commonsensical way, if pregnant women are subjected to all these tests and so forth, they are more likely to accept the process if they understand what motivates it, why it is all necessary from a medical point of view. So legitimation is not only present, it is as I said 'foregrounded', there are many explicit markers of purpose, the text is worded in a way which draws attention to the rationality of the procedure.

Higher-level semantic relations

In addition to relatively 'local' semantic relations between clauses and sentences, we can identify more 'global' or higher-level semantic relations over longer stretches of text, or even whole texts. One very common example is the 'problem–solution' relation (Hoey 1983, Hoey 2001, Winter 1982). For instance, many advertisements are built around this relation: the 'problem' is the needs or desires attributed to potential consumers, the 'solution' is the product (e.g. 'dry skin' may be the 'problem', Brand X skincream may be the 'solution'). Another important relation is the Goal–Achievement relation, which is common, for instance, in recipes which are organized in terms of a Goal (making a particular dish) and a method for Achievement (Hoey 2001).

The 'problem–solution' relation is also pervasive in policy texts of various sorts, for instance in Example 7. The problem and the existence of (though not the nature of) a solution are assumed in the heading, 'How can globalization deliver the goods?' This implies that globalization is not actually delivering the goods (producing beneficial outcomes), which is the 'problem', but the 'how'-question also implies that there are ways of solving it. The 'problem–solution' relation occurs again in the opening paragraph: the 'problem' is formulated in the first two sentences, the third sentence assumes that the expectations of the southern hemisphere can be met, i.e. that the 'problem' can be solved. There is then quite a complex recurrence of 'problem–solution' relations throughout the text.

As I pointed out in chapter 4, Example 7 is ambivalent in various ways. It is ambivalent in terms of what the 'problem' is – is it that globalization is not working, or that globalization is seen not to be working? Correspondingly, some 'solutions' appear to address the former (notably the structural change advocated in the penultimate paragraph, putting in place 'the fundamental structures of a market economy'), while other 'solutions' (those that involve the 'voices' of 'developing countries' being 'heard') seem to address the latter. Of course, some would argue that the real 'problems' of globalization are not actually addressed at all in this text, still less any 'solutions'.

Grammatical relations

Semantic relations are realized in a range of grammatical and lexical (vocabulary) features of texts – or to put it differently, there is a range of textual markers of these relations. Let us begin with grammatical relations between clauses within sentences – paratactic, hypotactic and embedded relations. Clauses are either *paratactically* related or *hypotactically* related (Eggins 1994, Halliday 1994, Quirk *et al.* 1972, 1995).

- *Parataxis*

    Clauses are grammatically 'equal' or 'coordinate' (e.g. 'the birds were singing *and* the fish were jumping' – the coordinating conjunction is italicized).

- *Hypotaxis*

    One clause, the 'subordinate' clause, is subordinated to another, the 'main' clause (e.g. 'the birds were singing *because* the sun was shining' – the second clause, with the conjunction 'because', is the subordinate one).

There is one further relation:

● *Embedding*

One clause functions as an element of another clause (its subject, for example), or as an element of a phrase (e.g. 'the man *who came to dinner*').

Let us illustrate these distinctions with the same two examples. In this case, I have identified grammatical relations in capitals between related clauses, and underlined embedded clauses. Conjunctions and other connectors are also again underlined.

Firemen Tackle Blaze

Night shift workers on a coating line at Nairn Coated Products, St George's Quay, Lancaster had to be evacuated HYPOTAXIS when fire broke out in an oven on Wednesday evening.

Four fire engines attended the incident PARATAXIS and firemen wearing breathing apparatus tackled the flames HYPOTAXIS which had started HYPOTAXIS when a break off in an oven caught fire under the infra red element.

The fire caused severe damage to 20 metres of metal trunking, and to the interior of a coating machine PARATAXIS and the coating room was smoke logged.

PARATAXIS But the department was running again by Thursday morning.

Examination

You will be weighed HYPOTAXIS so that your subsequent weight gain can be assessed. Your height will be measured, HYPOTAXIS since small women on the whole have a slightly smaller pelvis than tall women – HYPOTAXIS which is not surprising. A complete physical examination will then be carried out HYPOTAXIS which will include checking your breasts, heart, lungs, blood pressure, abdomen and pelvis. The purpose of this is to identify any abnormalities which might be present, PARATAXIS but which so far have not caused you any problems. A vaginal examination will enable the pelvis to be assessed HYPOTAXIS in order to check the condition of the uterus, cervix and the vagina. A cervical smear is also often taken at this time HYPOTAXIS to exclude any early pre-cancerous change which rarely may be present.

(Morris 1986)

Notice that clauses with 'relative pronouns' (*which* in this case, though *who*, *that*, etc. can also be relative pronouns) are taken as in hypotactic relations in some cases, and as embedded in others. Two types of relative clause are conventionally distinguished (Halliday 1994, Quirk *et al*. 1972): 'restrictive' or 'defining', and 'non-restrictive' or 'non-defining' – the former define or specify or delimit nouns in noun phrases (e.g. 'any abnormalities which might be present'), the latter are really equivalent to, for example, 'and this' ('which is not surprising' might be reworded as 'and this is not surprising') and are elements of sentences rather than elements of noun phrases.

In addition to these grammatical relations between clauses within sentences, the two examples have a number of cohesive markers of semantic relations between sentences. The first example has 'but' at the beginning of its final sentence, the second example has 'then', 'the purpose of this', and 'also'. The literature on 'cohesion' (Eggins 1994, Halliday and Hasan 1976, Halliday 1994, Martin 1992) includes under that rubric a variety of cohesive relations between sentences:

(a)   Reference relations: the definite article ('the'), demonstrative pronouns ('this', 'that', and personal pronouns ('he', 'she', 'it', 'they') are markers of reference back to earlier sentences, or forward to later ones.

(b)   Lexical (vocabulary) relations: predictable patterns of co-occurrence between words (such as 'weighed' and 'measured' at the beginning of the second example) constitute lexical 'chains' through texts.

(c)   Conjunctive relations between sentences are marked by conjunctions such as 'but' in the last sentence of the first example, or sentence connectors like 'therefore' or 'however'.

Explanatory logic versus logic of appearances

Let us look at Example 11, from the British Government's Green Paper (consultative document) 'The Learning Age', in terms of the distinctions above. I have indicated semantic relations between sentences and clauses in capitals for the first section of the extract, and underlined markers of semantic relations.

We are in a new age – the age of information and global competition. ELABORATION Familiar certainties and old ways of doing things are disappearing. ADDITION The types of jobs we do have changed ADDITION as have the industries in which we work and the skills they need. ADDITION

<u>At the same time</u>, new opportunities are opening up ADDITION <u>as</u> we see the potential of new technologies to change our lives for the better. ADDITION (CONSEQUENCE?) We have no choice but to prepare for this new age in which the key to success will be the continuous education and development of the human mind and imagination.

The rest of the section can be seen as an elaboration of the first sentence, and semantic relations between sentences and clauses within that elaboration are additive (though I have queried whether the final sentence might be seen as in a relation of consequence with those which precede it – see below). The representation of the 'new age' and of the changes it entails is basically an unordered list of appearances – unordered in the sense that they could quite easily be reordered (for instance, sentence 3 could precede sentence 2). Also, the appearances or evidences listed are quite diverse – changes in industries, jobs, skills, outlooks ('certainties'). A different way of representing these changes might include causal relations between changes in one area and changes in others (e.g. 'new skills are needed because industries have changed', 'familiar certainties are disappearing because old ways of doing things are disappearing').

The contrast here is between the 'logic of appearances' we actually have in this extract, and an 'explanatory logic', which as a developed analysis of social change might be an elaborate tracing of causal relations between other kinds of change, e.g. economic, educational and social psychological. We can see this contrast in terms of genre difference: the genre is actually in Martin's terms 'report' (generalized description – not description of concrete events or processes, but description of processes at a high degree of abstraction from the concrete, Martin 1992), whereas what I am saying is that it might have been 'exposition' (explanatory, not just descriptive, and a form of explicit argument – see chapter 4). Additive and elaborative semantic relations are predictable in a report.

Many contemporary policy texts show this tendency to prefer report and a logic of appearances over exposition and an explanatory logic, and it is worth considering why. A socio-economic analysis of the 'new age' would entail explanation, causality, and expository argument. Without analysis there can be no real understanding of the 'new age', and no real sense of its contingency – how changing things at one level could produce different possibilities. Analysis also introduces time depth, a sense of how changes over a certain period of time can produce effects subsequently. These features are absent in this example as in many contemporary policy texts. Many of these texts can be seen to limit policy options by portraying the socio-economic order as simply given, an unquestionable and inevitable horizon which is itself untouchable by policy and narrowly constrains options, essential rather than contingent, and without time depth. Moreover, these texts often appear to be promotional rather than analytical, concerned more to persuade people that these are indeed the only practicable policies than to open up dialogue. This form of report is what we might call 'hortatory report': descriptions with a covert prescriptive intent, aimed at getting people to act in certain ways on the basis of representations of what is. I shall return to these themes in chapter 6.

'Hortatory report' is a very common contemporary genre, not only in the domain of policy formation in government, but also for instance in the 'management guru' literature which gives persuasive reports on transformations in economies, societies and businesses with hortatory intent – to provide managers with blue-prints for transforming their own practice. Example 9 (below) is an extract from a recent book by a well-known management 'guru', Rosabeth Moss Kanter of the Harvard Business School. I have shown semantic relations between sentences and clauses (and similar relations between phrases in two cases) in the same way as above.

Companies that are successful on the web operate differently from their laggard counterparts. ELABORATION On my global e-culture survey, those reporting that they are much better than their competitors in the use of the Internet tend to have flexible, empowering, collaborative organizations. ADDITION The 'best' are more likely than the 'worst' to indicate, at statistically significant levels, that

- Departments collaborate (CONTRAST <u>instead of</u> sticking to themselves). ADDITION
- Conflict is seen as creative (CONTRAST <u>instead of</u> disruptive). ADDITION
- People can do anything not explicitly prohibited (CONTRAST <u>instead of</u> doing only what is explicitly permitted). ADDITION
- Decisions are made by the people with the most knowledge (CONTRAST <u>instead of</u> the ones with the highest rank).

ADDITION Pacesetters and laggards describe no differences in how hard they work (in response to a question about whether work was confined to traditional hours or spilled over into personal time), CONTRAST <u>but</u> they are very different in how *collaboratively* they work.

Working in e-culture mode requires organizations to be communities of purpose. ELABORATION Recall the elements of community sketched in chapter 1. ELABORATION A community makes people feel like members, not just employees – members with privileges but also responsibilities beyond the immediate job, extending to colleagues in other areas. ADDITION Community means having things in common, a range of shared understandings transcending specific fields. ELABORATION Shared understandings permit relatively seamless processes, interchangeability among people, smooth formation of teams that know how to work together even if they have never previously met, and rapid transmission of information. ADDITION In this chapter we will see how the principles of community apply inside organizations and workplaces, sometimes facilitated by technology but also independent of it. ADDITION <u>And</u> I will examine the challenges that have to be overcome to create organizational communities.

ADDITION The greater integration that is integral to e-culture is different from the centralization of earlier eras. ELABORATION Integration must be accompanied by flexibility and empowerment PURPOSE <u>in order to</u> achieve fast response, creativity, and innovation through improvization. ADDITION Web success involves operating more like a community than a bureaucracy. ELABORATION It is a subtle but important distinction. ELABORATION Bureaucracy implies rigid job descriptions, command-and-control hierarchies, and hoarding of information, ELABORATION <u>which</u> is doled out top-down on a need-to-know basis. ADDITION Community implies a willingness to abide by standardized procedures governing the whole organization, yes, but also voluntary collaboration that is much richer and less programmed. ADDITION Communities can be mapped in formal ways, CONTRAST <u>but</u> they also have an emotional meaning, a feeling of connection. ELABORATION Communities have both a structure and a soul.

This example is a report about types of company, in contrast to the report about contemporary social life in 'the new age' in the previous example. But here again, exposition and an explanatory logic are alternatives to the report and logic of appearances which actually characterize the text. Semantically speaking, we have a similar pattern of elaboration and addition in relations between clauses and sentences; in terms of grammatical relations, parataxis is predominant, hypotaxis is rare (notice the one Purpose relation, which is hypotactic). The example consists mainly of statements of fact, with a couple of normative statements (e.g. 'Integration must be accompanied by flexibility and empowerment'). Again, there is a hortatory element which is implicit rather than explicit – there are no direct injunctions to readers to act in certain ways. It depends upon assumed, implicit values (see chapters 3 and 10) within these apparent statements of fact – for instance, 'rapid transmission of information' is not explicitly evaluated as desirable in the second paragraph, but it is assumed to be desirable, a condition for success, and the implicit message is 'make your organization a community based on shared understandings if you want to succeed!'. The hortatory element also depends upon context: books of this sort are read by managers and executives with an eye to practical issues of how their companies might be improved.

Legitimation

I discussed above an extract from a piece of ante-natal literature in which the semantic relation of purpose was foregrounded. This is an example of legitimation in a particularly explicit form: ante-natal procedures are legitimated by a clear specification of what motivates them in the form of semantic relations of purpose which are explicitly marked by connectors ('so that', 'the purpose of this', 'in order to'). The rationality of the procedures is strongly foregrounded.

But this is only one of a number of strategies for legitimation. Four main strategies are distinguished by Van Leeuwen (undated, see also Van Leeuwen and Wodak 1999):

- *Authorization*

  Legitimation by reference to the authority of tradition, custom, law, and of persons in whom some kind of institutional authority is vested.

- *Rationalization*

  Legitimization by reference to the utility of institutionalized action, and to the knowledges society has constructed to endow them with cognitive validity.

- *Moral Evaluation*

  Legitimation by reference to value systems.

- *Mythopoesis*

  Legitimation conveyed through narrative.

The ante-natal example is an instance of Rationalization, with a strong emphasis on the utility of ante-natal procedures. Habermas (1984) has described modernization as a process in which specialized systems based upon 'instrumental' or 'means-ends' rationality separate themselves out from the rest of social life. The state, including the welfare state and state provision of welfare services such as healthcare, is one such system. Instrumental rationality assumes certain agreed ends, and legitimizes actions or procedures or structures in terms of their utility in achieving these ends. This means that Rationalization overlaps with Moral Evaluation, in the sense that the reasons and purposes given for the procedures evoke value systems which are taken for granted and constitute the 'generalized' motives which according to Habermas (1976) are now widely used 'to ensure mass loyalty'. In this case, the values evoked relate to the 'medicalization' of childbirth: great emphasis is placed upon warding off its risks and dangers – so a procedure designed to detect possible 'early pre-cancerous change' for instance is construed as self-evidently justified. A somewhat misleading feature of this classification of legitimation strategies is that all of them involve 'moral evaluation' in the sense of reference to value systems – so the strategy called 'Moral Evaluation' needs to be taken as moral evaluation without Authorization, Rationalization, or Mythopoesis. This is really the same as what I discussed as 'value assumptions' in chapter 3.

Rationalization is the clearest and most explicit form of legitimation, yet legitimation is also an issue in the two examples I discussed in the previous section, if perhaps less obviously so. I described above the first of these, the extract from the consultative document 'The Learning Age', as a 'report', a generalized description. In fact it makes a link between 'is' ('will' be) and 'must' (see the full extract in the Appendix, Example 11) – what the new age 'is', and what we 'must' do in response to it. This connects with my discussion in the previous section of why policy documents tend towards report rather than exposition: it is typical of many policy documents in a variety of social domains which portray particular policies as made inevitable by the way the world now is (Graham 2001a and b) – in the famous expression of former British Prime Minister Margaret Thatcher, 'there is no alternative' (widely referred to as the 'TINA' principle). Notice the slippage between description and prediction in the report – claims about what is the case alternate with predictions about what 'will' happen. The legitimation here applies to policies, to what we 'must' do, and these policies are legitimated by the claims about the 'new age'. In terms of the strategies of legitimation above, we might say that this is a form of Mythopoesis, though it rather stretches the category as Van Leeuwen describes it – it is not a narrative in the strict sense, it is rather the building up of a picture of the 'new age'. But like the narratives which Van Leeuwen describes it has characteristics of both the 'moral tale' and the 'cautionary tale' – the implication is that certain good things will happen if 'we' do implement the 'inevitable' policies (e.g. 'new opportunities' will open up), and certain bad things will happen if 'we' don't (e.g. we will not be able to 'compete'). Once again, Moral Evaluation is a part of the picture: 'being world leaders', 'competing', 'encouraging imagination and innovation', are desirable in the system of values which is evoked. Notice that there is also one instance of Rationalization (and the semantic relation of Purpose), in paragraph (4): 'To continue to compete, we must equip ourselves . . .'.

The other example discussed in the previous section is the extract from Kanter's managerial text. I suggested above that both examples are instances of 'hortatory report', they urge action on the basis of description, and they are correspondingly similar in terms of legitimation strategies. We can see this again as primarily Mythopoesis, building up a picture of the successful company, though in this case the action that is legitimated (changes in the management of companies) remains largely implicit. The Kanter text also quite extensively uses a strategy which we can see as combining Mythopoesis in something closer to Van Leeuwen's sense (the text is littered with short narratives like the one in the example below), and Authorization, though this is not illustrated in the extract in the Appendix. For instance:

> Changemasters find many ways to monitor external reality. They become idea scouts, attentive to early signs of discontinuity, disruption, threat, or opportunity. They can establish their own listening posts, such as a satellite office in an up-and-coming location, an alliance with an innovative partner, or investments in organizations that are creating the future. Reuters Greenhouse founder John Taysom began to see the potential of new technology when posted in Bahrain, because the peculiarities of transmitting financial information (Reuter's mainstay) suggested problems that technology could solve. Then he put himself in the middle of Silicon Valley and started tuning in. After a few strategic investments, the Reuters Greenhouse Fund opened for business with a philosophy that getting an inside look at a number of innovative companies would be the best way to learn about what was about to happen, not what had already been created.

This is typical of Kanter's book in legitimizing her claims through a short narrative about an authoritative figure or company ('Reuters Greenhouse founder John Taysom'), combining Mythopoesis with Authorization.

Equivalences and differences

Laclau and Mouffe (1985) theorize the political process (and 'hegemony') in terms of the simultaneous working of two different 'logics', a logic of 'difference' which creates differences and divisions, and a logic of 'equivalence' which subverts existing differences and divisions. I want to suggest first that this can usefully be seen as a general characterization of social processes of classification: people in all social practices are continuously dividing and combining – producing (also reproducing) and subverting divisions and differences. Social interaction, as Laclau and Mouffe suggest, is an ongoing work of articulation and disarticulation. My second suggestion is that this can be applied specifically to the textual moment of social events. Elements (words, phrases, etc.) are constantly being combined and divided in texts; prior combinations and separations are constantly being subverted. The point that texts are constantly combining some elements and dividing others is a rather obvious one. But what I am suggesting is that we see these processes as part of the textual moment of the social process of classification.

I pointed out earlier that the semantic relations between clauses and sentences in Examples 9 and 11 are predominantly relations of addition and elaboration, realized grammatically in the main by paratactic relations. In the case of the extract from the latter, 'The Learning Age', I showed above the semantic relations within the first section. If we consider this example from a process point of view, in terms of the relational 'work' that is being done, we might say that relations of meaning inclusion (the term used in semantics is 'hyponymy') are being set up: 'being in a new age' is elaborated in terms of 'familiar certainties and old ways of doing things disappearing', 'the types of job we do changing', 'industries and skills changing', 'new opportunities opening up'. These expressions can be seen as co-hyponyms of 'being in a new age', i.e. the meaning of the latter includes the meanings of the former, which are thereby made equivalent to one another (equivalent in sharing the property of being hyponyms of 'being in a new age'). Setting up such relations of meaning equivalence amounts to backgrounding the meaning differences between these expressions – in the present context, they are secondary. It amounts to building up meanings around the 'new age' which centrally include it being simultaneously a time of risk and a time of 'opportunity'. This textual process of meaning-making is an important element in the political process of seeking to achieve hegemony for neo-liberalism in so far as it contributes to building up a vision of the 'new age' through subverting the division between risk and opportunity, negative and positive (on the connection between vision and 'di-vision', or classification, see Bourdieu and Wacquant 1992). The effectivity of such hegemonic meaning-making is not guaranteed of course – it takes place within a struggle over meaning, and depends for instance on how pervasively these meaning relations are repeated in various types of texts, and how successfully alternatives are excluded.

In the Kanter text, in addition to relations of equivalence, there are also quite a few relations of difference – instances of the semantic relation of contrast, notably in the bullet-pointed list (where there are four instances of the contrastive conjunction 'instead of'). Within that list, relations of equivalence and difference are simultaneously built up. On the one hand, a relation of equivalence (co-hyponymy) between 'departments collaborating', 'conflict being seen as creative', 'people being able to do anything not explicitly prohibited', and 'decisions being made by the people with the most knowledge' are all hyponyms of 'being successful on the web'. And relations of equivalence between 'departments sticking to themselves', 'conflict being seen as disruptive', 'people doing only what is explicitly permitted', 'decisions being made by the people with the highest rank' are all hyponyms of 'being a laggard'. On the other hand, the two lists of co-hyponyms are in a (contrastive) relation of difference.

The process of 'texturing' equivalence and difference is clearer in dialogue, where one can sometimes see the 'work' that people are collaboratively doing to build new meaning relations and 'make meaning'. We can think of Example 10 in this way.

Ben: we thought you know maybe maybe I should be the facilitator for Grace's group or something where I'm away from the people a bit and um

Sally: yeah

Ben: just have a background in what's going on but just sort of keep them on the right track and let them they've got to really then rely on each other instead of relying on the supervisor to do the work

Grace: well I think kind of in the groups that are gonna come along that's what's gonna have to happen. I mean I know the the first ones that start off I think we have to go down this path to try to direct people onto the path and therefore we kind of will be in charge of the meeting but then we have to get people to start their own teams and us sort of just being a facilitator rather than

James: the team leader

[. . .] yeah

Grace: I mean it's hard to get started I think that's where people are having trouble and that's why they're kind of looking to you Ben and you know things like that

Peter: I'm not the only one I'm having trouble maintaining the thing

[. . .] yeah

Peter: I just can't maintain it at the moment you know a couple of days you know a couple of days crook there and you know just the amount of work that builds up it just goes to the back of the queue sort of thing it's shocking

James: so what you really want is the um you've got a a group you start a group and you want one of those people to sort of come out and [. . .] facilitate the group

Peter: just to maintain the group you know like just to keep it just keep the work flowing

Ben: what I'm trying to get across

Peter: cause

Ben: is I'm too close to those people because I

[. . .] yeah

> *Ben:* already go outside of the group and then I'm their supervisor outside
> on the on the floor where maybe if I was facilitating another group where
> I'm not I'm not above them you know I'm not their supervisor or
> whatever um I can go back to my job they can go back to theirs and they
> still um you know it's this their more their team than
>
> *Sally:* yours

What is in focus is 'facilitating' as part of the new management discourse which the company is trying to assimilate. The process of assimilating it can be seen in this extract – 'facilitating' is being assimilated through being worked into relations of equivalence and difference with elements of familiar (and essentially experiential, commonsensical) discourses. We can sum up these relations as follows.

facilitate/facilitator	team leader
keep them on the right track	relying on the supervisor
let them rely on each other	direct people onto the path
people start their own teams	be in charge
maintain the group	supervisor
keep the work flowing	

The left-hand column lists expressions which are worked into a relation of equivalence with 'facilitating' through semantic relations of addition and elaboration, the right-hand column lists another set of expressions equivalent to 'leading (the team)', and a relation of difference is set up between the two sets of expressions through semantic relations of contrast (which are realized by conjunctions such as 'instead of' and 'rather than'). Notice the distribution of expressions like 'sort of' and 'kind of' (hedging expressions): they can be linked to points in the dialogue where the work of setting up equivalences and differences is being done. One can on the one hand see what is going on here as a 'colonization' of local management language by the 'global' new management discourse, but looking at the work of setting equivalences and differences makes it clear that it is simultaneously an 'appropriation' of the new discourse by members of the local management community, taking it in by putting it in relation with what already exists. In other words, there is a dialectic of colonization and appropriation going on, and a global/local dialectic: an active process of reception of the colonizing 'global' discourse, which may have various different outcomes (Chouliaraki and Fairclough 1999).

Summary

We have distinguished a small number of major semantic relations between sentences and clauses (Causal, including Reason, Consequence and Purpose, Conditional, Temporal, Additive, Elaborative, and Contrastive/concessive), and their realization through Paratactic and Hypotactic grammatical relations. We also briefly discussed higher-level semantic relations such as the problem–solution relation. We used this framework to contrast an explanatory logic and a logic of appearances, where the former would involve an expository genre in which causal semantic relations and hypotactic grammatical relations are predominant, whereas the latter (evident in the examples we discussed) involves a genre of report in which additive and elaborative semantic relations, and paratactic grammatical relations predominate, in texts which we characterized as 'hortatory reports'. We linked this distinction to forms of legitimation, suggesting that such texts are characterized by legitimation through especially a form of Mythopoesis, rather than the clearest and most explicit form of legitimation, Rationalization. Finally we considered the idea that Laclau and Mouffe's identification of the simultaneous social logics of equivalence and difference might be 'operationalized' in text analysis, where relations of equivalence are set up as semantic relations of addition and elaboration (and lower-level semantic relations of synonymy and hyponymy), whereas relations of difference are set up as semantic relations of contrast.

6   Clauses

Types of exchange, speech functions and grammatical mood

Textual analysis issues

Types of exchange (knowledge exchange, activity exchange)
Speech functions (statements, questions, demands, offers)
Grammatical mood (declarative, interrogative, imperative)

Social research issues

Communicative and strategic action
Promotional culture
Public policy
Research interviews

In this chapter I shall continue to focus on Actional meanings, though now at the level of the clause or simple sentence. I shall begin with dialogue, and with a distinction between two primary types of exchange in dialogue: 'knowledge exchange', where the focus is on exchange of information, eliciting and giving information, making claims, stating facts, and so forth; and 'activity exchange', where the focus is on activity, on people doing things or getting others to do things. On the basis of this distinction, I shall differentiate a small number of primary speech functions, major categories of things people do with words, including Statements, Questions, Demands and Offers. Speech functions are related to the 'speech acts' which have been widely discussed in linguistic philosophy and linguistic pragmatics (Austin 1962, Levinson 1983, Mey 1993, Searle 1969, Verschueren 1999), but I shall focus on a small number of general functions rather than the plethora of different 'acts' distinguished in this literature. I have drawn upon though modified the approach of Martin (1992). Finally I shall come to grammatical mood, the realization of these meanings in the main 'sentence types', declarative, interrogative and imperative sentences.

The social research issues addressed in this chapter will include a return to Habermas's distinction between communicative and strategic action which I discussed in chapter 4, in relation to genre and purpose. Here my focus will be different: strategic action in texts includes giving an activity exchange the appearance of a (mere) knowledge exchange. I shall also discuss from a textual perspective the view of contemporary culture as **promotional culture** or 'consumer culture' (Featherstone 1991, Wernick 1991), working with Wernick's concept of a 'promoting message' in relation to the blurring of the distinctions between factual and evaluative statements, and factual statements and predictions. This bears upon the nature of contemporary policy formation in various domains, and characteristics of policy texts (Graham 2001a). Finally, I shall draw upon the discussion of Speech Functions and Grammatical Mood to consider certain aspects of research interviews in social science.

Exchanges

An 'exchange' is a sequence of two or more conversational 'turns' or 'moves' with alternating speakers, where the occurrence of move 1 leads to the expectation of move 2, and so forth – with the proviso that what is 'expected' does not always occur. Let us look again at the following simple dialogue (from Cameron 2001) as an example:

1 *Customer*: Pint of Guiness, please.
2 *Bartender*: How old are you?
3 *Customer*: Twenty-two.
4 *Bartender*: OK, coming up.

I shall distinguish two main categories of exchange, both of which are illustrated in this example:

A   Activity exchange (often oriented to non-textual action)
   Customer: Pint of Guiness, please.
   Bartender: OK, coming up.

B   Knowledge exchange
   Bartender: How old are you?
   Customer: Twenty-two.

Notice that the second exchange is inserted within the first exchange in the example – the second part of the activity exchange is delayed until the completion of the knowledge exchange. Activity exchanges are, as in this case, often oriented to non-textual action – doing things, or getting things done, rather than (just) saying things. Though is not necessarily so: 'Answer the question!' is the first part of an activity exchange whose second part is 'expected' to be textual action, i.e. giving an answer. But the focus in this case would be on answering as action, not just the answer as information.

There are two main types of activity exchange, which differ in whether the exchange is initiated by the person who is (or may be) the primary actor in the action which is at issue, or by the person who is not the primary actor. (For the moment I am referring only to the simplest case of two-participant dialogues.)

Actor-initiated activity exchange
>   Do you want a pint of Guinness? (Initiation)
>   Thanks. (Response)
>   (You're welcome) (Follow-up)

Other-initiated activity exchange
>   *Customer:* Pint of Guiness, please. (Initiation)
>   *Bartender:* OK, coming up. (Response)
>   (Thanks) (Follow-up)

In the first case, the exchange is initiated by someone who is offering to act, in the second case by someone who is asking for someone else (the Bartender) to act. I have labelled the moves as Initiation or Response, and included in both an optional (marked by round brackets) third 'move', a 'Follow-up' by the first speaker to the response from the second speaker.

A parallel distinction can be drawn between two types of knowledge exchange – one initiated by the person who has the knowledge (the 'knower'), the other by the person who wants the knowledge:

Knower-initiated knowledge exchange
>   I was twenty-two last birthday. (Initiation)
>   Oh really? (Response)

Other-initiated knowledge exchange
    Bartender: How old are you? (Initiation)
    Customer: Twenty-two. (Response)
    (I see) (Follow-up)

Speech functions

The primary speech functions are distinguished in terms of the different moves in the different types of exchange.

● *Activity exchange*

> Actor-initiated:
> > Do you want a pint of Guinness? (Offer)
> > Thanks (Acknowledgement)
> Other-initiated:
> > *Customer:* Pint of Guiness, please. (Demand)
> > *Bartender:* OK, coming up. (Offer)

● *Knowledge exchange*

> Knower-initiated
> > I was twenty-two last birthday. (Statement)
> > Oh really? (Acknowledgement)
> Other-initiated
> > *Bartender:* How old are you? (Question)
> > *Customer:* Twenty-two (Statement)

The primary speech functions I am distinguishing are: Demand, Offer, Question, Statement – Acknowledgement is a relatively secondary one. One point to note immediately about the terms here is that since I am making only primary distinctions at a general level, 'Demand' for instance includes things which are not 'demands' in the ordinary sense of the term. So, while 'pint of Guiness please' might conceivably be said in a 'demanding' way – though 'please' makes that rather implausible – it is more likely to be called a 'request', or indeed an 'order' in the specific sense of 'ordering' food or drink in restaurants or pubs.

These generalized speech functions could be elaborated and differentiated in terms of many different 'speech acts'. So Offer for instance would include promising, threatening, apologizing, and thanking, and Demand would include ordering, requesting, begging and so forth. But it is not my intention to move in the direction of 'speech act theory' in this book – readers may wish to refer to the literature within linguistic pragmatics on speech acts (for instance, Austin 1962, Levinson 1983, Mey 1993, Searle 1969, Verschueren 1999).

There are a number of significantly different types of Statement which it will be useful to distinguish – distinctions which I draw upon in analysis below.

- **Statements of fact ('realis' statements)**

    Statements about what is, was, has been the case (e.g. 'I met Violeta yesterday evening').

- **'Irrealis' statements**

    Predictions (e.g. 'I will meet Violeta tomorrow') (prediction), and hypothetical statements (e.g. 'I might meet Violeta (if she comes to England)').

- **Evaluations (e.g. 'Violeta is a fine person')**

    These may also be realized as exclamations such as 'What a fine person!'

Statements also may or may not be subjectively marked, which is a matter of 'modality' (see chapter 10): any of these examples might be initiated by a clause with a 'mental process' verb (see chapter 8) such as 'I think' or 'I believe' (e.g. 'I think Violeta is a fine person').

I have begun by referring to dialogue and given a conversational example, but I will assume that the different types of exchange and the speech functions apply to texts of any type, including written texts. The 'exchange' in the case of written texts is played out between the writing and the reading of the text, and there may therefore be considerable temporal and spatial gaps between the initiating and responding moves. Moreover, a written text and especially a mediated text (e.g. a book) will figure in a great many exchanges corresponding to its many readings. Written texts often consist in themselves of nothing but Statements, and responses to them may go on only in readers' heads, so it may seem somewhat tenuous to insist on the concept of exchange in such cases. Nevertheless, all texts imply and are oriented to dialogue in a broad sense, even a diary I write for myself inevitably involves choices in what sort of imaginary reader (be it an imaginary self) to address, and this generalization of the concept of exchange is one way to capture this.

Strategic and communicative action

Habermas (1984) has developed an account of modernity which centres upon communication. Central to the process of modernization is the separation out of 'systems' (notably the state, and the economic system – the market) from the 'lifeworld' (in one sense of that term – the world of ordinary experience). This specialization of systems depends upon a development and refinement of an 'instrumental rationality' in which action is strategic – people act (and act upon other people) in ways which are oriented to achieving results, greater 'effectivity' or 'efficiency' and so forth. Strategic action is contrasted with 'communicative action' – action which is oriented to reaching understanding, the mode of action which is salient in the 'lifeworld'. One can think of these two types of action in textual terms: people talk and write communicatively or strategically, or a mixture of the two. That in itself is not a problem in Habermas's view – the development and refinement of systems and strategic action including strategic ways of texturing is a *sine qua non* of modern life. What is problematic, and indeed potentially 'pathological', is the over-extension of strategic action as part of the 'colonization' of the lifeworld by systems.

Textual analysis can enhance these theoretical claims – or, to put it the other way round, we can 'operationalize' a Habermasian perspective in textual analysis. One level on which this can be revealing is in terms of exchange types and speech functions in clauses. Let us look at Example 2 (Appendix, pages 230–3) ('Festival Town Flourishes') in these terms. On the face of it, this is a text dominated by knowledge exchange – and specifically by knower-initiated knowledge exchange, and consisting of statements, mostly realis statements of fact, though with some predictions ('The town will soon house the General Consultate of the Slovakian Republic') and some evaluations ('Békéscsaba is an excellent choice in this region for investment . . .'). Yet the text is part of an actual and anticipated chain of events whose hoped-for outcome, for the local authority which has produced the text, is investment in the town. And this text in particular is clearly aimed at attracting investment – that is, its main orientation is to activity exchange, to other-initiated activity exchange and Demands on the part of the local authority for corporations to act by investing in the town, and Offers of things which are likely to attract corporations (e.g. a capable and flexible workforce). One can imagine a differently written text in which activity exchange was explicit – for instance this section:

> A capable workforce, improving infrastructure and flexible labor is readily available. In addition, the local education system offers qualified, multi-lingual professionals.

being written as something like:

Need a capable workforce, improving infrastructure, flexible labor and qualified, multi-lingual professionals? Invest in Békéscsaba, and we will give you them!

This is something akin to the distinction between 'hard-sell' and 'soft-sell' advertisements, and part of it is the distinction between directly addressing those to whom one is trying to sell (as in the rewrite) and not directly addressing them (see Myers 1999). Though notice the verb 'offer': the sentence in its original form is not an Offer, it is a Statement of fact, but a Statement of fact about what is on offer – whereas the re-written version *is* an Offer.

So why, one might ask, do we have a text which can be seen as primarily oriented to activity exchange actually written as if it were oriented to knowledge exchange, to giving information rather than 'selling' the town and soliciting investment? Such texts are in fact commonplace in contemporary social life. Universities trying to sell themselves to and attract potential students, medical practices trying to sell themselves to and attract patients, are more likely to produce texts of this sort than 'hard-sell' advertisements, and the same is true in many other fields, even in the sale of commodities such as soap powders. One can see why local authorities or universities, for instance, may tend to avoid more explicit advertising. Although both have been increasingly 'marketized', i.e. increasingly drawn into a market mode of operation which is difficult to resist, neither is simply a market type of organization, both have a difficult line to tread between acting in a market way and acting as governmental and educational organizations. But the communication here can be seen as strategic: for basically institutional reasons, activity exchange (Offers, Demands, 'selling', soliciting 'custom') is presented as if it were knowledge exchange. On one level, one can say that the 'Festival Town Flourishes' text is indeed knowledge exchange, is indeed giving information – but that is clearly not all it is doing, and it is giving information with a more primary purpose in view, successfully 'selling' the town and attracting investment (recall the discussion in chapter 4, including the comments on this example, of hierarchies of purpose, purposes which relatively explicit or implicit).

I said above that the text was mainly statements of fact, with a few predictions and evaluations. However, values and evaluation are clearly fundamental, and this suggests that the distinction between statements of fact and evaluations may not be as clear-cut as it may initially seem to be (Graham 2001a, Lemke 1995). The point is that the statements of fact in this text are pervasively evaluative, but implicitly so. We are in the territory of assumed values (see chapter 3). One need only ask 'why these 'facts' about Békéscsaba rather than the many others?' to see that the facts are selected for the values they convey, within the particular value system that is implicit (a value system appertaining to the world of international business and finance). So 'The town is 200 km south-east of Budapest and easily accessible from the capital by road and train within three hours' is not just stating facts, it is also implicitly evaluating the town as desirable for investors with respect to its position within communication networks.

Noting the implicit value-content of factual statements helps to make a link between the apparent orientation to knowledge-exchange and what I have suggested is a deeper orientation to activity-exchange. One might see evaluations, whether they are explicit or implicit, as a sort of halfway house between Statements and Demands. Values are motives for action, and while there is clearly a difference between Demands ('Invest in Békéscsaba') and evaluations ('Békéscsaba is a good town to invest in'), there is a sense in which the latter covertly invite action as mere statements of fact would not. The basis for the covertly hortatory character of the text becomes clearer.

In discussing explanatory logic and the logic of appearances in chapter 5, I referred to 'hortatory reports', and clearly there is a link between that discussion, which was focused on semantic relations between clauses and sentences, and what I am discussing now. Hortatory reports are also texts, on the level of the clause, which are apparently oriented to knowledge-exchange but actually oriented (also) to activity-exchange, and where factual statements are to a significant degree implicit evaluations. One finds the same exchange features and the same implicit evaluation in the extracts from The Learning Age (Example 11) and the management 'guru' text (Example 9) I discussed there. And the example I have discussed in this section, Example 2, can also be seen as hortatory report, and is like Examples 9 and 11 characterized predominantly by semantic relations of elaboration and addition.

One can see these relationships between apparent knowledge exchange which is actually (also) activity exchange, and apparent factual statements which are actually (also) evaluations, as a form of metaphor in an extended sense. We can include them in what Halliday (1994) calls **grammatical metaphor**, although they might more properly be called 'pragmatic metaphor' in the sense that it is a matter of one speech function apparently being another. I shall discuss 'grammatical metaphor' more fully in chapter 8.

Promotional culture

Habermas's rather abstract account of the relationship between strategic and communicative action can be made more concrete in terms of the concept of 'promotion' and the view of contemporary culture as 'promotional culture' (Wernick 1991). Wernick's understanding of contemporary culture as 'promotional culture' is summed up as follows: 'the range of cultural phenomena which, at least as one of their functions, serve to communicate a promotional message has become, today, virtually co-extensive with our produced symbolic world'. In other words, all sorts of texts (e.g. university prospectuses, various types of report such as the annual report of a company) which may be primarily doing other things (e.g. informing) are nowadays simultaneously promoting. A 'promoting message' is understood by Wernick to be one which simultaneously 'represents (moves in place of), advocates (moves on behalf of), and anticipates (moves ahead of)' whatever it is to which it refers.

The 'Festival Town Flourishes' text represents the town, advocates the town as a place to invest in, and one might say to some extent 'anticipates' the town in the sense that it projects the way it is onto the way it would be or will be as a centre of major international investment:

> Pap said Békéscsaba was situated on the cross-roads of the trans-European traffic network, serving as the nation's south-eastern gateway to central and eastern Europe. 'Because of its geographical position, Békéscsaba is an excellent choice in this region for investment and for locating businesses that want to penetrate the market in this part of the world,' he added.

Representing the town as a 'gateway' to central and eastern Europe from which businesses can 'penetrate the market' envisages it as an imaginary future hub of regional business activity.

Wernick's view of the 'promoting message' as simultaneously representing and advocating makes sense of the pervasive implicit value content of factual statements and the calculative selection of factual statements for the values they evoke. But seeing the representational and advocatory 'promoting message' as simultaneously 'anticipating' also points to another widespread feature of contemporary texts: the blurring of the distinction between statements of fact and predictions. We can connect this to what Bourdieu and Wacquant (2001) have identified as one significant feature of the texts of new capitalism: their 'performative power' in bringing into being what they purport to (merely) describe.

Let us look at the following extract from Example 5, Tony Blair's speech at the time of the attack on the World Trade Centre in New York and the initiation of the 'war on terrorism'.

> And, more than ever now, with every bit as much thought and planning, we will assemble a humanitarian coalition alongside the military coalition so that inside and outside Afghanistan, the refugees, four-and-a-half million on the move even before 11 September, are given shelter, food and help during the winter months.

The world community must show as much its capacity for compassion as for force. The critics will say: but how can the world be a community? Nations act in their own self-interest. Of course they do. But what is the lesson of the financial markets, climate change, international terrorism, nuclear proliferation or world trade? It is that our self-interest and our mutual interests are today inextricably woven together.

This is the politics of globalization. I realize why people protest against globalization. We watch aspects of it with trepidation. We feel powerless, as if we were now pushed to and fro by forces far beyond our control. But there's a risk that political leaders, faced with street demonstrations, pander to the argument rather than answer it. The demonstrators are right to say there's injustice, poverty, environmental degradation.

But globalization is a fact and, by and large, it is driven by people. Not just in finance, but in communication, in technology, increasingly in culture, in recreation. In the world of the Internet, information technology and TV, there will be globalization. And in trade, the problem is not there's too much of it; on the contrary there's too little of it.

The issue is not how to stop globalization. The issue is how we use the power of community to combine it with justice. If globalization works only for the benefit of the few, then it will fail and will deserve to fail. But if we follow the principles that have served us so well at home – that power, wealth and opportunity must be in the hands of the many, not the few – if we make that our guiding light for the global economy, then it will be a force for good and an international movement that we should take pride in leading. Because the alternative to globalization is isolation.

Confronted by this reality, round the world, nations are instinctively drawing together. In Quebec, all the countries of North and South America deciding to make one huge free trade area, rivalling Europe. In Asia, ASEAN. In Europe, the most integrated grouping of all, we are now 15 nations. Another 12 countries negotiating to join, and more beyond that.

Notice the rather perplexing mixture of factual statement and prediction about 'globalization' (paragraphs 4 and 5). In terms of factual statements, globalization 'is a fact', it is 'driven by people' (yet 'there's too little of it' in trade). But while it's 'a fact' in 'technology', it is a prediction for 'information technology' (there 'will be globalization'). And it is predicted to fail ('will fail and will deserve to fail') if it works only for the benefit of the few – if globalization can 'fail', then by implication it is a project or a plan rather than a 'fact'. And there is an alternative to globalization, 'isolation', which is again hard to reconcile with it being a 'fact'.

Such blurring of the distinction between fact and prediction (project, plan) is common in Blair's political language (Fairclough 2000b). And one can see the same thing happening here with 'the world community'. It is simultaneously assumed to exist (the first sentence of the second paragraph), and be able to act in certain ways, postulated as a possibility (there is an assumption in the second paragraph that the world 'can' be a community), and represented as in formation ('nations are instinctively drawing together', final paragraph).

Graham (2001a) suggests that the two features of 'promoting messages' I have discussed here, the slippage between fact and value, and between fact and prediction, are general features of contemporary policy texts. With respect to the second of these, he argues that 'policy authors strenuously, though perhaps invisibly, exercise the tense system to portray future and imagined states as if they actually existed in the here-and-now'. With respect to the first, he also identifies the link I discussed above between values and what I have called Demands, the implicit values of factual statements as covert Demands: 'The commands of contemporary policy are often implied in, disguised as, or buried under piles of ostensibly value-free, objective, pseudo-scientific facts'.

We can also connect these points on the 'promoting message' to the '**aestheti- cization** of everyday life' (Chouliaraki and Fairclough 1999, Featherstone 1991) which has been associated with 'promotional' or 'consumer culture. This includes an 'aestheticization' of events and of texts as part of events which is a significant aspect of the 'advocative' element in 'promoting messages'. A political speech by Tony Blair is an aesthetically designed event (Fairclough 2000b – see also chapter 10), and policy texts are often 'glossy' productions, just as for instance the self-promotional language of a CV goes along with meticulous attention to its physical appearance (font, lay-out, and so forth).

Grammatical mood

Speech function is related to grammatical mood, to the distinction between the main 'sentence types' (declarative, interrogative, imperative), though the relationship is not a straightforward one (see below).

- *Declarative*

  Subject precedes Verb (e.g. 'The book is on the table')

- *'Yes/no' Interrogative*

  Verbs precedes Subject (e.g. 'Is the book on the table?')

- ### *'Wh' Interrogative*

  Initial 'wh' word ('who', 'when', why', etc. – e.g. 'Where is the book?')

- ### *Imperative*

  No Subject (e.g. 'Put the book on the table')

Let us look at the relationship between speech function and grammatical mood in this following short dialogue, taken from Hodge and Kress (1988):

> *Max:*   A couple of questions very easy to answer for a radio programme we're doing. The first of the questions is *What* would you say language is?
> *Woman:*   Language . . . well it's the dialogue that people speak within various countries.
> *Max:*   Fair enough aaand *what* would you say it's made *out* of?
> *Woman:*   (*Pause, 8 seconds.*) It's made out of (*puzzled intonation*) . . .
> *Max:*   Hmmm.
> *Woman:*   Well I don't know you'd tell what's it's *made* out of . . . it's a person's *expression* I suppose is it?
> *Max:*   I haven't got the answers, I've only got the questions (*laughing*).
> *Woman:*   (*Simultaneously, small laugh.*)
> *Sid:*   That's not *bad* though.
> *Woman:*   Well it's an *expression*, it would be a person's expression wouldn't it?
> *Sid:*   That's a good answer.
> *Max:*   Thank you very much.

There are a number of declarative sentences (e.g. 'That's a good answer'), and a number of interrogative sentences (e.g. 'What would you say language is?'). Since we are now talking about a grammatical distinction, the difference is a matter of grammatical form. In declarative sentences, the order of grammatical elements is Subject followed by Verb (followed by other elements e.g. Object). One type of interrogative clauses (usually called 'yes/no' interrogatives because they expect a positive or negative answer) inverts the ordering of Subject and (part of the) Verb so that the latter precedes the former (e.g. 'Is that a good answer?'). Another type of interrogative (usually called 'wh-interrogatives') has an interrogative pronoun or adverb at the beginning of the sentence (these mainly begin 'wh' – 'who', 'what', 'why', 'when', 'where' 'how') and often also has the same inversion of the ordering of Subject and Verb, the Verb preceding the Subject. So in the case of 'What would you say language is?', 'what' is the initial wh-word (interrogative pronoun), and the modal verb 'would' is positioned before the subject 'you' (though the other part of the verb phrase, 'say', is not).

The clearly declarative sentences are Statements in terms of speech function, and the clearly interrogative sentences are Questions, but what are we to make of 'it's a person's *expression* I suppose is it?', and 'it would be a person's *expression* wouldn't it?'? These are declarative sentences, but with questions 'tagged onto' the end of them – what are usually known as 'tag-questions'. Notice how these are responded to, and what this tells us about how they are interpreted: the first is interpreted by Max as a question (that's the implication of him responding by saying that he hasn't got the answers), the second is interpreted by Sid as a '(good) answer', and therefore as a statement. What this suggests is that these sentences are, as their grammatical form would suggest, both Statements and Questions, providing information and at the same time asking for confirmation.

Apart from declaratives, interrogatives, and declaratives + tag-questions, the only other sentence type in this extract is what Halliday (1994) calls 'minor clauses', clauses which are 'grammatically incomplete', and in particular don't have verbs. The first is right at the beginning of the extract: 'A couple of questions very easy to answer for a radio programme we're doing'. The speech function of this would seem to be Statement – the interviewer seems to be telling the woman he's going to ask her some questions. The major sentence-type which is not represented here is the imperative: we don't having things like 'Answer the question!' Again, imperatives are distinct in their grammatical form: in particular, they don't have subjects. Notice that 'you must answer the question' is not imperative but declarative – it is grammatically different from 'Answer the question!', though they may have the same speech function (Demand). Imperatives are normally 'second-person', i.e. one can see 'you' as implicit, but one can take sentences such as 'let's answer the question!' as 'first person' imperatives.

The relationship between Grammatical Mood and Speech Function is a tendential one rather than a matter of simple correspondence. The strongest link is between declarative clauses and Statements – though as I have just said, minor clauses can also be Statements. Questions are usually interrogative, but there are also 'declarative questions' (compare 'how old are you?' and 'you're over eighteen?', the former is interrogative and the latter – despite the question mark – is declarative). Offers can be interrogative (Do you want a pint of Guinness?), imperative (Have a pint of Guinness!), or declarative (Here's a pint of Guinness). And while Demands are archetypically imperative (Give me a pint of Guinness), they can also be interrogative in the case of so-called 'question-requests' (Can I have a pint of Guinness), or declarative (I want a pint of Guinness). There are certain markers of Speech Function which narrow down the gap between it and Grammatical Mood. For instance a yes/no interrogative with 'please' (e.g. 'Can you open the window please?')

will be a Demand (a 'question-request') and not a Question. But determining the Speech Function of a clause often requires taking account of social contextual factors.

Speech function, grammatical mood and research interviews

The example I used in the previous section is a short interview – as it happens, for a radio programme. In terms of Speech Function, interviews, to state the obvious, have the characteristic organization – an aspect of their generic form – of Questions alternating with Answers which are generally Statements. Interviewers generally ask Questions, interviewees generally give Answers. This short extract does not quite fit this archetypal view of interview in that the tag-questions partly conform to the archetype of Answers (in so far as they are Statements) and partly do not (in so far as they are Questions) – notice that the interviewer's response to one of these, 'I haven't got the answers, I've only got the questions', might be taken as reminding the interviewee of the standard groundrules of interview, implicitly regulating the interviewee's contributions. In terms of Grammatical Mood, the Questions are both interrogative clauses.

Interviews vary in terms of how well they fit this archetype of interviewer and interviewee Speech Functions, but also in terms of how Questions in particular are realized in Grammatical Mood. Consider Example 1, the extract from an ethnographic research interview. Only one of the interviewer's Questions is an interrogative sentence ('And how does this relate to what is happening here?'). Notice that it is a 'wh' interrogative rather than a 'yes/no' interrogative – the former generally give interviewees greater latitude in terms of acceptable answers than the latter, and are in that sense 'open' as opposed to 'closed' questions. The others are minor clauses ('Bottom end?', 'But the good work you refer to?', 'And the other changes?') and an elliptical declarative clause ('Which means?'). One can relate these features of the Grammatical Mood of Questions to the particular nature of this type of research interview, in which the interviewer is concerned not so much to ask a (previously worked out) series of questions as to encourage the interviewee to keep talking and to get him to elaborate on what he has said. The Questions mainly figure as prompts. The particular nature of this type of research interview also explains properties of the manager's contributions. Although these are Answers, in that he does address the interviewer's Questions, they are clearly more than Answers – the manager is developing an extended account and argument about what's happening in the company, and in most cases having responded to the Questions he carries on with it. In some types of interview his contributions would be seen as problematic because they do not 'stick to the questions', here they are not, maybe one could say because there is an overarching question which obtains throughout the interview, something like 'what is your experience and view of what is going on in the company?'

Summary

The chapter began with a distinction between two types of speech exchanges, 'knowledge-exchanges' and 'activity-exchanges', which are associated respectively with the primary speech functions of Statement and Question, and Demand and Offer. Various types of statement were distinguished: statements of fact, predictions, hypothetical statements, and evaluations. We considered the idea that one can operationalize Habermas's distinction between 'strategic' and 'communicative action' in terms of 'grammatical metaphor', specifically focusing upon apparent knowledge exchanges which are covert activity exchanges, and apparent statements of fact which are covertly evaluations, and linking that to the 'hortatory report' genres discussed in the previous chapter. This can be specifically developed with respect to the view of contemporary culture as 'promotional culture', and the concept of a 'promotional message', which is associated with a slippage between fact and value, and between fact and prediction. Speech functions are realized in 'grammatical mood', though the relationship is a complex one. We differentiated three main grammatical moods (declarative, interrogative, imperative), as well as 'minor clauses'. One can differentiate types of research interview both in terms of the distribution of speech functions between interviewer and interviewee, and in terms of how interview questions are realized in grammatical mood (e.g. as 'declarative questions' rather than interrogatives).

Part III

Discourses and representations

7 Discourses

Text analysis issues

Discourses at different levels of abstraction
'Interdiscursive' analysis of articulation of discourses in texts
Equivalences and differences
Semantic relations between words (synonymy, hyponymy, antonymy)
Collocations

Social research issues

The 'new spirit of capitalism'
Classification

The identification and analysis of discourses is now a preoccupation across the humanities and social sciences. Foucault (1972, 1984) has been a decisive influence. Commenting on his own use of the word 'discourse', he writes:

> I believe I have in fact added to its meanings: treating it sometimes as the general domain of all statements, sometimes as an individualizable group of statements, and sometimes as a regulated practice that accounts for a number of statements.
>
> (Foucault 1984)

The analysis of discourse for Foucault is the analysis of the domain of 'statements' – that is, of texts, and of utterances as constituent elements of texts. But that does not mean a concern with detailed analysis of texts – the concern is more a matter of discerning the rules which 'govern' bodies of texts and utterances. The term 'discourse' is used abstractly (as an abstract noun) for 'the domain of statements', and concretely as a 'count' noun ('a discourse', 'several discourses') for groups of statements or for the 'regulated practice' (the rules) which govern such a group of statements. Foucault's work has been taken up in many different theories and disciplines, producing a rather bewildering range of overlapping and contrasting theorizations and analyses of 'discourses' (Dant 1991, Macdonell 1986, Mills 1997).

I see discourses as ways of representing aspects of the world – the processes, relations and structures of the material world, the 'mental world' of thoughts, feelings, beliefs and so forth, and the social world. Particular aspects of the world may be represented differently, so we are generally in the position of having to consider the relationship between different discourses. Different discourses are different perspectives on the world, and they are associated with the different relations people have to the world, which in turn depends on their positions in the world, their social and personal identities, and the social relationships in which they stand to other people. Discourses not only represent the world as it is (or rather is seen to be), they are also projective, imaginaries, representing possible worlds which are different from the actual world, and tied in to projects to change the world in particular directions. The relationships between different discourses are one element of the relationships between different people – they may complement one another, compete with one another, one can dominate others, and so forth. Discourses constitute part of the resources which people deploy in relating to one another – keeping separate from one another, cooperating, competing, dominating – and in seeking to change the ways in which they relate to one another.

Levels of abstraction

In talking about discourses as different *ways* of representing, we are implying a degree of repetition, commonality in the sense that they are shared by groups of people, and stability over time. In any text we are likely to find many different representations of aspects of the world, but we would not call each separate representation a separate discourse. Discourses transcend such concrete and local representations in the ways I have just suggested, and also because a particular discourse can, so to speak, generate many specific representations.

But discourses differ in their degree of repetition, commonality, stability over time, and in what we might call their 'scale', i.e. in how much of the world they include, and therefore in the range of representations they can generate. As in the case of genres (see chapter 4), it makes sense to distinguish different levels of abstraction or generality in talking about discourses. For instance, there is a way of representing people as primarily rational, separate and unitary individuals, whose identity as social beings is secondary in that social relations are seen as entered into by pre-existing individuals. There are various names we might give to this discourse

– for instance, the individualist discourse of the self, or the Cartesian discourse of the subject. It has a long history, it has at times been 'common sense' for most people, it is the basis of theories and philosophies and can be traced through text and talk in many domains of social life, and its 'scale' is considerable – it generates a vast range of representations. On a rather less general, but still very general, level, we might identify in the domain of politics a discourse of liberalism, and within the economic domain a 'Taylorist' discourse of management. By contrast, in Fairclough (2000b) I discussed the political discourse of the 'third way', i.e. the discourse of 'New Labour', which is a discourse attached to a particular position within the political field at a particular point in time (the discourse is certainly less than a decade old).

Example 9 is taken from a management 'guru' book which is the focus of Chiapello and Fairclough (2002). The background to that paper is the analysis by Boltanski and Chiapello (1999) of what they call the 'new spirit of capitalism' – or the ideology of what I have been calling new capitalism. Their analysis is based upon management texts rather like Example 9, and the objective of my paper with Chiapello was to see how their 'new sociology of capitalism' could be enhanced by using critical discourse analysis, allowing a more detailed account of how the 'new spirit of capitalism' is textured in management texts. We might see the 'new spirit of capitalism' as a new discourse which has emerged from combining existing discourses. Here is a brief illustration (not included in Example 9) of how such combinations are textured:

> Seven classic skills are involved in innovation and change: tuning in to the environment, kaleidoscopic thinking, an inspiring vision, coalition building, nurturing a working team, persisting through difficulties, and spreading credit and recognition. These are more than discrete skills; they reflect a perspective, a style, that is basic to e-culture.

The 'style' which is 'reflected' in this list is how the 'new spirit of capitalism' represents the 'leader' in business enterprises. The list works together into a relation of equivalence expressions which emanate from and evoke different discourses – listing is a texturing device for effecting the combination of discourses which constitute the new discourse. But one can see this process of combination as layered. Boltanksi and Chiapello (1999) suggest that the 'new spirit of capitalism' centrally articulates together 'inspirational' and 'connexionist' discourses (or what they actually call 'cités', or 'justificatory regimes') – leaders are people who combine vision with good networking, to put it rather crudely. The first three listed elements ('tuning in to the environment, kaleidoscopic thinking, an inspiring vision') emanate from the 'inspirational' discourse, whereas the fourth ('coalition building') emanates from the connexionist discourse. Yet the first three listed elements can themselves be seen to emanate from different discourses – 'tuning in' is a metaphorical use of an expression in technical discourse which evokes a discourse of personal relationships, perhaps a counselling discourse, where the quality of how one listens to others is in focus; 'kaleidoscopic thinking' evokes perhaps popular psychology texts on creative thinking; whereas 'inspiring vision' would seem to emanate from a discourse of art criticism). So the 'inspirational' discourse can itself be seen as an articulation of discourses.

Example 9 itself shows a similar texturing together of discourses, though in this case it is a matter of both equivalences within the 'new spirit of capitalism', and differences between it and the 'old' discourse (see the discussion of equivalences and differences in chapter 5). The texturing of the relationship of difference is effected through a range of contrastive or antithetical relational structures and expressions: *X instead of Y, X not just Y, X but also Y, X is different from Y, more like X than Y*. The clearest case is in the list in the centre of the extract, where what we might call the 'protagonist' discourse (the 'new spirit of capitalism') represented before the brackets is set off against the 'antagonist' discourse within the brackets. At the same time, elements in the list before the brackets are textured as equivalent, so are elements in the list within the brackets, and the different discourses from which these elements emanate are thereby articulated together.

The point of referring to different levels of 'abstraction' becomes clear as soon as we look in any detail at any of the discourses I have mentioned. They are all internally variable. Practically any treatment of Liberalism, for instance, is likely to on the one hand identify certain commonalities in Liberal representations of political life, but then go on to differentiate varieties of Liberalism. Even the discourse of the 'Third Way' is not homogeneous – one theme in the analysis I referred to is precisely how that discourse has varied and shifted in a rather short period of time. Why then talk about these heterogenous entities as 'discourses' at all? The answer cannot simply be based upon there being a certain commonality and continuity in the way the world is represented, as well as variation. It is also based upon the dialectical relationship between discourse and other elements of social life – that one distinguishes 'discourses' when particular ways (partly stable, partly variable) of representing the world are of social significance, perhaps in terms of the effectivity of discourse, its 'translation' into non-discoursal aspects of social life. Discourses can therefore be seen as not just ways of representing with a degree of commonality and stability, but such ways of representing where they constitute nodal points in the dialectical relationship between language and other elements of the social.

A further complexity is that discourses, except at the lowest level of generality, the level of the most specific and localized discourses, can themselves be seen as combinations of other discourses articulated together in particular ways. This is how new discourses emerge – through combining existing discourses together in particular ways. So, for instance, my analysis of the political discourse of the 'Third Way' saw it as a specific articulation of other discourses including social democratic and 'New Right' (Thatcherite) political discourses. The new is made out of a novel articulation of the old.

Texts and discourses

Different texts within the same chain of events or which are located in relation to the same (network of) social practices, and which represent broadly the same aspects of the world, differ in the discourses upon which they draw. For instance, Example 13 is an extract from a book written by two long-standing left-wing members of the British Labour Party on 'New Labour's' view of what it calls 'the global economy' and what they call 'capitalist globalization'. One difference between the representation of global economic change in this left-wing political discourse and the New Labour political discourse of the 'Third Way' is that 'transnational companies' are referred to as the agents dominating economic change – who 'divide and conquer'. In New Labour representations of global economic change, by contrast, these companies are not represented at all, and economic change ('globalization' and so forth) is represented as a process without social agents – as something which is just happening rather than something that people or companies or governments are doing (see Fairclough 2000b for comparative analysis of New Labour texts). Another significant feature of the left-wing discourse drawn upon in this extract is the semantic relations which obtain within it. Notice the different expressions used to represent transnational corporations – 'transnational companies', 'transnational capital', 'international capital'. Through rewording, a relation of equivalence, or synonymy, is textured between 'companies' and 'capital', between concrete and abstract. This sort of mapping of concrete, phenomenal forms of appearance ('companies') onto abstract, structural entities ('capital') is characteristic of a Marxist element which is evident in leftwing Labour discourse and which differentiates it from right-wing (and New Labour) discourse. Moreover, national governments (and the European Union) are represented as in a potentially antagonistic relationship to transnational companies/capital ('employing powers against' them, and acting in 'response' to them). This again is a characteristic of left political discourse – 'capital' is to be contested, fought against. And national governments are represented as potentially acting in alliance with trade union organizations (as well as non-governmental organizations more generally) on an international basis in accordance with 'internationalist' traditions – 'internationalism' here maintains its sense of the solidarity of labour, whereas in the discourse of New Labour is has come to refer to 'cooperation' between nation-states in the 'international community' (e.g. in bombing Yugoslavia). Notice also the concept of 'clientism', set up against 'employing powers against' or 'bargaining' with capital, which has no part in the political discourse of New Labour.

Texts also set up dialogical or polemical relations between their 'own' discourses and the discourses of others. In this case there is a critique of what New Labour says about 'partnership' and 'cooperation'. This is partly contesting the meanings given to these words within the discourse of New Labour, setting up a different discourse in which 'partnership' and 'cooperation' are articulated with 'trust', 'openness', 'respect'. And it is partly claiming (in an apparent allusion to New Labour's favoured 'not only but also' relations, e.g. 'cooperation as well as competition') that there is a covert hierarchy in New Labour discourse – 'enterprise' and 'competition' always comes before 'partnership' and 'cooperation'.

This dialogical/polemical relationship is one way in which texts mix different discourses, but their 'own' discourses are also often mixed or hybrid. An interdiscursive analysis of texts (see chapter 2) is partly concerned with identifying which discourses are drawn upon, and how they are articulated together. (We can see a text as drawing upon a discourse even if the realization of that discourse in the text is minimal – perhaps no more than a single word.) Let's look at Example 4 in this respect. Wodak, in the article from which the example is taken, traces the transformation of this text through successive versions in the course of meetings of the EU Competitiveness Advisory Group. Sentences 5–7 were added in later versions 'as a concession to the unions'. We can see this addition as a hybridization of discourses. The two main discourses here are, first, the neo-liberal discourse of economic change which represents 'globalization' as a fact which demands 'adjustments' and 'reforms' to enhance 'efficiency and adaptability' in order to compete; and, second, a political discourse which represents societies in terms of the goal of 'social cohesion' and threats to 'social cohesion'. These different discourses entail different policy priorities – policies to enhance competitiveness on the one hand, and social cohesion on the other. The discourse of social cohesion represents people in ways which are foreign to neo-liberal discourse – in terms of their feelings ('sense of unease, inequality and polarization'), and their 'hopes' and 'aspirations'. But sentence 7 is particularly significant in the way in which it articulates these discourses together by using vocabulary which works key categories within the two discourses into semantic relations – 'social cohesion' is reconstrued in economic terms as 'human quality' and 'the ability to work as a team' and as a 'source' of 'efficiency and adaptability'. Whereas the discourse of 'social cohesion' is a fundamentally moral and humane discourse which is oriented to people who have a 'sense' of belonging to a community, 'human quality' in particular reduces people to forces of production which rank along with others, such as information technology. Yet although these discourses can be seen as fundamentally incompatible in how they represent and imagine people, what we have here is a strategy of legitimizing the discourse of social cohesion in terms of the neo-liberal discourse.

Identifying and characterizing discourses

How do we go about identifying different discourses within a text? We can think of a discourse as (a) representing some particular part of the world, and (b) representing it from a particular perspective. Correspondingly, in textual analysis one can:

---

(1) Identify the main parts of the world (including areas of social life) which are represented – the main 'themes'.

(2) Identify the particular perspective or angle or point of view from which they are represented.

For instance, the themes of Example 7 (Appendix, pages 239–41) include: economic processes and change, processes of (global and national) governing, political protest (the misnamed 'anti-globalization' protests), and views of globalization (in 'the South'). Each of these themes is open in principle to a range of different perspectives, different representations, different discourses. In this case, economic processes and change (for instance the penultimate paragraph, on Ghana) are represented in the terms of the 'neo-classical', market-liberalization discourse of the 'Washington consensus' – in contrast for instance to Keynsian economic discourse. Governing is represented as 'governance', a term which is itself very much part of a neo-liberal discourse of governing which on the one hand represents governing as not only the business of governments but also 'the framework of global governance' (international agencies such as the World Trade Organization and the International Monetary Fund, which has been central in imposing the 'Washingtom consensus'), and on the other hand prescribes changes in governing in terms of 'transparency', 'accountability', and so forth. One can contrast this with more traditional state-centred discourses of governing.

I have suggested that discourses are distinguished both by their ways of representing, and by their relationship to other social elements. Focusing on the former we can specify ways of representing in terms of a range of linguistic features which can be seen as realizing a discourse.

The most obvious distinguishing features of a discourse are likely to be features of vocabulary – discourses 'word' or 'lexicalize' the world in particular ways. But rather than just focusing atomistically on different ways of wording the same aspects of the world, it is more productive to focus on how different discourses structure the world differently, and therefore on semantic relationships between words. One example is the relationship between 'transnational companies' and 'transnational capital' in Example 13, discussed above. The former is reworded as the latter in the text. One might see this as a local texturing of semantic relations – new semantic relations are indeed set up in texts, and that is part of the work of social agent (and the causal effects of agency, see chapter 2) in making meaning. But in this case a comparison of texts within this political tradition, including other texts of these authors, would suggest that the rewording draws upon and evokes the way of structuring the world associated with this discourse, rather than setting up a new relation. One might say that the text takes as given, presupposes, what one will find explicitly asserted and argued for elsewhere in texts which draw upon this discourse: that (transnational) companies are a phenomenal form of appearance of (transnational) capital. Semantically, we can say that 'companies' is a hyponym of 'capital', along with other 'co-hyponyms' such as 'trusts' and 'financial markets'. This presupposed structuring of the world, and this presupposed semantic relation, is both what allows the writers to reword 'companies' as 'capital' without having to make the relation explicit, and what allows readers to make sense of the text.

Another example of such a covert semantic relation is in the relationship between 'globalization' and 'economic progress' in sentences 1 and 2 of Example 4 – the coherence of the text depends upon a relationship of hyponymy between them, that 'globalization' is a hyponym of 'economic progress'. In Example 1, the employees of the company are classified into three groups – 'senior management', 'the bottom end' and 'us', where 'us' is middle management. These can be seen as co-hyponyms, and constitute a taxonomy, though it is not clear what the superordinate term is (i.e. what they are hyponyms of): perhaps 'workforce' is used in this way when the manager explains 'bottom end' in response to the interviewer's question: 'Of the workforce'. But 'workforce' is in contrast with 'managers' when the manager says 'take the power from the unions and give it back to the managers and give it back to the workforce', and perhaps a synonym of 'the bottom end'. These are not meaning relations one is likely to find in a dictionary, because they are specific to particular discourses. In addition to hyponymy ('meaning inclusion'), and synonymy ('meaning identity'), they include antonymy ('meaning exclusion'). For instance, in the discourse of social cohesion drawn upon in Example 4, the antonyms of 'social cohesion' include 'polarization' (in the text) as well as 'social exclusion' (not in the text).

What is at issue here is classification, preconstructed classificatory schemes or systems of classification, 'naturalized preconstructions . . . that are ignored as such and which can function as unconscious instruments of construction' (Bourdieu and Wacquant 1992), preconstructed and taken for granted 'di-visions' through which people continuously generate 'visions' of the world. When different discourses come into conflict and particular discourses are contested, what is centrally contested is the power of these preconstructed semantic systems to generate particular visions of the world which may have the perfomative power to sustain or remake the world in their image, so to speak.

The vocabularies associated with different discourses in a particular domain of social life may be partly different but are likely to substantially overlap. Different discourses may use the same words (for instance, both neo-liberal and 'anti-globalization' discourses use 'globalization'), but they may use them differently, and again it is only through focusing upon semantic relations that one can identify these differences. One way of getting at this relational difference is through looking at collocations, patterns of co-occurrence of words in texts, simply looking at which other words most frequently precede and follow any word which is in focus, either immediately or two, three and so on words away. Sometimes one is struck by collocations in particular texts. For instance, the word 'globalization' occurs in Example 7 in collocation with 'overpowering' ('fear that overpowering globalization will force the extinction of national cultures and traditions'). This is a text produced by an organization which has been strongly supportive of neo-liberalism, but which is giving voice to concerns about the negative effects of 'globalization', and drawing in discourses, as this collocation indicates, which one is unlikely to find in more conventional neo-liberal texts. But the most effective way of exploring collocational patterns is through computer-assisted corpus analysis of large bodies of text (McEnery and Wilson 2001, Stubbs 1996). For instance, in a corpus analysis of texts of New Labour and 'old' Labour (i.e. texts from earlier stages of Labour Party history), it emerged clearly that although the word 'work' was, rather obviously, rather common in both, its collocative patterns were different. 'Back to work', 'into work', 'desire to work', 'opportunities to work', 'Welfare-to-work' reflect common collocations in the New Labour corpus, whereas 'out of work', 'right to work', 'democracy at work', 'health and safety at work' reflect common patterns in the 'old' Labour corpus. Generalizing over the results, the focus in New labour is on getting people off welfare and into work, the focus in 'old' Labour is on improving conditions and relations in work, on unemployment as an infringement of the 'right to work' and a responsibility for Government (Fairclough 2000b).

Discourses are also differentiated by metaphor, both in its usual sense of 'lexical metaphor', words which generally represent one part of the world being extended to another, and what I shall call in the next chapter grammatical metaphor (e.g. processes being represented as 'things', entities, through 'nominalization'). Let me make some comments on lexical metaphor (see Goatly 1997). In Example 9, competition between companies is represented metaphorically as a race. The 'best' companies are 'pacesetters', like the runner who takes the lead and sets the pace in a race. The 'worst' companies are 'laggards', those who trail behind. Unlike 'pacesetter', 'laggard' is not specifically part of the vocabulary of racing, it broadens the metaphorical representation of companies as being like people to include other activities in which people are evaluated and graded in terms of performance (e.g. there are 'laggards' classrooms). Example 9 also explicitly elaborates a metaphorical representation of companies as 'communities' with 'members' (rather than just 'employees') who have 'shared understandings' and a 'feeling of connection', and so forth. Such metaphors differ between discourses – metaphor is one resource available for producing distinct representations of the world. But it is perhaps the particular combination of different metaphors which differentiates discourses: the two metaphors I have identified here are common ways of representing companies which turn up in various discourses, and it is perhaps the combination of these and other metaphors which helps to differentiate this particular managerial discourse. The influential work of Lakoff and Johnson (1980) on metaphors which are deeply embedded within cultures (e.g. the metaphorical representation of arguing as fighting) is also relevant here.

I referred above to semantic relations being presupposed. In fact, presuppositions and assumptions can more generally be seen as discourse-relative – the categories of assumption I distinguished in chapter 3 (existential assumptions, propositional assumptions, value assumptions) can all be seen as potentially tied to particular discourses, and as variable between discourses. Potentially, because there many assumptions which are more or less pervasively held throughout societies or social domains or organizations. I made the point in chapter 3, for example in discussing Example 4, that assumptions may be discourse-relative, so I shall not repeat the argument in detail here. I also suggested in Chapter 4, in discussing Argument as a genre, that arguments often rest upon assumptions which are discourse-specific and discourse-relative (see Gieve 2000).

I referred earlier to the two main discourses in example 4, the neo-liberal discourse, and the discourse of social cohesion. Despite the contrast between them, there is one thing they have in common: they represent real social processes and events in a highly abstract way. Although one can say that they are ultimately referencing concrete and particular events, if highly complex sets and series of such events, they represent the world in a way which abstracts away from anything remotely concrete. One corollary of this is that many of the elements of concrete events are excluded. Processes ('globalization', 'progress') and relations ('social cohesion') and even feelings ('hopes', 'aspirations') – I shall use 'processes' in a general sense to include all these – are represented, but the people involved are for the most part excluded ('people' in sentence 6 is an exception, but the representation here is again very general – in fact 'generic', see chapter 8), as are other elements of social events, such as objects, means, times, places. Processes are in fact 'nominalized', not worded with verbs as they most commonly are, but with noun-like entities called 'nominalizations' ('globalization', 'cohesion'), or what one might call 'process nouns', nouns with the verb-like quality of representing processes and relations and so forth ('progress', 'hope'). Syntactically, these process-expressions operate like nouns – so, for example, 'social cohesion' in (5) is the subject of a (passive) sentence. When processes are nominalized or worded as process nouns, their own subjects, objects and so forth tend to be excluded. Contrast Example 12 (Appendix, pages 248–9) with Example 4 (page 236). The sort of ethnographically oriented sociological discourse of the former represents events more concretely, and includes more elements of events (including the people involved in them) in its representations, than either the neo-liberal discourse or the discourse of social cohesion, both of which are oriented to abstraction from and generalization over events in mainly policy-formation contexts.

What these comments point to is that discourses are characterized and differentiated not only by features of vocabulary and semantic relations, and assumptions, but also by grammatical features. Discourses differ in how elements of social events (processes, people, objects, means, times, places) are represented, and these differences can be grammatical as well as lexical (vocabulary). The difference between a nominalization and a verb is a grammatical difference, so also is the difference between transitive and intransitive verbs, the difference between generic and specific noun phrases (e.g. generic, general and inclusive, reference to 'the police', as opposed to specific reference to 'this policeman'), and so forth. These are some of the ways in which discourses differ in the representation of social events (see chapter 8 for more detailed discussion).

Summary

We have seen that discourses are ways of representing the world which can be identified and differentiated at different levels of abstraction – so that for instance what Boltanski and Chiapello (1999) identify as the 'new spirit of capitalism' can be seen as a discourse at a high level of abstraction which develops as an articulation of discourses. Texts differ in the discourses they draw upon to represent particular aspects of the world, and they articulate different discourses together (hybridize or mix discourses) in various ways. Discourses can be differentiated in terms of semantic relations (synonymy, hyponymy, antonymy) between words – how they classify parts of the world – as well collocations, assumptions, and various grammatical features.

8 Representations of social events

Textual analysis issues

Clause elements: processes, participants, circumstances
Exclusion or inclusion of elements of social events
Abstract or concrete representations of social events
Representation of processes, and process types
Representation of social actors
Representation of time and space
Grammatical metaphor (e.g. nominalization)

Social research issues

Governance
Recontextualization
The universal and the particular
Agency
'Space–times'

My focus in this chapter is on Representational meanings in the clause (see **types of meaning** in the Glossary of key terms). What can be represented in clauses includes aspects of the physical world (its processes, objects, relations, spatial and temporal parameters), aspects of the 'mental world' of thoughts, feelings, sensations and so forth, and aspects of the social world. I shall be concentrating on the latter. I shall approach it in terms of the representation of social events, though of course the social world can also be represented in a more generalized and abstract way in terms of structures, relations, tendencies and so forth. Different levels of abstraction and concreteness in representations are distinguished below.

In terms of social research issues, I shall return to the question of governance (and genres of governance) which was introduced in chapter 2, though now in terms of an analytical framework for seeing representation as recontextualization. I shall also return to the discussion of the universal and particular in chapter 3, in terms of ways of referring to social actors (particularly 'generic' reference). I shall discuss the question of agency (see **structure and agency** in the Glossary of key terms), specifically how texts represent agency, e.g. whether actions are represented in ways which specify or conversely elide the agency of actors, and what the social and political significance of this textual 'choice' may be. And finally I shall draw upon the work of the geographical theorist David Harvey (Harvey 1996a) on the social construction of time and space (space–time), and consider how Harvey's perspective might be 'operationalized' in textual analysis in a way which enriches analysis of representations of time and space in texts.

The clause from a representational perspective

All three main types of meaning (Action, Representation, Identification) are simultaneously at issue in clauses, and each gives a particular perspective on the clause, and particular analytical categories (see the 'multifunctional' analysis of clauses in Halliday 1994). In chapter 6, I was looking at the clause in terms of Actional meanings, and this included looking at categories of speech function (Statement, Demand, etc.) and at Grammatical Mood (declarative, interrogative, imperative). The perspective and the categories are different when one looks at Representational meanings: from this perspective, clauses can be seen as having three main types of element: Processes, Participants, and Circumstances. For instance, in 'Laura saw Fiona in Lancaster', there is a Process ('saw'), two Participants ('Laura', 'Fiona'), and a Circumstance ('in Lancaster'). Processes are generally realized as verbs, Participants as Subjects, Objects, or Indirect Objects of verbs, Circumstances as various types of adverbial elements, such as time or place (as in this case) adverbials. We can differentiate different types of each element (e.g. different Process types), and clauses differ in terms of the **Process types**, Participants and Circumstances selected. See below for more details.

Exclusion, inclusion and prominence

Social events bring together various elements. Let us say in very broad terms that they include:

Forms of activity
Persons (with beliefs/desires/values . . . histories)

> Social relations, institutional forms
> Objects
> Means (technologies . . .)
> Times and places
> Language (and other types of semiosis)

We can look at texts from a Representational point of view in terms of which elements of events are included in the representation of those events and which are excluded, and which of the elements that are included are given the greatest prominence or salience. Rather than seeing such a procedure as comparing the truth about an event with how it is represented in particular texts (which raises problems about how one establishes the truth independently of particular representations), one can see it in terms of comparison between different representations of the same or broadly similar events (see Van Leeuwen 1993, 1995, 1996 for such an approach to Representational meaning).

For instance, the packet of a well-known brand of cigars carries the following short text:

> Finest grade cigar tobaccos from around
>   the world are selected for Hamlet.
> Choice leaves, harvested by hand, are dried,
>   Fermented and carefully conditioned.
> Then the artistry of our blenders creates this
>   Unique mild, cool, smooth smoking cigar.
>
> HAMLET
> Fine cigars

Elements of the social events represented which are included are the forms of activity (selecting, harvesting, drying tobacco leaves, etc.) and the objects of these forms of activity (tobaccos, leaves, cigars). It is the forms of activity in particular which are given most prominence: this short text represents quite a lot of activities. Persons are partially included ('our blenders') but partially excluded: the persons who select, harvest, dry, ferment and condition the tobacco leaves are excluded. Also excluded are the social relations and institutional forms, means (except 'by hand'), times and places, and language of the types of events (harvesting, and so forth) represented. One can connect these exclusions to the grammatical forms of clauses: in the first four lines we have passive clauses with material Processes (e.g. 'are selected') and, in terms of Participants, ('passive') Subjects (e.g. 'choice leaves'), but not Agents (not e.g. 'by local peasants'), and without time or place Circumstances.

Compare an imaginary sentence (which I have made up) from a novel:

> As noon approached, Pedro began vigorously cutting leaves at the southern edge of the field which he knew the overseer would inspect first and most thoroughly.

This includes forms of activity (e.g. 'cutting'), objects (e.g. 'leaves'), persons ('Pedro', 'the overseer'), social relations (the relation between worker and overseer), time ('as noon approached') and place ('at the southern end of the field'). Of course, many other, different, representations of the tobacco industry could be found. One can appreciate what is socially significant about the representation on the 'Hamlet' packet if one brings into the picture one of the most controversial features of contemporary capitalism: the production of goods for the markets of relatively rich countries through poorly-paid labour and bad working conditions in relatively poor countries. This has been widely regarded as part of an exploitative and unjust international division of labour. The marketing of goods such as cigars in relatively rich countries can therefore be a rather delicate matter, and it as hardly surprising if the production process tends to be represented in ways which occlude the relations and circumstances of production, and even the workers who produce – an occlusion of agency.

It is too reductive, however, to see only a political motivation for these exclusions – if that were the case, why refer to the production process at all? One might say that the production process is represented as part of the focus on building up an image of the product as a quality product. The quality of the materials and the care and discrimination which goes into their selection and processing are explicit ('fine', 'unique', 'carefully', 'choice', etc.) or implicit ('by hand', 'selected') in the vocabulary, and expressions of distinction ('Finest grade cigar tobaccos', 'Choice leaves', 'the artistry of our blenders') are given prominence through being located in the initial ('thematic') position in clauses. What matters here are the objects (raw materials, products) and the activities applied to them, not the persons who carry them or the social relations of production.

Concrete and abstract representations of events

Social events can be represented at different levels of abstraction and generalization. We can usefully distinguish three levels of concreteness/abstraction:

> Most concrete: representation of specific social events
> More abstract/generalized: abstraction over series and sets of social events
> Most abstract: representation at the level of social practices or social structures

The 'Hamlet' advertisement is written at the intermediate level of abstraction, representing not concrete, specific social events but a series of repeated social events. My made-up sentence by contrast represents a specific, concrete event. The European Union policy paper (Example 4) on the other hand represents the social world in an abstract way. It represents globalization as a process of social change in terms of relations between economic processes ('destruction of obsolete activities and creation of new ones'), social psychological change ('a widespread sense of unease, inequality and polarization'), and policy initiatives ('implement the necessary reforms') represented in corporatist terms as undertaken by government, employers and trade unions.

Notice that, as with the 'Hamlet' advertisement, the question of agency arises with the economic processes. 'Economic progress' is represented as a process without human, social, agents. The second sentence includes several nominalizations and process nouns (see below for explanation of these terms): 'progress', 'destruction', 'activities', 'creation'. One can see each of these as referencing and generalizing over complexes of events involving persons – so it seems reasonable ask: who is 'progressing' (and who is not 'progressing') economically? who is doing things which are 'obsolete'? (and why are they 'obsolete?), who destroys, who creates? One can see social agents of economic processes as excluded here – it is a 'game' without social players. At the same time, agency is shifted to abstract processes and entities. It is 'economic progress' (or perhaps 'the pace' – the reference is not very clear) that 'imposes deep and rapid adjustments'; it is 'a global economy' that makes 'demands'; and there is a risk that 'resources' will 'leave' for other parts of the world. Notice that the movement of 'resources' is represented as an intransitive process (as opposed to a transitive process, e.g. 'people will move resources'), and that 'resources' are personified (like people, they are liable to travel in search of better opportunities).

When representations are generalized or abstract, we need to look particularly closely at how things are being classified, at the 'classification schemes' which are drawn upon to impose a 'di-vision' on the social – a division, a classification, which constitutes a particular 'vision' (Bourdieu and Wacquant 1992). Classification schemes being drawn upon in this case include an implicit division between economic 'progress' and its (unnamed) other (perhaps 'stagnation', 'recession'); 'social cohesion' and social fragmentation (or 'polarization'); a division of the world according to affording of 'opportunities' into (more or less) 'promising' and 'unpromising' parts; and the tri-partite classification of significant actors in the policy domain ('government', 'trade-unions', 'employers'). One can see differences between discourses as partly a matter of different 'key words' in their vocabularies (e.g. 'progress', 'social cohesion'), but it is actually more productive to see these differences as differences in classification schemes.

Representation as recontextualization

We can incorporate the questions discussed above (exclusion/inclusion/prominence, and abstract/concrete representation) within a broader view of the representation of social events as *recontextualization*, a concept I discussed in chapter 2 in connection with genres of governance. In representing a social event, one is incorporating it within the context of another social event, recontextualizing it. Particular social fields, particular networks of social practices, and particular genres as elements of such networks of social practices, have associated with them specific 'recontextualizing principles' (Bernstein 1990). These are specific 'principles' according to which they they incorporate and re-contextualize social events. These principles underlie differences between the ways in which a particular type of social event is represented in different fields, networks of social practices, and genres. Elements of social events are selectively 'filtered' according to such recontextualizing principles (some are excluded, some included and given greater or lesser prominence). These principles also affect how concretely or abstractly social events are represented, whether and how events are evaluated, explained, legitimized, and the order in which events are represented. In summary:

- *Presence*

    Which elements of events, or events in a chain of events, are present/absent, prominent/backgrounded?

- *Abstraction*

    What degree of abstraction/generalization from concrete events?

- *Arrangement*

    How are events ordered?

- *Additions*

    What is added in representing events – explanations/legitimations (reasons, causes, purposes), evaluations?

Van Leeuwen (1993) develops a similar view of representation in terms of the Deletion, Addition, Substitution, and Rearrangement of elements.

Compare Examples 12 and 4 (Appendix pages 248–9, and 236) in these terms. Both include representations of the broadly social psychological effects of economic change on people as employees, as workers. Example 12 is taken from what the author describes as an 'essay' pursuing a single 'argument' about the effects of the new 'flexible' capitalism on 'character', focusing on the 'concrete experience of individuals' gathered through 'exploring the daily life around me, much as an anthropologist might'. Although the details of persons, places, circumstances are changed to preserve anonymity, the author's aim is to 'reflect the sense' of what he has observed. The social events represented are a series of meetings and conversations amongst a group of IBM programmers who have been made redundant, in which a series of events (and, through abstraction, social practices and structures) associated with the men's loss of employment were represented. In terms of 'presence', persons and places are particularly prominent in the author's representation of these meetings, and the relation between types of activity, persons, and places is made prominent. Events are not located in time, and there is presumably a chain of events in which these meetings are located which is not specified (e.g. how did the programmers come to start having these regular meetings?). There is a low level of abstraction, events are represented concretely, but with generalization over a series of events – this is a characterization of a series of meetings the author experienced. The question of Arrangement does not really arise, because the focus is on one recurrent event, and not in terms of a narrative account of its unfolding through time, but in terms of a more analytical description of key features (how people sit, who does the most talking, how people distribute themselves within the café). Part of this can be seen as making social agents into 'characters' (Bal 1997). In terms of 'Additions', an element of evaluation is 'added' in the representation of the meetings (for instance in the selection of detail e.g. 'white-shirted, dark-tied'), but not explanation or legitimation. One can see that the recontextualizing principle for this form of sociological writing would accentuate the specificity of concrete events (in this case, a regular pattern of events), their locations, and the persons involved.

Example 4, the EU policy document, represents by contrast highly complex series and sets of economic and social events, past, present and predicted, at a high level of abstraction – there is not only generalization over complex series and sets of events (e.g. destruction of 'obsolete activities'), and abstraction of facets which cut across sets and series of events (e.g. 'social cohesion'), but also the most abstract level of structural relations (e.g. the structural relation between social cohesion and economic 'efficiency' and 'adaptability' in sentence 7). The only element of events consistently present and prominent is forms of activity (material – 'destruction', mental – 'aspirations'), sometimes with persons ('people', 'governments', etc.) or objects ('obsolete activities'), more often without. Particular series or sets of events (e.g. the destruction of 'obsolete activities') are not located in time and place – indeed indifference to place ('in all countries') is thematized. But time becomes important in the arrangement and ordering of these highly abstract representations of events in relation to each other in the text: in particular, in organizing a relationship between 'realis' and 'irrealis', the actual world (past/present) and the predicted and prescribed world of policy (e.g. between 'globalization' ('progress', 'destruction', 'creation') and 'adjustments' and 'reforms'). These relationships are also in some cases causal relationships – for instance, 'Failure to move quickly and decisively will result in loss of resources' sets up a cause–effect relation between (present) failure and (future, predicted) loss. Additions include evaluations, legitimations, explanations (e.g. sentence 3 legitimizes sentence 4; and 'a disjunct between the hopes and aspirations of people and the demands of a global economy' is negatively evaluated – a textual cue to this negative evaluation is 'risk').

I discussed 'genres of governance' in chapter 2, seeing them as genres associated with networks of social practices which are specialized for regulating and controlling ('governing') other (networks of) social practices. Policy documents of this sort are one genre of governance. When other social practices are recontextualized within policy documents, it is predictable (an aspect of the recontextualizing principle at work in such documents) that there will be a high degree of abstraction from and generalization across concrete events, and that causal and temporal relations will be specified between these abstractions, as in this example. Such policy documents are important in linking scales – generalising over many local cases (and – a standard critique – thereby suppressing difference) to make claims which hold and have policy implications nationally or internationally.

Representation of processes and associated participants and circumstances

We can distinguish a small number of main Process Types, which differ in their key, defining, Participants, and in the types of Circumstance associated with them (compare the accounts in Halliday 1994 and Van Leeuwen 1995):

Process type	Key participants	Circumstances
Material	Actor, Affected	Time, Place, Purpose, Reason, Manner, Means
Verbal	Actor	
Mental	Experiencer, Phenomenon	Time, Place, Reason
Relational (1)	Carrier, Attribute	
Relational (2)	Token, Value	
Existential	Existent	

With regard to Circumstances, Process types fall into two main groups: Material and Verbal processes allow a wider range of Circumstances than Mental, Relational and Existential processes. There are two main types of Material Process: transitive (Actor + Process + Affected, e.g. 'Globalization increases choice and liberty'), and intransitive (either Actor + Process, e.g. 'John ran', or Affected + Process, e.g. 'societies have been changing', depending on whether the process is a 'doing' or a 'happening'). Transitive material processes can be active or passive (the latter with the option of having or not having passive 'agents' – e.g. 'Choice and liberty are increased', without an agent, or 'Choice and liberty are increased by globalization', with an agent). Here is an illustrative analysis of part of Example 12. I have simplified the analysis somewhat by just analysing the parts which are underlined:

1 The River Winds Café, not far from my neighbours' old offices, is a cheery hamburger joint, (RELATIONAL-1, CARRIER+PROCESS+ATTRIBUTE)

2 formerly tenanted during daylight hours only by women out shopping or (MATERIAL, (AFFECTED)+PROCESS+ACTOR (passive agent)

3 sullen adolescents wasting time after school. (MATERIAL, ACTOR+PROCESS+AFFECTED)

4 It is here that (RELATIONAL-2, TOKEN+PROCESS+VALUE)

5 I've heard these white-shirted, dark-tied men, sort out their histories. (MENTAL, EXPERIENCER+PROCESS+PHENOMENON)

6 who nurse cups of coffee (MATERIAL, ACTOR+PROCESS+AFFECTED)

7 while sitting attentively as if at a business meeting, (MATERIAL, (ACTOR)+PROCESS)

8 these white-shirted, dark-tied men sort out their histories. (MATERIAL, ACTOR+PROCESS+AFFECTED)

9 One knot of five to seven men sticks together; (MATERIAL, ACTOR+PROCESS)

10 they were mainframe programmers and systems analysts in the old IBM. (RELATIONAL-1, CARRIER+PROCESS+ATTRIBUTE)

11 The most talkative among them were Jason, a systems analyst . . . and Paul, a younger programmer (RELATIONAL-2, VALUE+PROCESS+TOKEN)

12 who had been with the company nearly twenty years, (RELATIONAL-1, CARRIER+PROCESS+CIRCUMSTANCE)

13 whom Jason had fired in the first downsizing wave. . . . (MATERIAL, AFFECTED+ACTOR+PROCESS)

There are two Process Types not exemplified here, Verbal and Existential. Sentence 8 might be rewritten as a Verbal process (<u>these white-shirted, dark-tied men talk about what has happened to them</u>) and sentence 1 as an Existential process (<u>There is a café</u> not far from my neighbours' old offices called the River Winds Café).

Metaphorical (non-congruent) representations of processes

Halliday (1994) extends the concept of 'metaphor' from its conventional application to the meanings of words to grammar. One can distinguish, in the case of representation, between 'congruent' (or 'non-metaphorical') and 'metaphorical' representations. This is a helpful distinction, but also a problematic one. It is problematic because 'congruent' can be interpreted as making claims about how events or practices or structures 'really' are, independently of particular representations of them. Alternatively, 'congruent' can appeal to a rather loose notion of how events and so forth are represented most 'normally', in the 'unmarked case'. That remains problematic, but it does capture a useful distinction between, for instance, representing processes *as* processes, as opposed to representing processes as entities, which is one of the more significant forms of metaphorical representation. For instance, as I pointed out above there is a sense in which one can say that 'economic progress', 'destruction (of obsolete activities)', 'activities', and 'creation (of new ones)' all ultimately reference complex sets and series of events which involve people doing things or things happening to people. The latter can be taken as appealing to 'congruent' representations – thus 'employees in the factory produce steel girders' is congruent, whereas 'activities' is not, it is a grammatical metaphor, processes being metaphorically represented as entities which operate semantically like any other entities (e.g. they can be destroyed). Entities, things (as well as persons) are congruently represented linguistically as nouns, whereas as processes are congruently represented linguistically as verbs with associated subjects, objects and so forth. 'Activities' and 'progress' are 'process nouns' – they are part of the nominal (noun) vocabulary of English but belong to a particular sub-category with a special connection with verbs (and thus processes). 'Destruction' and 'creation' are usually called by contrast 'nominalizations' – there is a transparent link between 'destruction' and 'people destroy things', 'creation' and 'people create things', such that it is easy to see the former in each case as a 'nominalization' of the latter, the conversion of a verb into a noun-like word, and semantically of a process into an entity.

Nominalization characteristically involves the 'loss' of certain semantic elements of clauses – both tense (so 'destruction' can cover 'was destroyed', 'is destroyed', 'will be destroyed', etc.) and modality (so distinctions between 'is', 'may be', 'should be' and so forth are 'lost'). It also may involve the exclusion of Participants in clauses – so in this case none of the process nouns or nominalizations has an agent (what would most commonly be the grammatical subject in a clause). As I pointed out earlier, there is no specification of *who* progresses, acts, destroys or creates. Nominalization is a resource for generalising, for abstracting from particular events and series or sets of events, and in that sense it is an irreducible resource in scientific and technical discourse (Halliday and Martin 1993) as well as governmental discourse (Lemke 1995). As I noted above, such generalization and abstraction, for instance in the genres of governance, can erase or even suppress difference. It can also obfuscate agency, and therefore responsibility, and social divisions. In this case, for instance, the question of who makes progress, who doesn't, who destroys and might be held responsible for destruction, whose livelihoods, etc. are destroyed.

Representations of events, activities, processes, entails choice (not usually conscious choice, of course) amongst the process types, and here again one sees certain choices as congruent and others as metaphorical. For instance, the processes (verbal phrases underlined) in 'The pace <u>has become</u> swifter and the game <u>has taken on</u> planetary dimensions' can both be seen as type-1 relational processes – 'taken on' is equivalent to 'come to have' (the two main sub-types of this relational process are 'being' and 'having'). Both 'speed-up' and 'globalization' are represented as things that have come about, rather than things that are the effects of causal agents (for instance, international agreements between governments, policies of business corporations). In a different discourse, certain forms of Marxist or anti-globalization discourse, they may well be represented as effects of causal agents, and the process types may be material. (See Example 13, Appendix pages 249–50.)

Example 12 includes a number of representations of the unemployment of the programmers, including: 'they lost their jobs', 'they were let go', 'the dismissed employees', and 'dismissal'. One of these ('they were let go') contains a complex verb with a transitive element ('let') and an intransitive element ('go'), and it is a passive clause without an agent, so that the agent of 'let . . . go', the agent responsible for them becoming unemployed, is elided. This is semantically interesting in that what one might see as the congruent material transitive Agent–Process–Affected relation (as in, e.g. 'the management fired them') is metaphorically construed as the programmers being allowed ('let') to act ('go'). In the case of 'they lost their jobs', one might see the congruent material transitive process with the programmers as Affected metaphorically construed as a material transitive process with the programmers as Agent (as if the men were the agents of their own unemployment). 'Dismissed' is a reduced passive (compare 'they were dismissed') functioning as modifier of a noun (rather like an adjective), and 'dismissal' is a nominalization – one might see the process type as congruent in these cases, but the agents are elided.

Tracing the precise nature and distribution of grammatical metaphors can be seen as one productive way into researching effectivity of texts within a particular social order, and in processes of social change. For example, Graham (2001a) suggests that 'process metaphor', the metaphorical construal of processes in the material world, is a particularly significant aspect of a highly influential genre in new capitalism, policy formation: 'In the policy genre, process metaphor is a deceptively powerful tool for construing future human *activity* (*time*) as a pseudo-spatial, fact-like *object* (*space*)'.

Representations of social actors

Just as there are choices in the representation of processes, so also there are choices in the representation of **social actors**. Social actors are usually Participants in clauses, though they may not be (they may be within Circumstances instead), and not all Participants are social actors – they may be physical objects for instance (compare 'the car hit Mary', 'the car hit a rock' – both 'Mary' and 'a rock' are objects of the verb, i.e. Participants, but only 'Mary' is a social actor).

We can chart the choices available in the representation of social actors in terms of the following variables (Van Leeuwen 1996 identifies many more variables):

● *Inclusion / exclusion*

Already discussed above in more general terms with respect to the representation of social events. We can distinguish two types of exclusion of social actors

a)   suppression – i.e. not in the text at all
b)   backgrounding – i.e. mentioned somewhere in the text, but having to be inferred in one or more places

● *Pronoun / noun*

Is the social actor realized as a pronoun ('I', 'he', 'we', 'you', etc.) or as a noun?

● *Grammatical role*

Is the social actor realized as a Participant in a clause (e.g. Actor, Affected), within a Circumstance (e.g. in a preposition phrase, for instance 'She walked <u>towards</u> John'), or as a Possessive noun or pronoun ('<u>Laura's</u> friend', '<u>our</u> friend')

● *'Activated' / 'passivated'*

Is the social actor the Actor in processes (loosely, the one who does things and makes things happen), or the Affected or Beneficiary (loosely, the one affected by processes)?

● *Personal/impersonal*

Social actors can be represented impersonally as well as personally – for instance referring to the police as 'the filth' is impersonalizing them.

● *Named/classified*

Social actors can be represented by name (e.g. 'Fred Smith') or in terms of class or category (e.g. 'the doctor'). If the latter, they can be referred to individually (e.g. 'the doctor') or as a group ('the doctors', 'doctors').

● *Specific/generic*

Where social actors are classified, they can be represented specifically or generically – for instance 'the doctors' may refer to a specific group of doctors (e.g. those who work in a particular hospital), or to the class of doctors in general, all doctors (e.g. 'the doctors see themselves as gods').

I have italicized all the representations of social actors in this extract from Sennett's *The Corrosion of Character* (see Example 12), and marked exclusions with '^'.

Lippmann has often been on *my* mind in attending to *a group of middle-aged programmers I*'ve come to know, *men who* were recently downsized^ at an American IBM office. Before *they* lost their jobs, *they* rather complacently – subscribed to the belief in the long-term unfolding of *their* professional careers. As *high-tech programmers, they* were meant to be *the masters of the new science*. After *they* were let go^, *they* had to try out different interpretations of the events which wrecked *their* lives; *they* could summon no self-evident, instant narrative which would make sense of *their* failure. . . .

The River Winds Café, not far from *my neighbours'* old offices, is a cheery hamburger joint, formerly tenanted during daylight hours only by *women* out shopping or *sullen adolescents* wasting time after school. It is here that *I*'ve heard *these white-shirted, dark-tied men*, who nurse cups of coffee while sitting attentively as if at a business meeting, sort out *their* histories. *One knot of five to seven men* sticks together; *they* were *mainframe programmers* and *systems analysts* in the old IBM. The most talkative among them were *Jason, a systems analyst who* had been with the company nearly twenty years, and *Paul, a younger programmer whom Jason* had fired in the first downsizing wave.

The main social actors included are the programmers and the author ('I'). Those who did the firing (the senior managers?) are excluded. Social actors are Participants (e.g. '*they* were mainframe programmers'), or Possessives ('*my neighbours'* old offices', '*their* lives'), and they are realized as nouns and pronouns (the first person 'I', and 'they' used anaphorically to refer back to a noun previously used). Programmers are both activated (mainly in 'sorting out their histories') and passivated (mainly in having 'been downsized'). Representation is personal except for 'knot'. Programmers are both classified (as 'programmers' etc.) and named (e.g. 'Jason'), and reference is to groups when there is classification. Reference is specific rather than generic.

Social actors in Example 4 are shown according to the same conventions:

1   But (globalization) is also a demanding^ process, and often a painful^ one.
2   Economic progress has always been accompanied by ^ destruction of obsolete ^activities and ^ creation of new ones.
3   The pace has become swifter and the game has taken on planetary dimensions.
4   It imposes deep and rapid ^ adjustments on *all countries* – including European countries, where industrial civilization was born.
5   ^ Social cohesion is threatened by a widespread ^ sense of ^ unease, ^ inequality and ^ polarization.
6   There is a risk of a disjunct between the hopes and aspirations of *people* and the demands of a global economy.
7   And yet ^ social cohesion is not only a worthwhile social and political ^ goal; it is also a source of ^ efficiency and ^ adaptability in a ^ knowledge-based economy that increasingly depends on human ^ quality and the ^ ability to work as *a team*.
8   It is more than ever the duty of *governments, trade-unions and employers* to work together
    •   to describe the stakes and refute a number of mistakes;
    •   to stress that *our countries* should have high ambitions and they can be realized^; and
    •   to implement the necessary reforms consistently and without delay.
9   ^ Failure to move quickly and decisively will result in ^ loss of resources, both human and capital, which will leave for more promising parts of the world if Europe provides less attractive opportunities.

The main social actors are 'people', and what one might group together as the 'movers', those who make things happen (governments/trade unions/employers).

Both are extensively excluded. Where social actors are included, they occur as Possessives (the duty of *governments, trade-unions and employers*), within Circumstances (on *all countries*) and once as Participant, the Carrier in a type-1 Relational process (*countries* should have high ambitions). Representation is both personal (e.g. 'governments' – a collective noun, but still personal) and impersonal ('countries'). Social actors are classified, not named. Reference is mainly generic (e.g. 'governments', 'people'), though 'our countries' is specific.

And here, thirdly, is an extract from Example 1 (Appendix, pages 229–30):

'Well, *I* was going to say, how do *you* change this sort of negative ^ culture? *We* have done a lot here. But *my* greatest fear is that *they* are going to destroy all the good work that *we* put onto this site if *they* keep pushing and pushing and pushing *the bottom end* like *they* are doing. *I* believe that *people* will react in such a way shortly that *they* will destroy everything.'

'Bottom end?'

'Of *the workforce*; pushing *them* by getting rid^, *I* mean. How the hell can *you* preach this ^ flexibility, this personal and business development at the same time as *you* are getting rid^? As *someone* said to *me* yesterday, *an operator*, "Why am *I* in here now doing the best *I* can getting this ^ product out when tomorrow morning *you* can give *me* a brown envelope?" *I* had no answer.'

'But the good ^ work *you* refer to?'

'Take ^ IR. There has been a coordinated plan to take the power from *the unions* and give it back to *the managers* and give it back to *the workforce* as well. That was going fairly well. But these continuing rounds of ^ redundancies will give the ^ opportunity to say "*We* told *you* so; *we* knew that was the ground plan all along." *The union people* can say, "*You* should have listened to *us* all the time."'

'And the other changes?'

'Developing Organisational Capability, winning ^ culture, Business Improvement Plan, ^ empowering, and all that: *I* am totally committed to all of this principle. These changes are the way forward. But what *the company* is doing is going contrary to what all this is about. This is dangerous – raising ^ expectations and then smashing them. *I* believe *the senior management* has a moral responsibility to *its workforce* and to employ^. *The firm* is an integral part of the society *we* live in.'

'Which means?'

'All *business* has got to keep faith with all of *those it deals with* if *it* is going to deserve to survive.'

The main social actors are the manager ('I'), middle managers ('we'), the company/ senior managers, the workforce, trade unions. The main exclusion is the workforce, and, since the workforce sometimes is included, it is a case of 'backgrounding'. Social Actors function as Participants, Possessives, and within Circumstances. There is quite a range a pronouns: 'I' (the manager being interviewed), 'we' (middle managers), generic 'you' (i.e. 'you' as a colloquial alternative to the more formal and mainly upper class 'one', e.g. 'how do you change this sort of negative culture?'), specific 'you' (i.e. addressing one or more specific people, e.g. 'But the good work *you* refer to?'), non-anaphoric 'they' (i.e. referring to a known group in the context in an 'us and them' way, rather than referring back to a previously used noun) to refer to senior management, anaphoric 'they' / 'it'. The picture in terms of activation and passivation is quite complex, but the workforce are passivated more than other social actors (e.g. 'pushing *them* by getting rid ^'). It is also only the workforce that are represented impersonally ('the bottom end', 'the workforce'). Social actors are classified, never named, and apart from 'an operator' and the pronouns 'I' and specific 'you', reference is to groups rather than individuals. Reference is sometimes specific ('what *the company* is doing') and sometimes generic ('the firm', meaning firms in general), and perhaps ambivalent in some cases ('I believe *the senior management* has a moral responsibility' – the senior management of this company, or senior management in general?).

Let me pull together some comparisons and some comments on more socially significant choices in the representation of social actors. I have already commented earlier on inclusion and exclusion. There are many motivations for exclusion, such as redundancy or irrelevance, but exclusion may be politically or socially significant. For instance in Example 12, what are we to make of the agentless passive clauses ('men who were recently downsized^', 'After they were let go^') and what one might argue is the metaphorical substitution of an intransitive process ('they lost their jobs') for a transitive one ('someone fired them')? There is room for argument, but one question which at least merits discussion is whether these ways of excluding the agents or agencies who actually fired the men are symptomatic of a view of redundancy as something which happens to people rather than something which is done to people – a calamity rather than a crime, to put it in rather dramatic terms. I commented on exclusions in Example 4 earlier, so I shall say no more about it. In Example 1 the main exclusion, backgrounding, is the workforce. The intransitive or elliptical use of 'getting rid' is particularly striking – perhaps the backgrounding in this case is a matter of delicacy, euphemism, avoidance of calling a spade a spade.

Pronouns are usually worth attending to in texts. One obvious point is the 'us and them' division associated with the non-anaphoric 'they' in Example 1. The first person plural pronoun, 'we', is important in terms of Identificational meanings (see Part 4), how texts represent and construct groups and communities. A more general point about Example 1 is that the main 'we-community' is middle managers, the group of managers to which the interviewee belongs (though it is not clearly defined as a group), and a division is set up between middle managers and senior managers – indeed this is represented as a deeper division than that between middle managers and the workforce. 'We' is used 'exclusively' here, to include broadly middle managers, but excludes senior managers and also, for instance, the interviewer. As is often the case, 'we' shifts meaning through the text. In the reported speech (actually in part a representation of imaginary rather than real speech), the 'we-community' is the unions – though there is a characteristic vagueness about whether it includes trade-unionists generally or just the union leadership. 'We' is also used inclusively at the end, loosely referencing everyone and anyone ('the society *we* live in'). The communities constructed as 'we' are often elusive, shifting and vague.

It is interesting to contrast 'we' with generic 'you' in Example 1. There is a 'you'-community constructed here as well as a (middle-management') 'we-community'. The manager includes himself within both, but they are different. The 'you-community' is more extensive than the 'we-community', but it does not include anyone and everyone – it references the community of managers, but the wider community of managers, not just the (middle-)managers in this company. In chapter 3, I discussed how the dialectic of the particular and the universal is textually enacted. The 'we-community' here references the particular, the 'you-community' references the universal, managing as a universal process (and as a global process, as opposed to the local process in the company). Generic reference in general is associated with the universal, for instance the oscillation between particular and universal in Example 1 (e.g. 'the firm', representing firms universally). At the same time, generic 'you' is a mainly colloquial pronoun (in contrast to 'one') which references ordinary practical experience, and the 'you-community' is in that sense the community of practical management, the community of the 'ordinary manager', with which this manager is associating himself.

The significance of 'activation' and 'passivation' is rather transparent: where social actors are mainly activated, their capacity for agentive action, for making things happen, for controlling others and so forth is accentuated, where they are mainly passivated, what is accentuated is their subjection to processes, them being affected by the actions of others, and so forth. The programmers in Example 12 are represented as the victims of processes within IBM, and the workers are mainly represented similarly in Example 1. Contrast this with a 'class struggle' view of industrial relations which implies a clash of agencies. Impersonal representation of social actors (e.g. 'the bottom end', 'the workforce' in Example 1) can dehumanize social actors, take the focus away from them as people, represent them, for instance, as in this case, instrumentally or structurally as elements of organizational structures and processes. The opposite extreme to impersonalization is naming – representing individuals by name.

Representations of time and place

A general distinction within representations of both time and place is between representations of location (e.g. 'at 9pm', 'in Lancaster') and representations of extent (duration, distance – e.g. 'for 3 hours', 'for 3 miles'). Various linguistic features contribute to the representation of time: the tense of verbs (past, present and future time, e.g. 'played', 'plays', 'is going to play'); the aspect of verbs, the distinction between progressive and non-progressive ('is playing', 'plays') and between perfect and non-perfect ('has played', 'plays'), adverbials (e.g. 'today', 'yesterday', 'tomorrow'), and conjunctions and prepositions which mark temporal (as well as spatial) relations (e.g. while, before, after; between, in front of, behind, etc.).

According to Harvey (1996a), space and time are social constructs – they are differently constructed in different societies, change in their construction is part of social change, and constructions of space and time are contested (for instance within class struggles in workplaces). Moreover, constructions of space and constructions of time are closely interconnected, and it is difficult to separate them, so that it makes sense to focus on their intersection in the construction of different space–times. In any social order, there will be different co-existing space–times (the relationship between the 'global' and the 'local' which I have referred to at various points is primarily a relationship between space–times), and one matter for analysis is how these different space–times are connected to each other. Harvey gives the example of trade union militancy in specific places or localities, and the way the specificity of place is connected with the national and international space–times of social movements. Such connections are made routinely in daily life in events and the ways in which events are chained together, and are built into social practices and networks of social practices.

Space, time, and 'space–times' are routinely constructed in texts. Having said this, one must be careful not to reduce these constructions to texts, because aspects of the physical environment such as urban design and the architectural design of buildings are also at issue. But texts are nevertheless very significant in the processes discussed in the previous paragraph, and it therefore makes sense to ask how we might 'operationalize' perspectives such as Harvey's in the analysis of texts. One aspect of this is the chaining of texts as part of the chaining of events discussed in chapter 2, and genre chains. In discussing 'genres of governance' in that chapter, I suggested that such genres contribute to linking different 'scales' of social life, the local, national, regional, and global, which is centrally a matter of linking different 'space–times'. But the construction and interconnection of space–times is also routinely going on within particular texts, and is a focus for analysis of texts.

Take for instance the following extract from Example 1. Textual elements which are germane to the construction of time have been italicized, those germane to the construction of space underlined:

'Well, I *was going to say*, how *do* you *change* this sort of negative culture? We *have done* a lot <u>here</u>. But my greatest fear *is* that they *are going to destroy* all the good work that we *put* onto <u>this site</u> if they *keep pushing and pushing and pushing* the bottom end like they *are doing*. I *believe* that people *will react* in such a way *shortly* that they *will destroy* everything.'

Notice the movement between different temporalities which is realized in the shifting tense and aspect of verbs and in one case an adverb ('shortly'): from the complex 'future-in-the-past' ('was going to say'), to simple present tense ('do . . . change'), to present perfect ('have done'), to present ('is'), to future ('are going to destroy'), to past ('put'), to present progressive ('keep pushing', 'are doing'), to simple present ('believe'), to 'future ('will react . . . shortly', 'will destroy'). One can identify three different space–times here: the space–time of the interview itself (the first 'future-in-the-past' verb represents the manager's future intention at an earlier point in the interview, before the interviewer's question), the 'local' space–time of the workplace, and the 'global' space–time of management. The space–time of the workplace is constructed as a relationship between past (the 'good work' that has been done), present (what 'they' are doing, what the manager believes and fears – notice that the present perfect ('have done') differs from the past ('put') precisely in that it links the past and present), and future (people will react, everything will be destroyed). One can ask of any organization or institution (workplaces, trade unions, families) how relations between past, present and future are constructed, and how they are 'textured' in texts, and how they change as part of social change (e.g. New Capitalism).

The 'global' space–time of management is realized in a particular way of using the simple present tense ('do . . . change') which is sometimes called the 'timeless present' – it represents not the present time, but an undelimited timespan, the temporality of 'management as such', management as a process which exists outside and beyond any specific site of management and is in that sense 'global', located everywhere and nowhere. Notice that whereas the 'local' space–time of the workplace is specified spatially ('here', 'this site'), the 'global' space–time of management is not. Notice also that the 'global' space–time of management is linguistically marked not only by verb tense but also by generic 'you' – the 'you-community' belongs in global space–time. This indicates that the representation of space–times cannot be reduced to the representation of time and space, that particular spatio-temporalities are interlinked with particular social relations and social identities.

The movement between the 'local' space–time of the workplace and the 'global' space–time of management recurs throughout this text. We can see the manager as using it as a vantage point from which to assess and evaluate what has been going on within his own particular company. This, of course, is how 'expert systems' (Giddens) are pervasively positioned in relation to the local and 'practical' sites and locations of social life. What textual analysis can show is how that relationship is routinely organized and sustained and reproduced in text and talk.

The construction of space–time in Example 4 (the European Union policy document) is different.

1 But (globalization) *is* also a demanding *process*, and *often* a painful one.

2 Economic *progress has always been* accompanied by destruction of *obsolete* activities and creation of *new* ones.

3 The *pace has become* swifter and the game *has taken on* planetary dimensions.

4 It *imposes* deep and *rapid* adjustments on all countries – including European countries, where industrial civilization was *born*.

5 Social cohesion *is threatened* by a widespread sense of unease, inequality and polarization.

6 There *is* a risk of a disjunct between the hopes and aspirations of people and the demands of a global economy.

7 And yet social cohesion is not only a worthwhile social and political goal; it *is* also a source of efficiency and adaptability in a knowledge-based economy that *increasingly depends* on human quality and the ability to work as a team.

8 It *is more than ever* the duty of governments, trade-unions and employers to work together
   • to describe the stakes and refute a number of mistakes;
   • to stress that our countries *should have* high ambitions and they can be realized; and
   • to implement the necessary reforms consistently and *without delay*.

9 Failure to move *quickly* and decisively *will result* in loss of resources, both human and capital, which *will leave* for more promising parts of the world if Europe *provides* less attractive opportunities.

There is again a relationship between a 'local' space–time and a 'global' space–time, though the example makes it clear that what is 'local' is relative – the 'local' here is in fact regional, 'Europe', used in the common but contentious way to reference the European Union. The 'global' space–time is the space–time of 'globalization' itself. We have again the present tense for an undelimited timespan (for instance in sentences 4, 5, and 6), though in this case combined with spatial specifications ('all countries', 'widespread', 'global', 'in a knowledge-based economy') which accentuate the spatial universality of globalization and its consequences. The present perfect and the adverb 'always' in sentence 2 accentuate the temporal universality of the consequences of 'economic progress', and the present perfect verbs in sentence 3 frame globalization within a process of temporal (in 'pace') and spatial change ('increasingly' and 'more than ever' in sentences 7 and 8 also represent change).

The relationship between the 'global' space–time and the 'European' space–time is that the latter is framed by the former. The 'global' space–time is constructed as actual and real in a sequence of factual statements, which frame and ground the construction of the 'European' space–time in sentences 8 and 9 as an imaginary, projected space–time within the domain of policy. Modality is significant: the 'global' space–time is the domain of what 'is', whereas the 'European' space–time is the domain of what 'must' be. Obligational modality is however mainly implicit. In sentence 8, one can see 'it is the duty of governments . . .' as a metaphorical equivalent of 'governments . . . must', though there is also one explicit obligational modality ('should'). Sentence 9 is most directly prediction (future in terms of tense), but it triggers assumptions which are normative statements ('we must move quickly and decisively', 'Europe must provide more attractive opportunities'). This sort of relationship between the global 'is' and the regional or national 'must' is pervasive in texts which represent globalization.

Summary

We have seen that in terms of their Representational meanings and their grammatical and lexical realization, clauses have three main elements: Processes, Participants, and Circumstances. When we look at clauses as representing social events, we can compare them (and, more globally, texts) in terms of which elements of social events are included or excluded, and which included elements are given greatest salience. We can also compare them in terms of how concretely or abstractly (with what degree of generalization) social events are represented. We can connect these distinctions with the view of representation as 'recontextualization', and of particular networks of social practices and associated genres as having particular 'recontextualizing principles' which tend to favour particular inclusions and exclusions, degrees of concreteness or abstraction/generalization, as well as characteristic ways of arranging, explaining, legitimizing and evaluating events. Thus, for instance, genres of governance have a predictable tendency to represent events through generalization and abstraction. I differentiated six main types of Process (Material, Mental, Verbal, two types of Relational, Existential), and suggested that particular events can be 'congruently' or 'metaphorically' represented by different process types, or by 'nominalization' of processes. The representation of social actors

(Participants) involves a number of choices, including activated/passivated, personal/ impersonal, named/classified, and specific/generic, as well as exclusion or inclusion, and using pronouns as opposed to nouns. These choices are socially significant for instance with respect to the representation of agency. Finally, we discussed the representation of time and space (Circumstances), suggesting that Harvey's analysis of 'space–times' can be operationalized in textual analysis by seeing space–times and relations between space–times as routinely textured in texts.

Part IV
Styles and identities

9 Styles

Text analysis issues

Styles: levels of abstraction
Dialogicality
Linguistic realizations of styles

Social research issues

Social identity and personal identity (personality)
Agency
Social 'characters'
Public space

Styles are the discoursal aspect of ways of being, identities. Who you are is partly a matter of how you speak, how you write, as well as a matter of embodiment – how you look, how you hold yourself, how you move, and so forth. Styles are linked to identification – using the nominalization rather than the noun 'identities' emphasizes the process of identifying, how people identify themselves and are identified by others. And I have used the term Identification for one of the three major types of meaning in texts. The process of identification is partly a textual process, and although Styles/Identification are not discrete from Discourses/Representation or Genres/Action (their relationship is on the contrary dialectical – see chapter 2 and below), it is different, and we need to make an analytical distinction between them.

In so far as the process of identification does involve the constitutive effects of discourse, it should be seen as a dialectical process in which discourses are inculcated in identities (see chapter 2). A practical sense of this process is evident in a memorandum which Philip Gould, one of Tony Blair's key advisers, produced

('Consolidating the Blair identity') when Blair became leader of the Labour Party in 1994. 'What he must do is build on his strengths, and build an identity as a politician that is of a piece with the political positions he adopts. He must be a complete, coherent politician who always rings true.' In the terms I am using, one can interpret this as saying that Blair needs to inculcate within his way of being aspects of the political discourse of New Labour (the 'Third Way'), especially this discourse as an imaginary, as a vision of society (Fairclough 2000b). One consequence of this dialectical view is that Identificational meanings (as well as Actional meanings) in texts can be seen as presupposing Representational meanings, the assumptions on which people identify themselves as they do (so in Blair's case, these would include imaginaries of what government should be, what leadership should be, and so forth).

Social identity and personal identity (personality)

Identification is a complex process. Part of its complexity arises from the fact that a distinction needs to be drawn between personal and social aspects of identity – **social identity and personality**. Identity cannot be reduced to social identity, which partly means that identification is not a purely textual process, not only a matter of language. Recent post-structuralist and post-modern theory has closely associated identity with discourse, and identity (or 'the subject') is often said to be an effect of discourse, constructed in discourse. There is some truth in that, but only some. It is problematic partly because people are not only pre-positioned in how they participate in social events and texts, they are also social agents who do things, create things, change things (see chapter 2). But it is also problematic because it fails to recognize the importance of our embodied, practical engagement with the world, which begins before children even learn languages and continues throughout our lives, in processes of identification, specifically in the formation of 'self-consciousness', a continuous sense of the self (Archer 2000). Self-consciousness is a precondition for social processes of identification, the construction of social identities, including social identification in discourse, in texts.

Distinctions are also needed, however, within social identity, which lead to an elaboration of the concept of agency (see **structure and agency** in the Glossary of key terms). I shall follow Archer (2000) here. People are involuntarily positioned as Primary Agents because of what they are born into and initially have no choice about – peasantry or gentry, working-class or middle-class, male or female, their positions within society's distribution of resources, as Archer puts it. Few people in contemporary societies remain within the limits of these positionings, but their capacity to transform them depends upon their reflexivity and their capacity to become Corporate Agents capable of collective action and shaping social change. Achieving social identity in a full sense is a matter of being capable of assuming social roles but personifying them, investing them with one's own personality (or personal identity), enacting them in a distinctive way. People's full development as social agents is dialectically interconnected with their full development as personalities, neither of which is guaranteed. Becoming a personality is a matter of being able to formulate one's primary and ultimate concerns, and to balance and prioritize one's social roles in terms of these. Of course, this is itself a socially constrained process – part of the dialectic between social identity and personal identity or personality is that the former constrains the latter.

Of course, a person's social identity includes diverse social roles, though it is doubtful whether this 'role theory' way of putting it can adequately grasp the internal complexity and heterogeneity of social identity, which has been a major theme in post-structuralist theory.

Levels of abstraction

The discussion of levels of abstraction in Chapter 7, the chapter on discourses, carries over to styles. But in this case, we need to take account of the dialectic of social identity and personality discussed above. MacIntyre (1984) suggested that a significant part of what makes a culture distinctive is its stock of 'characters', its culturally most salient identities. He gave the contemporary examples of the Manager and the Therapist. These 'characters' are seen to exist at a rather high level of abstraction and generalization, they have a considerable continuity over time (though major social changes entail changes in the stock of 'characters'), they are pervasive through social life. Identifying the 'characters' of new capitalism and tracing textual processes of identification of these 'characters' is one issue which I shall take up below. But clearly there are various styles of being a Manager or a Therapist, on a less abstract level. And on the concrete level of social events, one needs to address Archer's question of how personalities, or personal identities, invest the 'character' of Manager, Therapist, Politician, etc. in distinctive ways – Blair for instance may be in some ways a typical modern politician, but he is also a distinctive modern politician whose personality has invested the role of political leader in a distinctive way.

Styles and texts

Let me trace some implications of the above for text analysis. First, agency as a causal force (chapter 2) in shaping events and texts is not undifferentiated – the effectivity of agency depends upon both the nature of the event and its relationship to social practices and social structures, and the capacities of the agent. Second, there are implications for dialogue and for social difference (see chapter 3). One might say that dialogue in the richest sense is communication between people as social agents and as personalities. One question that can be asked in textual analysis is to what extent people address each other on this basis, and to what extent there is mutuality and symmetry between those co-involved in social events, or conversely to what extent considerations of communicative strategy (see chapter 4) result in a reduction of the difference of the other and a lack of dialogicality. We can link this for instance to questions of citizenship and public sphere (Fairclough 1999, Touraine 1997): effective citizenship and effective public space dialogue (the dialogue of citizens on matters of social concern) depend, one might argue, on dialogue in this rich sense. Thirdly, identification in texts is both a matter of individuality and collectivity, an 'I' and a 'we', or rather potentially multiple 'I's and/or 'we's. For instance, Tony Blair in Example 5 (I discuss this example in some detail in chapter 10) speaks as a member of an inclusive 'we'-community (those, for instance, who 'feel powerless' in the face of globalization), an exclusive 'we'-community ('we' the Alliance against Terrorism), and as an individual, an 'I', or one might say more than one 'I' (the 'I' that 'realizes why people protest against globalization' is perhaps not the same 'I' as the one who issues ultimata to the Taliban).

Characteristics of styles

Styles are realized in quite a range of linguistic features. First, phonological features: pronunciation, intonation, stress, rhythm. Second, vocabulary and metaphor – one area of vocabulary which varies with identification is intensifying adverbials such as 'dreadfully', 'awfully', 'frightfully', and so forth, as well as swear-words which function in a similar way ('bloody', 'sodding', etc.). Messages about both social identity (e.g. social class) and personality are carried by the variable selections people make from words of this sort (including whether and how much, and how obscenely, they swear). Style also involves an interplay between language and 'body language' – for instance, Tony Blair's identity as a politician is partly a matter of his facial expressions, his gestures, his stance, and so forth – as well as, for example, his hairstyle and clothing. To what extent one should include such things within discourse, or language, is a contentious matter. 'Body language' is based in the physical materiality of bodies, yet it is clearly 'semioticized' in the sense that various gestures have relatively stable meanings. But then, all sorts of aspects of the material world can be 'semioticized', including landscapes, buildings, and so forth. This is not a reason for reducing them to language or discourse, but for recognizing the dialectical nature of the relationship between discourse and the non-discursive world. The latter 'internalizes' the former (Harvey 1996a).

In the next chapter, I shall be focusing on a few aspects of textual meaning which contribute to identification, centrally around the categories of modality and evaluation. I shall see both in terms of commitments which people make in their texts and talk which contribute to identification – commitments to truth, to moral obligation, to necessity, to values. I shall also discuss pronouns, seen as incorporated within a broad view of modality, which are of obvious significance here (e.g. whether texts include personal pronouns, and if so which – 'I', 'we', generic 'you', etc.).

Summary

In this brief chapter we have discussed Styles as analytically distinct from, though dialectically interconnected with, Genres and Discourses. I have also presented a dialectical view of the relationship between social identity and personality, and argued that Styles can be identified at different levels of abstraction like Genres and Discourses. Though in the case of Styles these levels of abstraction are related to ways in which personalities invest social identities and roles. We have discussed ways in which the theoretical complexities of identity can be more concretely focused in textual analysis. Finally we have looked at some of the range of linguistic realizations of differences in Style.

10 Modality and evaluation

Text analysis issues

Modality
Evaluation
Personal pronouns

Social research issues

'Characters' of new capitalism
Heterogeneity of social identity
Informalization of public identities
Social identity and personality
Aestheticization of public identities
The public sphere, citizens and experts

In this chapter I shall continue to discuss Identification in texts with a focus on modality and evaluation, though other textual features relevant to Identification will also be discussed as they arise in relation to the social research issues. Both modality and evaluation will be seen in terms of what authors *commit* themselves to, with respect to what is true and what is necessary (modality), and with respect to what is desirable or undesirable, good or bad (evaluation). My assumption is that what people commit themselves to in texts is an important part of how they identify themselves, the texturing of identities.

The social research issues I shall take up in this chapter include, first, the question of the significant 'characters' of new capitalism in MacIntyre's sense (1984 – see the discussion in chapter 9), in terms of how they identify themselves in texts. I shall contrast the Politician (represented by Tony Blair, Example 5, Appendix, pages

237–8) and the Manager, or rather Management Guru (Rosabeth Moss Kanter, Example 9, Appendix, pages 244–5). The second issue is how one addresses the internal heterogeneity of social identity from a text analytical perspective, and I shall address this issue in terms of the 'various Mr Blairs' one can identify (Fairclough 2000b). This will include the question of the societal informalization (Misztal 2000) of public identities, the pervasive tension, for instance, in contemporary politicians between being 'ordinary' people (Sennett 1974), and being in various ways extraordinary (figures of public authority). The third issue is the relationship between social identity and personality which I discussed in chapter 9, and the question of how textual analysis might contribute to researching it. The fourth issue is the aestheticization (Chouliaraki and Fairclough 1999, Harvey 1990) of identities, especially in public life, which is partially reflected in the pervasive preoccupation with 'image'. And the fifth and final issue is public sphere and 'citizenship', how people identify themselves as citizens in contemporary society, especially in relation to various types of Expert.

Modality

In chapter 6, I distinguished four major Speech Functions, two associated with Knowledge Exchanges (Statement, Question), two associated with Activity Exchanges (Demand, Offer). The question of modality can be seen as the question of what people commit themselves to when they make Statements, ask Questions, make Demands or Offers. The point is that there are different ways of doing each of these which make different commitments. This is most obvious with Statements, so I shall focus on them initially. For instance, in Example 9, the author makes Statements about what makes an e-company successful, including: 'Companies that are successful on the web operate differently from their laggard counterparts'. She might have written: 'Companies that are successful on the web seem to operate differently from their laggard counterparts' or 'Companies that are successful on the web often operate differently from their laggard counterparts', or 'Companies that are successful on the web may operate differently from their laggard counterparts'. What she actually wrote commits her to the truth of the proposition more than any of these alternatives. The differences between them are differences in modality.

According to Halliday (1994), 'modality means the speaker's judgement of the probabilities, or the obligations, involved in what he is saying.' And according to Verschueren (1999), 'modality . . . involves the many ways in which attitudes can be expressed towards the 'pure' reference-and-predication content of an utterance, signalling factuality, degrees of certainty or doubt, vagueness, possibility, necessity, and even permission and obligation.' Hodge and Kress (1988) refer to the 'stance' speakers or writers take towards representations, their degree of 'affinity' with them. All of these formulations, like my own, see modality in terms of a relationship between speaker or writer, or 'author', and representations.

The suggestion is not that this is a 'private' relationship between a rational self and the world. Modality is important in the texturing of identities, both personal ('personalities') and social, in the sense that what you commit yourself to is a significant part of what you are – so modality choices in texts can be seen as part of the process of texturing self-identity. But this goes on in the course of social processes, so that the process of identification is inevitably inflected by the process of social relation. Let us go back to the sentence from Example 9. In writing 'Companies that are successful on the web operate differently from their laggard counterparts', Kanter not only makes a strong commitment to the truth of the proposition, she does so as an internationally famous management 'guru' giving authoritative information about e-business to managers who read her book as a possible blueprint for change. The texturing of identity is thoroughly embedded in the texturing of social relations.

As I suggested in chapter 2, the three major aspects of meaning in texts, Action, Representation and Identification, are dialectically related, and this is particularly clear in the case of modality. How one represents the world, to what one commits oneself, e.g. one's degree of commitment to truth, is a part of how one identifies one-self, necessarily in relation to others with whom one is interacting. Putting it differently, identities are relational: who one is is a matter of how one relates to the world and to other people. One can see a 'guru' identity, a specific form of the 'character' of Expert, being constructed in Kanter's text, partly through choices in modality, but it is an identity-in-relation – in relation to the business world which is represented, and to the managers and executives who are addressed. This means that choices in modality are significant not only in terms of Identification, but also in terms of Action (and the social relations of Action), and Representation. Modality can be seen as initially to do with 'commitments', 'attitudes', 'judgements', 'stances' and therefore with Identification (which is why I deal with it in this section of the book), but it is also to do with Action and social relations, and Representation. The same is true of Mood. It can be seen as primarily to do with types of Action, Exchange Types and Speech Functions (see chapter 6), but experts, for example, who overwhelmingly use declarative clauses to make Statements identify themselves differently from experts who use interrogative clauses to ask Questions, so Mood is also significant for Identification. It can be one contributory element in different ways of being an expert. This dialectical property of textual choices means, in the case of modality, that, for instance, a modal choice of avoiding a strong commitment to truth, such as saying 'he may be there' when one knows he is or is not there, can be primarily motivated by the social relations of Action, as a matter of discretion maybe – though that in itself gives a 'message' about one's identity.

We can move towards social research issues, and the transformations of new capitalism, by noting that there are social limits on modality choices which go beyond the social relations of particular texts or talk. We can ask: who is able to commit themselves to strong truth claims about this or that aspect of the world? Predictions are a good example: who is it that is able to commit themselves to strong truth claims about what *will* happen? Of course, anyone might make predictions, but the question is rather: who has the socially ratified power of prediction? And who identify themselves in part through exercising this power of prediction? One group with precisely that power is management gurus – though there are no instances in Example 9. Another group is politicians and governments. There are quite a few predictions in Example 11, the extract from the Government consultation paper on the 'Learning Age' – e.g., 'The information and knowledge-based revolution of the twenty-first century will be built on a very different foundation – investment in the intellect and creativity of people'. There is a name for this kind of prediction – 'futurology'. The power of futurological prediction is a significant one, because injunctions about what people must do or must not do now can be legitimized in terms of such predictions about the future, and extensively are. Another group who have predictive power is perhaps priests, though that is rather a different matter.

Exchange types, speech functions and types of modality

I linked modality to exchange types and speech functions at the beginning of the chapter. In fact there are different types of modality which can be associated with the different types of exchange and speech function. In summary:

● *Knowledge exchange ('epistemic' modality)*

    Statements: 'author's' commitment to truth'
        Assert: The window is open
        Modalize: The window may be open
        Deny: The window is not open

    Questions: author elicits other's commitment to truth
        Non-modalized positive: Is the window open?
        Modalized: Could the window be open?
        Non-modalized negative: Isn't the window open?

● *Activity exchange ('deontic' modality)*

>Demand: 'author's' commitment to obligation/necessity
>>Prescribe: Open the window!
>>Modalize: You should open the window
>>Proscribe: Don't open the window!
>Offer: author's commitment to act
>>Undertaking: I'll open the window.
>>Modalized: I may open the window
>>Refusal: I won't open the window

One thing to note here is that this view of modality goes beyond cases of explicit modalization, i.e. cases where there is an explicit marker of modality. The archetypical markers of modality are 'modal verbs' ('can, will, may, must, would, should', etc.), though there are in fact many other ways in which modality is marked (see below). But in the case of Statements, modalized cases are seen here as intermediate between Assertion and Denial, which are typically realized as positive Statements (e.g. 'Conflict is seen as creative') and negative Statements (e.g. 'Conflict is not seen as creative') without modal verbs or other modal markers. All of these fall within the broad category of modality. The rationale for this is fairly obvious: in terms of commitments to truth, 'Conflict may be seen as creative' or 'Conflict could be seen as creative' are intermediate between Assertion and Denial. In the case of Demands, modalized forms (e.g. 'you should open the window', 'you must open the window') are seen as intermediate between Prescriptions (e.g. 'Open the window!') which are typically realized as positive imperative clauses, and Proscriptions (e.g. 'Don't open the window!') which are typically realized as negative imperative clauses. Questions are seen in terms of the author eliciting the commitment to truth of others. Again, the range of modalities includes non-modalized questions ('Is the window open?', 'Isn't the window open?') as well as modalized questions ('Could the window be open?'). The same is true for Offers.

Modality is a very complex aspect of meaning, and the framework above excludes much of its intricacy. For instance, Demands can be realized as 'question-requests', as clauses which are Interrogative in their Grammatical Mood (e.g. 'Will you open the window?') and have the form of modalized Questions. There are also distinctions of tense ('can', 'could'; 'will', 'would') which overlap with the distinction between hypothetical and non-hypothetical (e.g. 'I will open the window', 'I would open the window if asked').

In the following short dialogue (which I used in chapter 6 in connection with Grammatical Mood), I have underlined expressions relevant to the marking of modality.

> *Max:* A couple of questions very easy to answer for a radio programme we're doing. The first of the questions is *What <u>would you say</u>* language <u>is</u>?
> *Woman:* Language . . . well it'<u>s</u> the dialogue that people speak within various ountries.
> *Max:* Fair enough aaand *what* <u>would you say</u> it'<u>s</u> made *out* of?
> *Woman:* (*Pause, 8 seconds.*) It'<u>s</u> made out of (*puzzled intonation*) . . .
> *Max:* Hmmm.
> *Woman:* Well <u>I don't know you'd tell</u> what's it'<u>s</u> *made* out of . . . it'<u>s</u> a person's *expression* <u>I suppose is it</u>?
> *Max:* I <u>haven't got</u> the answers, I'<u>ve only got</u> the questions (*laughing*).
> *Woman:* (*Simultaneously, small laugh.*)
> *Sid:* That'<u>s not</u> bad though.
> *Woman:* Well it'<u>s</u> an *expression*, it <u>would be</u> a person's *expression* <u>wouldn't it</u>?
> *Sid:* That'<u>s</u> a good answer.
> *Max:* Thank you very much.
>
> (Hodge and Kress 1988, p. 125)

The modality here is epistemic, with the Speech functions of Statement and Question. The first thing to note here is the way in which the interviewer words his questions. Rather than 'what is language?' and 'what is it made out of?', he asks 'what would you say language is?', 'what would you say it's made out of?' Hypothetical modality ('would you say') is used in a way which makes the questions more tentative, as if the interviewer was hypothesizing about asking the question rather than actually asking it ('if I were to ask you what language is, what would you say'). This is perhaps because of the social distance between a younger male interviewer and an older female interviewee. The woman's first answer is an Assertion ('it's the dialogue that people speak in various countries'), but her response to the second question is modally more complex. First, she comments on the question, herself using hypothetical modality, but it is marked not only with a reduced form of 'would' ('you'd') but also with a mental process clause ('I don't know' – see chapter 8) which gives a subjective marking to the modality, i.e. explicitly marks the commitment of the person who is speaking. This might have been worded just as a negative hypothetical modal verb ('you wouldn't tell'). The answer, when it comes, begins as an apparent Assertion, but then is subjectively modalized ('I suppose'), and made into a tag question ('is it?'), so there is mixture between making a truth commitment and eliciting a truth commitment, the latter weakening the former. Max's response consists of a Denial ('I haven't got the answers') followed by an Assertion ('I've only got the questions'), and Sid's two contributions are also Assertions. The woman's final turn shows the same shifts from categorical Assertion as her previous turn – from 'it's an expression' to hypothetical 'it would be a person's expression' and then again a question tag ('wouldn't it?'). These modal markings can be interpreted as a reluctance on the part of the woman to commit herself strongly to truth claims. Readers may wish to compare these points with Hodge and Kress's fuller analysis (1988: 125–7).

Levels of commitment

In modalized clauses, both epistemic and deontic, one can distinguish different levels or degrees of commitment to truth on the one hand and obligation/necessity on the other (Halliday 1994). Schematically:

	Truth	*Obligation*
High	certainly	required
Median	probably	supposed
Low	possibly	allowed

The examples I have given here are 'modal adverbials' ('certainly', etc.) in the case of epistemic modality, and participial adjectives ('required', etc.) in the case of deontic modality. But part of the diversity of modal verbs is that some are higher in terms of degree of commitment than others. Compare for epistemic modality: 'he certainly opened the window', 'he probably opened the window', 'he possibly opened the window'; 'he must have opened the window', 'he will have opened the window', 'he may have opened the window'. And for deontic modality: 'you are required to open the window', 'you are supposed to open the window', 'you are allowed to open the window'; 'you must open the window', 'you should open the window', 'you can open the window'.

Markers of modalization

I have already indicated some of the range of markers of modalization. They include most centrally the modal verbs, but also as we have seen modal adverbs such as 'certainly', participial adjectives such as 'required', mental process clauses such as 'I think'. In fact it is possible to take a very inclusive view of what may mark modalization – Hodge and Kress (1988) are more inclusive than most of the literature on modality. Corresponding to modal adverbs, there are also modal adjectives such as 'possible' or 'probable' which appear in separate modalizing clauses such as 'it is possible' (e.g. 'it is possible that he opened the window'). There are various verbs apart from the modal verbs which can be seen as markers of modalization, such as verbs of appearance ('seem', 'appear' – 'he seems to have opened the window'). Other types of adverb can also be markers (e.g. 'in fact', 'obviously', 'evidently'), including adverbs like 'usually', 'often', 'always' which mark what Halliday distinguishes as a separate modality of 'usuality' (1994).

Beyond, these cases, one might also include, as Hodge and Kress do, 'hedges' such as 'sort of' or 'kind of' (e.g. 'they're *kind of* looking to you Ben', which comes from Example 10). Intonation and other aspects of oral delivery are also relevant to a speaker's degree of commitment – whether things are said in a hesitant, tentative, confident or assertive tone. One might even include reported speech – attributing a statement to others (e.g. 'I'm told that they're looking to you Ben') is a way of lowering one's own commitment to it.

The sort of commitment an author makes, and therefore how an author identifies himself or herself, also depends upon the intersection between modality and other categories in clauses. These include Speech Function and Grammatical Mood – I have already pointed out that modality works differently in, for example, Statements and Questions. They also include 'person': the difference between subjectively marked modalities (e.g. 'I think the window is open') and modalities which are not subjectively marked (e.g. 'The window's open') is that the former are 'first person' statements ('I-statements') whereas the latter are 'third-person' statements. 'First person' statements can also be plural, 'we-statements' (e.g. 'we will not walk away' in Example 5, discussed below) – like the 'power of prediction', the power of making statements on behalf of others, or indeed on behalf of 'all of us' (as when Blair says in the same text 'we feel powerless') is a power which has an uneven social distribution, and is important for identification. Another category which significantly intersects with modality is process type (see chapter 8) – for instance, making strong truth claims about the mental processes of others (e.g. the manager in Example 1, talking about people in Liverpool: 'They are totally suspicious of any change') is also assuming a power which is important in identification.

Evaluation and values

I am going to use 'evaluation' in a general sense to include not only the type of Statements which I called 'evaluations' in chapter 6, but also other more or less explicit or implicit ways in which authors commit themselves to values (see Graham 2002, Hunston and Thompson 2000, Lemke 1998, Martin 2000, White 2001, forthcoming). We can distinguish the following categories:

Evaluative statements ('evaluations' in chapter 6)
Statements with deontic modalities
Statements with affective mental process verbs
Value assumptions

Evaluative statements

In chapter 6 I distinguished the following categories of Statement: statements of fact ('realis' statements), predictions and hypothetical statements (both 'irrealis'), and evaluations. Evaluative statements (evaluations) are statements about desirability and undesirability, what is good and what is bad (e.g. 'this is a good book', 'this is a bad book', 'this book is wonderful', 'this book is awful').

Evaluative statements are in the most obvious case realized as relational processes ('type 1' relational processes in the terms of Chapter 8) as in these examples. In these cases, the evaluative element is in the attribute, which may be an adjective (e.g. 'good'), or a noun phrase (e.g. 'a bad book'). Alternatively, evaluative statements may be realized as other processes where the evaluative element is the verb – rather than saying 'he was a coward', one might say 'he chickened out'. They can also be realized as other types of process with evaluative adverbs (e.g. 'The author has put this book together *dreadfully*', 'The author has summed up the arguments *wonderfully*' – material and verbal processes respectively). Exclamations (which can be seen as a separate if minor Grammatical Mood) are an alternative to evaluative statements (e.g. 'What a wonderful book!' instead of 'This book is wonderful').

I said above that evaluative statements are statements about desirability or undesirability. With words such as 'good', 'bad', 'wonderful', 'dreadful', desirability is quite explicit. But evaluative statements also evaluate in terms of importance, usefulness and so forth (see Lemke 1998), where desirability is assumed. So evaluative statements such as 'this is an important book', 'this is a useless book' imply that the book is desirable or undesirable – it is generally taken as self-evident that what is 'important' or 'useful' is desirable. When we move away from such transparent cases, evaluative statements quickly become discourse-relative – for instance, 'she's a communist' may be an evaluative statement, but only relative to a particular discourse. Many other words which figure in evaluations, such as 'brave', 'cowardly', 'honest', 'dishonest', have complex meanings which include an evaluative element – for instance, a 'brave' person is a person who is for instance prepared to take personal risks, whereas an 'honest' person is someone who, for instance, does not tell lies, but both are also by implication 'good' persons. In these cases, it is difficult to imagine the words being used in evaluative statements (e.g. 'she's a coward') without having these evaluative meanings – though classification of people into 'brave' and 'cowardly' is not universally accepted, and its evaluative implications can be subverted (e.g. 'Good soldiers have the common sense to be cowards'). Evaluations are often embedded within phrases (e.g. 'This *awful book* costs a fortune') rather than made as statements. We can say that 'this awful book' presupposes the evaluative statement 'this book is awful'.

Evaluation come on a 'scale of intensity' (White 2001). Evaluative adjectives and adverbs as well as 'affective' mental process verbs cluster in semantic sets of terms which range from low to high intensity. For instance: 'I like/love/adore this book', 'this book is good/wonderful/fantastic', 'it's badly/dreadfully/appallingly written'. The same is true of other types of verbs ('the soldiers killed/massacred/slaughtered/butchered the villagers').

Statements with deontic modality or affective mental processes

Statements with deontic (obligational) modalities are linked to evaluation. For instance, when Tony Blair says (Example 5 – see below for discussion of this example) that 'The values we believe in should shine through what we do in Afghanistan', he implies, in more general terms, that acting on the basis of values is desirable, a good thing to do.

There is also a distinctive category of explicit evaluations with mental processes, specifically affective mental processes (e.g. 'I *like* this book', 'I *hate* this book'). Let's call them 'affective evaluations'. These are generally subjectively marked evaluations, i.e. they explicitly mark the evaluation as that of the author, and they are therefore comparable to subjectively marked modalities (e.g. '*I think* she has arrived'). But they can also appear as relational processes where the attribute is affective – compare 'This book fascinates me', 'This book is fascinating'.

Assumed values

Already in these rather transparent cases I have been referring to values which are implicit or assumed (see **assumptions** in the Glossary of key terms). But I am reserving the category of 'assumed values' for cases without the relatively transparent markers of evaluation (evaluative statements, deontic modalities, affective mental process verbs) above, where values are often much more deeply embedded in texts.

If we use the metaphor of 'depth', one stage 'down' are evaluations which are triggered in texts by words such as 'help': for instance if I write 'this book helps to . . .', whatever follows 'helps to' is likely to be positively evaluated (for instance 'clarify the debate about globalization'). Even 'deeper' are assumed values which are not 'triggered' in this way, but depend upon an assumption of shared familiarity with (not necessarily acceptance of) implicit value systems between author and interpreter (of course that familiarity may not in fact be shared). I discussed this point in chapter 3 – for instance, to say that social cohesion is 'a source of efficiency and adaptability' is to imply that it is desirable relative to a neo-liberal discourse within which 'efficiency' and 'adaptability' are primary 'goods'.

Characters of new capitalism: the Guru and the politician

I shall approach the issue of 'characters' by comparing in terms of modality and evaluation Examples 5 and 9 (Appendix, pages 237–8, and 244–5), which are authored by representatives of two prominent contemporary 'characters', the Politician and the Expert (more specifically, the management expert or 'guru'). In the following extract from Example 5, I have underlined expressions which are significant for modality, focusing for the most part on main clauses rather than subordinate and embedded clauses (though including the latter where they are of particular interest).

The values we <u>believe</u> in <u>should</u> shine through what we <u>do</u> in Afghanistan.

To the Afghan people we <u>make</u> this commitment. The conflict <u>will not</u> be the end. We <u>will not</u> walk away, as the outside world <u>has done</u> so many times before.

If the Taliban regime changes, we <u>will</u> work with you to make sure its successor is one that is broad-based, that unites all ethnic groups, and that offers some way out of the miserable poverty that is your present existence.

And, more than ever now, with every bit as much thought and planning, we <u>will</u> assemble a humanitarian coalition alongside the military coalition so that inside and outside Afghanistan, the refugees, four-and-a-half million on the move even before 11 September, are given shelter, food and help during the winter months.

The world community <u>must</u> show as much its capacity for compassion as for force.

The critics <u>will</u> say: but how can the world be a community? Nations act in their own self-interest. <u>Of course</u> they <u>do</u>. But what <u>is</u> the lesson of the financial markets, climate change, international terrorism, nuclear proliferation or world trade? It <u>is</u> that our self-interest and our mutual interests <u>are</u> today inextricably woven together.

This <u>is</u> the politics of globalization.

I <u>realize</u> why people protest against globalization.

We <u>watch</u> aspects of it with trepidation. We <u>feel</u> powerless, as if we were now pushed to and fro by forces far beyond our control.

But <u>there's a risk</u> that political leaders, faced with street demonstrations, <u>pander</u> to the argument rather than answer it. The demonstrators <u>are</u> right to say there's injustice, poverty, environmental degradation.

But globalization <u>is</u> a fact and, by and large, it <u>is</u> driven by people.

Not just in finance, but in communication, in technology, increasingly in culture, in recreation. In the world of the Internet, information technology and TV, there <u>will</u> be globalization. And in trade, the problem <u>is not</u> there's too much of it; on the contrary there'<u>s</u> too little of it.

The issue <u>is not</u> how to stop globalization.

The issue <u>is</u> how we use the power of community to combine it with justice. If globalization works only for the benefit of the few, then it <u>will</u> fail and <u>will</u> deserve to fail. But if we follow the principles that have served us so well at home – that power, wealth and opportunity must be in the hands of the many, not the few – if we make that our guiding light for the global economy, then it <u>will</u> be a force for good and an international movement that we <u>should</u> take pride in leading.

Because the alternative to globalization <u>is</u> isolation.

In terms of Speech Function, most of this extract is made up of Statements, but there is one Question ('But what is the lesson of the financial markets, climate change, international terrorism, nuclear proliferation or world trade?'). This is rhetorical in the sense that Blair answers it himself, but it does (along with other features to which I refer) give the sense that Blair is dialoguing with others rather than just delivering a monologue. There are quite a number of questions of this sort in the speech as a whole.

Most statements are 'realis' statements, statements of fact (e.g. 'This is the politics of globalization'), but some are 'irrealis', either hypothetical (e.g. 'If the Taliban regime changes' – I have not marked modality features for these clauses) or predictions ('there will be globalization'). I referred earlier to the power of prediction, which Blair has, or at least lays claim to.

Starting with epistemic modality, most Statements are Assertions or Denials. The only case of modalization is: '<u>there's a risk</u> that political leaders, faced with street demonstrations, <u>pander</u> to the argument rather than answer it'. I am treating 'there's a risk' as a marker of modalization, so that this is roughly equivalent to 'political leaders <u>may</u> . . . pander to the argument'. In the case of predictions, I am treating 'will' as a future tense auxiliary verb, so that e.g. 'there will be globalization' is an Assertion rather than a modalized Statement. So broadly speaking, Blair is making strong commitments to truth. The relation of Assertions to Denials is also significant for dialogicality. There are three points at which a Denial (or Denials) is followed by an Assertion – for instance, 'The issue <u>is not</u> how to stop globalization. The issue <u>is</u> how we use the power of community to combine it with justice'. Implicitly, Blair is entering a dialogue, or perhaps a polemic, with those who take different views (e.g. that the issue is somehow to stop globalization).

There are a variety of types of process in these Statements. Blair makes strong commitments to the truth of statements about material processes ('We <u>will not</u> walk away'), mental processes ('We <u>feel</u> powerless'), verbal processes ('we <u>make</u> this commitment'), and relational processes ('the alternative to globalization <u>is</u> isolation'). Quite a few of the statements are 'first person' statements either singular (e.g. 'I <u>realize</u> why people protest against globalization') or plural ('we <u>watch</u> aspects of it with trepidation'), as well as 'third person' (e.g. 'The issue <u>is not</u> how to stop globalization'). Mental process statements have first-person subjects. Statements represent the world at varying levels of abstraction or generalization, and some are highly abstract, a long way from concrete events and circumstances and processes (e.g. 'the alternative to globalization <u>is</u> isolation').

Turning to deontic modality, there are three instances, all modalized. Modalization is high in one case ('The world community <u>must</u> show as much its capacity for compassion as for force'), median in the two others (including 'The values we believe in <u>should</u> shine through what we <u>do</u> in Afghanistan').

What can we conclude from these points about modality about the 'character' of the Politician in the case of Blair? First, that this is a relatively dialogical 'character', engaging with others rather than simply delivering a monologue. Second, that this 'character' assumes the power of prediction. Third, that he makes strong commitments to truth, and moves between strong commitments to what is the case ('realis' statements), strong predictions, and moral statements using deontic modalities. He talks authoritatively about what is, what will be, what should be, and binds these together. Fourth, that he oscillates between speaking impersonally, speaking personally ('I'-statements) and speaking on behalf of communities, either the 'world-community' (which is, one might argue, in effect an exclusive 'we'-community of major states such as those leading the 'alliance against terrorism'), or an inclusive 'we'-community of common experience ('we all'). Fifth, that he strongly commits himself to truths not only about the processes and relations of the material world, but also most significantly about mental processes, about what 'we' feel, for instance. Sixth, that he strongly commits himself to the truth of statements which are in some cases very generalized and abstract. What I am suggesting is that these features of modality, these forms of commitment, are part of the process of self-identification of the Blair political 'character'.

Let us turn to evaluation. There are two evaluative statements in the extract ('The demonstrators are right to say there's injustice, poverty, environmental degradation', 'it (globalization) will be a force for good' – since the context is hypothetical, one should maybe formulate the evaluative statement as 'globalization may be a force for good'). There are also a number of statements with deontic modalities which contribute to evaluation (including 'The values we believe in should shine through what we do in Afghanistan'). We should also note the purpose clause ('so that . . . the refugees . . . are given shelter, food and help during the winter months'), which implies that giving refugees shelter and so forth is desirable (see the discussion of legitimation and moral evaluation in chapter 5). There are also a number of expressions which trigger positive (e.g. 'make sure') or negative ('there's a risk that') evaluations, and beyond that a number of assumed values which are not triggered textually. These include the assumption that 'isolation' is not desirable ('Because the alternative to globalization is isolation') – notice that as the 'alternative' to what is undesirable, 'globalization' is implicitly valued as desirable.

I have set out in a summary form below the main values Blair commits himself to in this extract – what is constructed as desirable, and what is constructed as undesirable (the list is not exhaustive).

- *Desirable*

    Action being informed by values
    Making commitments
    A regime being broad-based, uniting ethnic groups, offering a way out of
        poverty
    Acting on the basis of thought and planning
    Refugees being given shelter, food and help
    Compassion in international affairs
    Politicians answering arguments
    Speaking out about injustice, poverty, environmental degradation
    Recognizing facts
    Change being driven by people
    Combining globalization with justice
    Power, wealth and opportunity being in the hands of the many, not the few
    Globalisation

- *Undesirable*

    Walking away from a difficult situation
    Politicians pandering to arguments
    Injustice, poverty, environmental degradation
    Globalization working only for the few
    Isolation

Blair refers explicitly to values (as well as 'principles') in this extract – 'The values we believe in should shine through what we do in Afghanistan'. In committing himself to these values, he is identifying himself in the sort of way that politicians generally do – as a moral 'character' (e.g. action being informed by values), politically enlightened (e.g. a regime being broad-based, uniting ethnic groups, offering a way out of poverty), humane (compassion in international affairs), democratic (change being driven by people), and realistic (recognizing facts).

Now some comparisons between Blair and Kanter (Example 9). Kanter's text does not have the dialogicality of Blair's, it is more monological. Although there are only predictions with respect to what is going to happen in the chapter ('we will see how the principles of community apply inside organizations and workplaces'), there is some of the same oscillation between factual statements with epistemic modality (e.g. 'The greater integration that is integral to e-culture is different from the centralization of earlier eras'), and moral statements with deontic modality ('Integration must be accompanied by flexibility and empowerment'). The texts are similar in making strong commitments to truth, though there are rather more modalized statements in Kanter's (e.g. 'those reporting that they are much better than their competitors in the use of the Internet tend to have flexible, empowering, collaborative organizations', where I take 'tend to' as a marker of 'usuality' similar to 'often') which suggests some 'academic caution' about over-generalizing results. (Kanter is a senior academic and her book is based upon a large-scale research project.) But the texts both include commitments to the truth of very abstract and generalized statements (e.g. 'Shared understandings permit relatively seamless processes . . .'). Kanter's text is more impersonal than Blair's, though there are personal statements relating to the reading and writing of the text itself (e.g. 'In this chapter we will see how the principles of community apply inside organizations and workplaces . . .'). The process types in strongly modalized Statements are mainly relational, with a few material (e.g. 'Companies that are successful on the web operate differently . . .') or verbal ('Pacesetters and laggards describe no difference . . .') ones. There are no mental processes (apart from 'In this chapter we will see . . .', which refers to the chapter itself).

Let me turn to evaluation. I have reproduced the beginning of Example 9 below:

> Companies that are successful on the web operate differently from their laggard counterparts. On my global e-culture survey, those reporting that they are much better than their competitors in the use of the Internet tend to have flexible, empowering, collaborative organizations. The 'best' are more likely than the 'worst' to indicate, at statistically significant levels, that
>
> * Departments collaborate (instead of sticking to themselves).
> * Conflict is seen as creative (instead of disruptive).
> * People can do anything not explicitly prohibited (instead of doing only what is explicitly permitted).

- Decisions are made by the people with the most knowledge (instead of the ones with the highest rank).

Pacesetters and laggards describe no differences in how *hard* they work (in response to a question about whether work was confined to traditional hours or spilled over into personal time), but they are very different in how *collaboratively* they work.

One striking feature of this extract is that although Kanter is reporting research results, she does so in a highly evaluative way. There are quite a number of evaluative statements, though they are realized in ways which are in a broad sense embedded. Direct evaluative statements can be seen as presupposed. 'Companies that are successful on the web' presupposes that some companies are successful on the web, where 'successful on the web' is a discourse-relative evaluative expression. 'Their laggard counterparts' presupposes that their counterparts are laggards. The successful companies and their 'laggard counterparts' ('anaphorically') referred back to as the 'best' and the 'worst' are presupposed to be the best and the worst respectively – an explicit ranking in terms of desirability which is only somewhat mitigated by the fact that 'best and 'worst' are in 'scare-quotes'. Anaphoric reference (reference back in the text) again triggers the evaluative presupposition that the two types of company are respectively 'pacesetters' and (again) 'laggards'.

In addition to these embedded evaluative statements, there are assumed values. Within this discourse, having 'flexible, empowering, collaborative organizations' is desirable – but notice the mixing of the value assumption and a modality ('tend to have') which reduces commitment to truth in a standardly cautious academic way. There are also assumed values in the wording of the bullet-pointed results – in this discourse, collaboration, creative conflict and so forth are assumed to be desirable. The following sentence also reports research results in a value-'loaded' way, again evoking the virtue of working collaboratively.

I have summarized some of the most striking desirables and undesirables in Kanter's text:

- *Desirable*

    Having flexible, empowering, collaborative organizations
    Working collaboratively
    Creative conflict
    People being free to act (do anything not prohibited)
    Decisions being based on knowledge
    Companies being communities

People feeling like members
Having shared understandings
Having teams that know how to work together
Transmitting information rapidly
Voluntary collaboration
Companies having a soul

● **Undesirable**

Departments sticking to themselves
Seeing conflict as disruptive
Only doing what is permitted
Decisions being made on the basis of rank
People feeling like employees
Bureaucracy
Rigid job descriptions
Command-and-control hierarchies
Hoarding information

Let me briefly draw some conclusions about similarities and differences between the 'characters' of Politician and Expert as they are represented in these cases – of course the aim is not to make generalizations about these 'characters' on the basis of such limited data, but to show how text analysis might contribute to a full-scale study of them. These are different forms of public authority and identity. Both characters talk/write authoritatively about what is the case, often in a very abstract and generalized way, though the complexity of Kanter's identity as both 'guru' and academic is perhaps indicated by the higher number of modalized statements; and both move between authoritative truth statements and authoritative moral statements. So both assume the power to tell others what is and what should be. But it is only the politician that dialogues polemically with others, and speaks personally, and on behalf of others including the mental processes ('feelings') of others. (Kanter only writes personally of herself with respect to her writing, and on behalf of others, with respect to their reading of her chapter).

Turning to evaluation, the first thing to say is that the language of the Expert no less than that of the Politician is grounded in values (being an expert, even a scientist, does not mean being free of values, even if it is widely construed that way – see Wynne 2001). Indeed, Kanter's values are, if anything, more on the surface than Blair's, in that the text contains a numbers of evaluative statements, though they are embedded. There is a clear contrast in terms of the breadth of value commitments – Blair commits himself to a wide range of general values, whereas Kanter commits herself to a more specifically located set of organizational values.

The various Mr Blairs: mixed identities

Tony Blair has sometimes been accused of trying to be 'all things to all men', though in a sense that is something any politician must be – politicians have to address and carry along diverse constituencies, and that is increasingly so as political allegiances become more volatile. Blair the Politician can be seen as not a unitary 'character', but a 'character' composed of a number of diverse Tony Blairs. In part this is a matter of audience – for instance Blair the 'decision maker' addressing a business audience, Blair the 'citizen' addressing a 'civil society' audience, Blair the 'leader' addressing a Labour Party audience (Donadio 2002). But one can also see Blair shifting between these various identities in a single speech or interview (Fairclough 2000b).

For example, my comments on the modality of Example 5 above could be interpreted as pointing to heterogeneities and contradictions – that the Blair 'character' is a contradictory character, on the one hand speaking with impersonal authority, or on behalf of the 'world-community', about what is the case (epistemic modality), what will be (predictions), what should be (deontic modalities), yet on the other hand speaking personally ('I'-statements) and on behalf of an inclusive 'we'-community of common experience ('we all'). On the one hand making authoritative statements about the processes and relations of the material world, but on the other hand about what 'we' (all) feel.

One might argue that for any contemporary politician there is a tension between the public figure, the leader, and the 'normal person', I've argued elsewhere (Fairclough 2000b) that in the case of Blair, the public figure is always anchored in the 'normal person', and that is clear even in the speech from which Example 5 was taken, when Blair was making a major speech about the 'War on Terrorism' in his capacity of one of the dominant if not the dominant statesman within the 'world community'. Elsewhere, the 'normal person' is a more salient element of the mix of identities:

> *Frost*: and how do you deal with that problem of that problem which you rightly mentioned of the of the way some of the strongest elements of the press are ranged against this policy on Europe I mean . the Murdoch press e:m the Telegraph Group the Mail Group I mean right there you have a huge preponderance e:m how does that affect your policy making or does it just affect your policy presentation or does it just affect the fact that you don't read those papers
>
> *Blair*: (laughs) no it means that you've got to go over their heads to a large extent . and and reach the people . and let's have an honest debate . about the euro I mean before Christmas we had some of the most ludicrous

> stories about what Europe was planning to do with our taxes and our
> lifestyle and all the rest of it there is a big big question . about Britain's
> future . and the future direction of the country and . I believe that Britain
> cannot stand apart from Europe Britain has got to be part of Europe I
> believe that . as I say the test on the euro is that it has to be . in our national
> economic interest . but what we cannot do . is stand aside as a matter of
> principle

This is an extract from a television interview between Blair and Sir David Frost in
April 1998. There are two markers of subjective modality with the first person
singular pronoun and a mental process verb (both 'I believe'). Notice also 'I mean',
which might also be taken as marking subjective modality, and the other first person
pronoun in 'as I say'. Other pronouns are also significant: the 'we' (which occurs
several times, in 'let's', 'we had', 'our taxes', 'our lifestyle', 'what we cannot do')
is inclusive, 'all of us', and there is also one instance of generic 'you', the 'you' of
common experience. Overall, Blair the 'normal person', Blair speaking as an
ordinary citizen and a member of the community, is more salient here than in
Example 5. But there are also other features which reinforce this – using the
conversational word 'ludicrous' and the phrase 'and all the rest of it', and features
of accent (pronouncing 'got to' with a glottal stop instead of a 't' in the 'Estuary
English' way) and delivery (an affective elongation of the first syllable of 'ludicrous'),
as well as features of 'body language' (an engaging grin and a laugh in response to
the joke at the end of Frost's question, an oscillation of his head from side to side
as he says 'ludicrous'). We can see here the 'informalization' (Misztal 2000) of
identities which has been such a marked feature of recent public life, the public
appropriation of the private and the 'ordinary' (Sennett 1974), the 'conversationalization' of public language (Fairclough 1992).

Social identity and personality

Blair the Politician is not just a man filling a social role, it is also a personality,
a particular personal investment of the 'character' of Politician. One can approach
this partly in terms of idiosyncracies – for instance, the rather peculiar side-to-side
movement of the head I referred to just above (which is picked up by satirists) seems
to be idiosyncratic. But one can also see Blair's personality as partly the product of
the distinctive way in which he weaves together the various Mr Blairs – the 'normal
person', the 'tough' leader, the international statesman, the man of principle,
conviction and 'values'. With respect to the presence of the 'normal person' in the
mix, any politician these days has to deal with the tension (as I said above) between

being 'ordinary' and being extraordinary (a leader, a public figure), but politicians differ, and project different personalities, precisely in how they manage that tension, what the mix is, what other distinctive elements there are in the mix. One element for instance which we could see Blair as having learnt from Margaret Thatcher is the 'conviction politician', the man of principle and indeed passion, an element which not all politicians have (or cultivate).

The 'aestheticization' of public identities

The 'aestheticization' of politics (Harvey 1990) has been traced back to the Nazi period, for instance the aesthetic management of the massive rallies which the Nazis organized in Germany in the 1930s. More recently, analysts have pointed to a more pervasive 'aestheticization' of social life, the private lives of consumers as well as public life (Chouliaraki and Fairclough 1999, Featherstone 1991, Lury 1996). The preoccupation with 'image' is an aspect of this, and one can trace it across politics, more recently education (the 'image' of a successful academic, for instance – see Bourdieu 1998), and into the individualism of consumerized private life. Part of the identification of 'characters' such as the Politician or the Manager or, more generally, the Expert is the construction of an aesthetic, and again this is a process which is partly textual.

If we stick with the case of Tony Blair, the quotation from his adviser Philip Gould which I used in chapter 9 points to a process of building the image of the political leader which is an inevitable part of modern politics. Whenever Blair makes a political appearance, certainly an important political speech, one needs to see it amongst other things as an aesthetically worked event, and part of the identification of Blair as the construction of an aesthetic. To do so of course entails going beyond the transcript of what was said on a particular occasion and looking at the occasion as a whole. This includes the visual design of the location in which a speech is delivered, the way in which the location and Blair himself as the central point of it is filmed, the 'spin' that is put on the event by 'spin doctors' who aim to shape the media coverage which both precedes it and follows it. And also the embodiment of Blair (which I have begun to discuss above) including his stance, his gestures, his facial expressions, the movement of his head and his hands, and so forth. But the language also needs to be seen within this frame of aestheticiaztion – it too is designed in part for aesthetic effect. We can see this as part of what is entailed in looking at political language as 'rhetoric', including for instance the syntactic and lexical patterning of the language but also the rhythm of it as speech.

In part, a rhetorical perspective takes us back to aspects of traditional rhetoric. For example the 'parallelism' (Leech and Short 1981) at the beginning of Example 5 is a standardly recognized rhetorical or stylistic device:

> Don't overreact some say. We aren't.
>
> We haven't lashed out. No missiles on the first night just for effect.
>
> Don't kill innocent people. We are not the ones who waged war on the innocent. We seek the guilty.
>
> Look for a diplomatic solution. There is no diplomacy with Bin Laden or the Taliban regime.
>
> State an ultimatum and get their response. We stated the ultimatum; they haven't responded.
>
> Understand the causes of terror. Yes, we should try, but let there be no moral ambiguity about this: nothing could ever justify the events of 11 September

There is grammatical parallelism here, a series of imperative sentences ('Don't overreact', 'Don't kill innocent people', etc.) followed by a series of (mainly) declarative sentences – making a simulated dialogue as I pointed out in chapter 3. We also need to consider, as I said above, the delivery, including the rhythm. But Blair's aesthetic is very much tied into his personality, because personality in modern politics is a partly given, partly developed and worked upon, a matter of 'image'. So the distinctive mix of different styles I referred to above is also a part of the aesthetic.

Citizens and experts and the public sphere

The relationship between the public and various types of experts has attracted interest in a number of areas of social research, including sociology (Giddens 1991), media studies (Livingstone and Lunt 1994, see also Fairclough 1995b) and science studies (Wynne 2001). We can see this concern as connected with questions and worries about citizenship in contemporary society, and the contemporary standing and health of the public sphere, a theme I have touched on in earlier chapters (Calhoun 1992, Habermas 1989, Habermas 1996, Sennett 1974).

I want to discuss citizens and experts as contemporary 'characters' with respect to a meeting organized somewhere in England to discuss farm trials of genetically-modified (GM) foods taking place in the area (Example 15, Appendix, pages 252–5). This is based upon a real case which has been anonymized, which was an agreed condition of recording it.[1] These trials are designed to test whether GM crops have more adverse environmental effects than non-genetically-modified equivalents. The meeting had the format of many similar public meetings. It was chaired by a well-known local figure, there were several speakers who were given the floor in the first part of the meeting, and in the second part of the meeting members of the audience were invited to put questions to the speakers. The speakers were experts of different types – a government official with expert knowledge of the farm trials, a representative of a company which produces GM seed for farmers who is a scientist, and a representative of an organization which promotes organic farming who has expert knowledge of the implications of GM agriculture for organic farming.

Let me begin with the experts. Here is an extract from the government official's opening speech, in which he is talking about 'the consultation process' and the European Union Directive which controls it:

One of the issues which occurs very frequently at public meetings such as this is the issue of consultation and I'd like to spend just a little bit of time explaining the constraint under which the consultation process currently has to operate. We have a Directive at the moment which dates back to 1990 and under that Directive there is very limited scope for consultation about individual sites where GM crops might be grown. The legislation requires that the applications submitted to the Government have to be judged on their merits and once a consent has been granted it can only be revoked on valid scientific grounds. There is always scope for new scientific evidence to be considered.

The process of informing people about prospective FSE sites is that there is information advertized in local newspapers. We publish a news release every time there is to be a new sowing round and we identify in our news release the particular sites to six-figure grid references. We also write to all parish councils like this one to say where the sites are and to provide as much relevant background information as we can. And we always say that we are willing to come and address meetings like this to explain what the programme is all about.

And here is an extract from the opening by the representative of the GM seed company:

Why would the farmer be interested in this technology? Okay, well I've already talked about yield and I'll come back to that yet again in a second. But what's great about this is you can use a particular sort of herbicide called Liberty. Now normally with oilseed rape what you do as a farmer is you go in and you put a thin layer of herbicide onto the soil, okay. This is what they call a pre-emergence herbicide. And what happens is that as the weeds come through they come into contact with the herbicide and they die. Okay? . . .

Liberty is different, no point spraying it on the soil, it's just about inactivated on contact. What that means is you have to spray it onto the weeds. There is no point spraying it onto the soil and letting the weeds come through it. The weeds just carry on growing. Okay? If that's the case what we're looking at now is rather than a 'just in case' it's an 'if we actually need it'. So the farmer will come along, look and see those weeds in that crop and say 'ok, do I need to spray?' and 'if so how much do I need to spray?' So there are weeds in that field and he'll make that decision. So we're moving away from the idea of 'oh well I'll spray it just in case anything comes through' to 'if we need to we'll use it'. And that's a very exciting thing for a farmer.

It's worth noting initially what these two experts represent themselves as doing in these opening presentations. The government official represents himself as 'explaining' things, whereas the company scientist says that he aims to give people 'a feeling for what it's all about'. These are two different styles of being an expert. They do have some things in common – one is authoritative modality, categorical (non-modalized) assertions (and one or two denials e.g. 'There is no point in spraying it onto the soil'). But there are also striking differences. Both extracts are knowledge exchanges, but the company scientist shows a more interactive orientation to the audience by checking (with 'okay') that the statements he has made have been understood. Moreover, this extract begins with a question – in contrast with the more monological style of the official, who basically just makes statements, the company scientist simulates a question–answer exchange, which also contributes to a more interactive orientation. Notice also that the company scientist, but not the government official, uses explicit evaluative statements alongside statements of fact ('what's great about this', 'that's a very exciting thing for a farmer'). He also dramatizes his presentation by 'doing' the voice of the farmer. Another contrast is semantic relations between sentences and clauses: in the first extract, they are basically elaborative and additive, whereas in the second there is much more complex set of relations (elaboration, contrast, conditional, consequence). Together with other features, this adds to the interactive engagement which the company scientist achieves, in contrast with the government official: 'discourse markers' which mark functional relations between utterances ('well', 'now'), and several 'thematic equative' constructions (Halliday 1994) which give a denser information structure by separating a clause into two parts which are in an equative relationship (compare 'you go in and you put a thin layer of herbicide onto the soil' with what we actually have here – 'what you do' is (equative verb) 'you go in and you put a thin layer of herbicide onto the soil').

These are, as I said, two different styles of expertise. The government official's style is a more traditional one, tied to the authority of bureaucracies. The company scientist's style is by contrast linked to the increasing mediation of expertise, in the sense that experts now increasingly depend upon the projection and broadcasting of their expertise through mass media. It's not that government officials are unaffected by this development, it is perhaps rather that, unlike other types of expert, they have not so far been affected deeply enough to radically change their style. They have not had to put so much work into acquiring the capacity to 'communicate' (be clear, engaging, persuasive etc.) with large public audiences, or into public relations. What is noteworthy about this newer style of expertise is the complicity between science, business and media: there is now apparently nothing scandalous, as there once would have been, about someone speaking with the expertise of a scientist on behalf of a business, and using the 'skills' of public relations in doing so. But perhaps such complicities do contribute to a pervasive public distrust of experts (Wynne 2001).

The format of the meeting as I briefly described it above goes to the heart of contemporary controversy over public 'participation' in general and in policy-making over genetically-modified foods in particular. In the meeting, members of the audience are asked by the chair to limit themselves to asking questions, which assumes that what is at issue is 'information' rather than 'consultation', experts 'informing' the public or 'explaining' things to them, the public seeking clarification of this information by asking questions. But in fact, members of the audience do not limit themselves in this way – many of their contributions make claims or statements, develop arguments, and challenge speakers rather than just asking questions. We might look at what happens in a meeting of this sort in terms of people negotiating citizenship – as an occasion (a rather novel one for some of the audience) where people see themselves as involved in a process of public deliberation over matters of common public concern with a view of having an influence on the process of policy making.

This is an extract from a contribution from the floor which the speaker prefaces by saying he has a 'three-part question'. This is the first of the three parts – 'point one':

First of all much use is being of the word consultation. To the gentleman from DEFRA I'd like to say we had a referendum in our village last year which said that we didn't want GM trials in our village. We had another survey carried out this year, the majority of people said that we didn't want it in our village.

> It's falling on deaf ears, stony ground. Our views are not taken into account although you from Government say yes, it's a dialogue with the deaf I feel. Basically, no consultation, no notice taken of us. Point one.

The first point is that the speaker here is clearly not asking a question, he is making statements – giving the government official information, then making judgements about the consultation process. There are attempts especially by the chair to restrict people to asking questions, but generally they are not restricted in this way. Secondly, although one might see 'I'd like to say' as somewhat mitigating the force of the assertion in the second sentence, what we basically have here is strong commitment to truth, a modality of assertions and denials. One might say that the speaker is prepared to strongly commit himself to truths and judgements as a citizen (so such strong commitments are not the exclusive prerogative of experts). The third point is that the claim that there is (in the words of the government official) a 'consultation process' is explicitly contested.

The following is a more extended exchange involving two male members (M1, M2) of the audience as well as the Government official. I have omitted the latter's extended account of the notification procedure.

> *M1*:   There are two or three problems or concerns really. One really is the lack of time the parish has been given with respect of when we know. We don't know when the site is to be. We only know when the site is to be drilled. The County Council has put a motion through that we would ask DEFRA to let us know when the site is agreed, and then we could have a meeting like this if you like before it all gets out of hand. The other thing is there's a massive increase in nose problems through spores that are in the air now. Years ago we used to have hay fever problems at hay time, now we seem to get them – Is there any difference between the spores of genetically modified crops and the conventional crop? I think those are two major concerns that locally are causing problems. I don't know whether there's an answer to both but there certainly is an answer in time delay and there may be an answer to the other.
>
> *M2*:   Could I just make a point as well? I mean the first part of that, this year the first we knew about these crops was in the newspaper.
>
> *M1*:   Exactly.
>
> *M2*:   And when we did draw some information off the Internet, it was the day they'd stated for sowing. So that's when the Parish Council knew –

M1: The County Council has asked the Government to – if we can know – when the site is decided upon then we need the information. And I think that will give us a reasonable length of time to evaluate whether it is or isn't going to be a problem.

Government Official: Can I [unclear word]. Well, I think that I said that our practice is to write to all Parish Councils when a trial site is proposed and we did that –

M1: No, that isn't what happened –

Government Official: Could I just say what we do? [Extended account of the notification procedure – omitted.] So we do our very best to make sure that the people know.

M1: At what point do you know which site you are going to use?

M1 begins by making statements about two problems, and then asking a question about the second of them, after which he refers to them as 'concerns' which cause 'problems' and speculates on whether there are 'answers'. One might see an ambivalence in exchange type here. M1 would seem to be asking for more than answers to questions, i.e. more than information, he would seem to be asking for solutions to problems – which would make this an action exchange. This is one potential tension in interactions between experts and citizens – the former being oriented to 'information' (and knowledge exchanges), the latter being oriented to action (exchanges). The meeting in this case is predefined in terms of knowledge exchanges, yet the audience do in some cases manage to shift the focus onto action.

What is also noteworthy here is the shift away from the normative expectation of one speaker from the floor at a time. M1 and M2 are working collaboratively to elaborate a problem and its solution. What is perhaps interesting here is the assumption ('we could have a meeting like this if you like before it all gets out of hand', 'give us a reasonable length of time to evaluate whether it is or isn't going to be a problem') that local people should have an input in policy making (see also the complaint in the previous extract that 'our views are not taken into account'), which is actually not possible in the terms of the European Union Directive. People as citizens seem to assume they should have a say in what happens, whatever the official procedures lay down. A further point is that M1 actually interrupts the government official to challenge what he is saying. In these various ways, people are, one might say, seeking to act as citizens through stretching and breaking the procedural rules of the meeting.

What seems to most upset the audience is precisely the lack of real consultation, but another theme is that experts simply do not know what the possible consequences and effects of GM crops may be (see Wynne 2001). One way of seeing what goes on in a meeting like this – the ways in which people, usually unostentatiously but persistently, breach the 'rules' about 'questions' to get across the points and criticisms and challenges they want to get across – is, in terms of the dialectics of discourse (see chapter 2), that distrustful representations of experts are enacted in the ways in which people interact with them as citizens on occasions like this.

Summary

We began this chapter by presenting a framework for analysing epistemic and deontic modality which draws upon the distinctions between Exchange Types and Speech Functions discussed in chapter 6. We then discussed categories of explicit and implicit evaluation, and went on to use these two analytical perspectives to address a range of social issues. The first of these was the 'characters' of new capitalism: we compared the styles of Politician and Expert in terms of commitments to truth, necessity, and values. From there we went on to discuss mixed identities, heterogeneities and contradictions in the identity and style of politicians, and the question of how textual analysis with a focus on modality and evaluation might contribute to researching the tension between social identity and personality, and aestheticization of public identities. Finally, we returned to the issue of the public sphere, in terms of the relationship between experts and citizens.

Note

1 The example is taken from a European Union funded research project on the construction of citizenship in the context of approval procedures for GM crop trials ('Participation and the Dynamics of Social Positioning – the case of Biotechnology. Images of Self and Others in Decision-making Procedures'). My colleagues in the British team for this 8-nation project are Simon Pardoe and Bron Szerszynski. I am indebted to both of them in my analysis of this example (see Fairclough *et al.* forthcoming).

Conclusion

I have two objectives in this concluding chapter. The first is to draw together and summarize the various aspects of textual analysis which have been introduced and discussed in the course of the book. I shall do this in the form of a set of questions which one can ask of a text. I shall also illustrate how the various analytical issues and perspectives and categories can be brought together in analysing a particular text – specifically, Example 7 from the Appendix.

My second objective is to set out a brief 'manifesto' for the Critical Discourse Analysis research programme to which this book is a particular contribution. I have emphasized from the beginning of the book that textual analysis is just one of the concerns of this wider research endeavour, but it will, I hope, help readers to get textual analysis into perspective and into proportion by concluding the book with a slightly fuller sketch of the overall research programme. As I said in chapter 1, this does not mean that this book is only of relevance or value to people who are working within this research programme – much of what has been said about textual analysis could be applied within a very wide spectrum of social research.

Textual analysis

In the following checklist, I have summarized in the form of questions the main issues in textual analysis discussed in previous chapters, and indicated in which chapters they were discussed.

- *Social events (chapter 2)*

    What social event, and what chain of social events, is the text a part of?
    What social practice or network of social practices can the events be referred to, be seen as framed within?
    Is the text part of a chain or network of texts?

- **Genre (chapter 2, chapter 4)**

  Is the text situated within a genre chain?

  Is the text characterized by a mix of genres?

  What genres does the text draw upon, and what are their characteristics (in terms of Activity, Social Relations, Communication Technologies)?

- **Difference (chapter 3)**

  Which (combination) of the following scenarios characterize the orientation to difference in the text?

  a) an openness to, acceptance of, recognition of difference; an exploration of difference, as in 'dialogue' in the richest sense of the term

  b) an accentuation of difference, conflict, polemic, a struggle over meaning, norms, power

  c) an attempt to resolve or overcome difference

  d) a bracketing of difference, a focus on commonality, solidarity

  e) consensus, a normalization and acceptance of differences of power which brackets or suppresses differences of meaning and over norms

- **Intertextuality (chapter 3)**

  Of relevant other texts/voices, which are included, which are significantly excluded?

  Where other voices are included? Are they attributed, and if so, specifically or non-specifically?

  Are attributed voices directly reported (quoted), or indirectly reported?

  How are other voices textured in relation to the authorial voice, and in relation to each other?

- **Assumptions (chapter 3)**

  What existential, propositional, or value assumptions are made?

  Is there a case for seeing any assumptions as ideological?

- **Semantic/grammatical relations between sentences and clauses (chapter 5)**

  What are the predominant semantic relations between sentences and clauses (causal – reason, consequence, purpose; conditional; temporal; additive; elaborative; contrastive/concessive)?

Are there higher-level semantic relations over larger stretches of the text (e.g. problem–solution)?

Are grammatical relations between clauses predominantly paratactic, hypotactic, or embedded?

Are particularly significant relations of equivalence and difference set up in the text?

- *Exchanges, speech functions and grammatical mood (chapter 6)*

What are the predominant types of exchange (activity exchange, or knowledge exchange) and speech functions (statement, question, demand, offer)?

What types of statement are there (statements of fact, predictions, hypotheticals, evaluations)?

Are there 'metaphorical' relations between exchanges, speech functions, or types of statement (e.g. demands which appear as statements, evaluations which appear as factual statements)?

What is the predominant grammatical mood (declarative, interrogative, imperative)?

- *Discourses (chapter 7)*

What discourses are drawn upon in the text, and how are they textured together? Is there a significant mixing of discourses?

What are the features that characterize the discourses which are drawn upon (semantic relations between words, collocations, metaphors, assumptions, grammatical features – see immediately below)?

- *Representation of social events (chapter 8)*

What elements of represented social events are included or excluded, and which included elements are most salient?

How abstractly or concretely are social events represented?

How are processes represented? What are the predominant process types (material, mental, verbal, relational, existential)?

Are there instances of grammatical metaphor in the representation of processes?

How are social actors represented (activated/passivated, personal/impersonal, named/classified, specific/generic)?

How are time, space, and the relation between 'space–times' represented?

● *Styles (chapter 9)*

What styles are drawn upon in the text, and how are they textured together? Is there a significant mixing of styles?

What are the features that characterize the styles that are drawn upon ('body language', pronunciation and other phonological features, vocabulary, metaphor, modality or evaluation – see immediately below for the latter two)?

● *Modality (chapter 10)*

What do authors commit themselves to in terms of truth (epistemic modalities)? Or in terms of obligation and necessity (deontic modalities)?

To what extent are modalities categorical (assertion, denial etc.), to what extent are they modalized (with explicit markers of modality)?

What levels of commitment are there (high, median, low) where modalities are modalized?

What are the markers of modalization (modal verbs, modal adverbs, etc.)?

● *Evaluation (chapter 10)*

To what values (in terms of what is desirable or undesirable) do authors commit themselves?

How are values realized – as evaluative statements, statements with deontic modalities, statements with affective mental processes, or assumed values?

An example

I have reproduced Example 7 below. My comments on it are certainly not exhaustive, my aim rather is to show how one might combine some of the analytical resources introduced in the book in analysing a particular text.

How Can Globalization Deliver the Goods: The View from the South

Globalization is now a loaded term in many parts of the world. It is often associated more closely with the social challenges facing the southern hemisphere rather than with economic opportunities. What are the critical issues that need to be addressed in order for globalization to meet the expectations of the southern hemisphere?

Globalization is often more closely associated with the social challenges facing the southern hemisphere than with the economic opportunities. The future success of globalization requires that developing countries be fully involved in the management of the global economy and that their voices be heard.

Recent demonstrations have made it clear that the priorities and agendas of the developing world must be heard. The United States and Europe can no longer set the global agenda on their own. But the integration of environmental and labour standards into the framework of global governance may not be as easy as the protestors thought. Many in the developing world see these issues as potential excuses for trade barriers.

In terms of global governance, the establishment of the Group of 20 was a step in the right direction. In the Group of 20, unlike the Group of 7, both industrial and developing countries have a say in economic coordination. But, economics are not the only concern. Cultural homogenization worries many. There is fear that overpowering globalization will force the extinction of national cultures and traditions, especially in the southern hemisphere. Others disagree with this notion, saying societies have been changing for all eternity. Globalization increases choice and liberty, while national group identity does the opposite. In a world with close contact between differing cultural identities and ethnic practices, governors must be careful not to steer diversity down the destructive paths of the past. There is also concern that globalization means more for the rich, and less for the poor. But it must be made clear that the benefits of overall growth should reach all, and that economies that are more transparent tend to have lesser income inequalities.

Nonetheless, it is true that some countries are falling behind. Ghana, for example, has strictly followed structural adjustment programmes for 15 years, yet still struggles to attract investment and grow. It is common to blame globalization, but some say such growth won't come by solely focusing on macroeconomic variables. Rather, the fundamental structures of a market economy, freely moving prices and guaranteed contracts and property, must first be in place.

While addressing these concerns, and helping globalization meet the expectations of the southern hemisphere, leaders will make things easier by striving for good governance. More transparency, more accountability, and more participation by all involved will help make the process seem more humane.

Example 7 comes from a section of the World Economic Forum website which itself includes three different types of text – a summary of a session of the annual meeting of the Forum (the text above), selected quotations from the session, and extracts from emails sent to the website by people from various countries in response to the debate. We can see from this part of the complex *chain of events* of which this example is a part – a meeting, the production and distribution of a summary of the meeting presumably by staff of the World Economic Forum, and a plethora of events in places scattered across the world in which people watched recordings of the debate or read accounts of it, perhaps had discussions about it, perhaps read related literature, and wrote responses to the website. One could extend this network of events to include preparatory events for the meeting within the World Economic Forum and within the diverse other organizations represented in the debate, and events following from the meeting. What would, I think, emerge from tracing this network of events is the importance and the impact of meetings of the World Economic Forum – and the importance of what one might call the power of summary, the power of producing a ratified report of what went on, as in Example 7.

We can see the example in terms of a *network of social practices* and, as part of that, a *genre chain*. The World Economic Forum is a sort of international 'think tank' which assembles leading figures in government, business, and civil society, is oriented to discerning, predicting and ultimately directing the processes of 'globalization', and has been widely regarded as rather effective in doing so. It has no formal or official status, and is not a democratically accountable organization. Until a few years ago, it received relatively little public attention, but its meetings now attract protests and demonstrations (e.g. in New York in 2002). At the same time, it has developed its own publicity machine including a sophisticated 'interactive' website, and opened up its meetings to critics of globalization. What the example points to is a net-working of one unaccountable but influential corner of the practices of global governance, and civil society. One can therefore see Example 7 in terms of the issues about the 'public sphere' which I have discussed in earlier chapters. The main part of Example 7, the summary of the debate, can be seen as part of the publicity which mediates the connection between the organization and civil society. The genre chain includes debate, official report, email 'letters', press and broadcast report, and no doubt other types of report and discussion within the organizations involved and represented.

The *genre* of the summary has more of the character of a genre internal to an organization (and in that sense an 'official' report) than a conventional mediating genre. It is not a news report, it is not an account of what happened in the course of the debate, it is rather on the face of it a summary of arguments of the sort which might be made within an organization for purposes of record. I say 'on the face of it' because there is an ambivalence about the activity here, about what is going on. Is the activity simply a matter of recording the arguments in the debate, or is it an intervention in the argument in its own right, a polemic which covertly counters arguments against the form of globalization which the World Economic Forum has advocated, a 'discussion' in Martin's (1992) sense? I discussed aspects of the argumentation in chapter 4 (pages 81–3). One effect of using the form of intra-organizational summary produced by unidentified officers of the organization is to retain a large measure of organizational control of the process of 'going interactive', setting up an interactive website and apparently opening up to civil society.

With respect to *difference*, what we have on the face of it is basically scenario (a), an exploration of different points of view (which is what gives it the character of a 'discussion' in Martin's sense). But as I also suggested in the analysis in chapter 4, there is an obfuscation of difference, because points of view and claims are not clearly attributed to voices, and we seem to have something rather more like scenario (b), a polemic, in that a protagonist–antagonist relation appears to be set up between an unidentified protagonist (representing the leadership of the World Economic Forum?) contesting the claims of the South (antagonist). Again, see the discussion in chapter 4 for details.

Turning to *intertextuality*, one might argue that one set of excluded voices are those whose critique of globalization is more radical than anything here – the closest is the 'concern that globalization means more for the rich and less for the poor', but there are certainly plenty of voices in 'the South' (as well as elsewhere) which represent globalization as, for instance, a new form of imperialism which is inherently geared to the exploitation of the countries of 'the South' by corporations based in North America, Europe and East Asia: even an American 'empire'. What is not clear, but could be established, is whether such voices were excluded just from the summary of the debate, or from the debate itself. With respect to attribution, where claims are attributed they are attributed non-specifically (e.g. 'some say', 'others disagree', there is a fear that'), and in a number of cases they are not attributed at all (e.g. 'leaders will make things easier by striving for good governance'), contributing to the obfuscation of difference referred to above, and the sense that there is an unidentified protagonist voice refuting certain claims. There is no direct reporting (quoting) of voices – where voices are attributed they are indirectly reported (which raises questions about the relationship between what was actually said and how it is summarized here).

There are a number of significant *assumptions*, including most obviously the propositional assumption (triggered by the 'how'-question of the heading) that globalization *can* deliver the goods (and can meet the expectations of the southern hemisphere). Other propositional assumptions include: that 'the South' has a view; that the southern hemisphere does have expectations of globalization – and that there is a unity of view and expectations in 'the South'; that the United States and Europe have been setting the global agenda on their own; that the protestors thought it would be (relatively) easy to integrate environmental and labour standards into the framework of global governance. Amongst many existential assumptions, note: there is such a thing as 'the South' and 'the developing world' – these are taken for granted as classificatory categories. This categorization is not uncontentious: some would argue that many parts of the undeveloped (or underdeveloped) world are not significantly 'developing', and 'the South' has come to replace the largely discredited 'Third World'. There are also many value assumptions, including the assumption that globalization 'delivering the goods' and 'meeting the expectations of the southern hemisphere' are desirable, so too 'choice and liberty' and 'transparency', 'accountability', 'participation' (triggered by 'help to'), whereas 'trade barriers' are undesirable (triggered by 'excuses for'). The text is clearly positioned within a neoliberal value system.

Semantic relations between clauses and sentences are predominantly of two types: elaborative, and contrastive/concessive. A pattern repeated several times is the development of a claim over two or more clauses or sentences in an elaborative relation, which is in a contrastive/concessive relation with another claim (which may also be developed over two or more clauses in an elaborative relation). For example:

> Recent demonstrations have made it clear that the priorities and agendas of the developing world must be heard. ELABORATIVE The United States and Europe can no longer set the global agenda on their own. CONTRASTIVE But the integration of environmental and labour standards into the framework of global governance may not be as easy as the protestors thought.

Both of these semantic relations (elaboration, contrast) are frequent in this text. The contrastive/concessive relation is marked by the conjunctions 'but' (four times), 'yet', and 'while' (twice). One can also see a contrastive relation between the sentence beginning 'others disagree with this notion' and the sentence which precedes it (in the fourth paragraph), although in this case it is not marked by a conjunction. There are also a few instances of other semantic relations – purpose ('What are the critical issues that need to be addressed <u>in order for</u> globalization to meet the expectations of the southern hemisphere?'), and addition ('There is <u>also</u> a concern that globalization means more for the rich, and less for the poor'). The text is also characterized by the 'higher-level' problem–solution semantic relation, as I pointed out in chapter 5 (page 91). *Grammatical relations* between clauses are predominantly paratactic.

The predominant *type of exchange* is knowledge exchange, and the predominant *speech function* is statement. There are two questions, the first part of the title ('*How Can Globalization Deliver the Goods*: the View from the South'), and the last sentence of the opening paragraph. These are of course questions which are answered as well as asked in the text, but they give it a somewhat dialogical appearance. Most statements are 'realis' (statements of fact), but there are also 'irrealis' predictions, notably the two sentences of the final paragraph ('leaders *will make* things easier by striving for good governance', 'more transparency . . . *will help* make the process seem more humane'). The most obvious metaphorical relation is between statements of fact and evaluations – a number of statements of fact can be read as implicit evaluations (e.g. 'Globalization increases choice and liberty'). But one might ask whether there is also a metaphorical relation between knowledge exchange and action exchange – whether some of the apparent statements are also demands, and whether therefore in Habermas's terms this is a covertly strategic text, what I called in chapters 5 and 6 a 'hortatory report'. Grammatical mood is predominantly declarative, apart from the two questions, which are interrogative.

I made some comments on the *discourses* of this example in chapter 3 (see page 43). Major themes include: economic change ('globalization'), processes of (global and national) governing, views of globalization (in 'the South'), political resistance to globalization. One point to notice is that both economic change and governing are represented not only in relatively specialist terms, but also in lay terms – the former as 'delivering the goods', the latter as the 'voices' of developing countries 'being heard', and developing countries 'having a say'. One of the emails picks up 'voices being heard' and describes it as 'patronizing', treating developing countries as 'client states'. The expression actually occurs in a relation of equivalence: 'requires that <u>developing countries be fully involved in the management of the global economy</u> and that <u>their voices be heard</u>'. The first expression can be referred to the representation of governing in terms of a specialist discourse of 'governance' (which involves governing being represented as 'managing'). The second is, as I said, a lay or ordinary language expression; it evokes a discourse of 'participation' which is generally ambivalent about whether those whose voices are 'heard' (or 'have a say') have any real influence over policy making.

The articulation of these two discourses together here might on the one hand be seen as a common strategy of 'translating' specialist language into ordinary language for a non-specialist audience. But it might also on the other hand be seen in terms of an ambivalence and contradiction in the proposal to 'involve' developing countries in global management – that perhaps what is envisaged is an 'involvement' which does not affect the power of an elite group of states to 'set the global agenda'. Indeed, the issue of 'participation' seems to be central for this example on more than one level. One might contentiously put it in terms of the question: is either the envisaged participation of 'the South' in 'global governance', or the apparent opening up of the World Economic Forum's deliberations to the 'participation' of civil society, of more than cosmetic significance? Is 'participation' just a cultivation of surface democratic forms beneath which the same exclusive relations of power can carry on? Is the 'participation' only in the discourse, only textual, and therefore merely rhetorical?

Economic change is represented in terms of a neo-liberal market-liberalization discourse. This includes a predictive narrative that a 'structural adjustment programme' will lead to 'attracting investment' and 'growth' (not actualized in the case of Ghana, which is referred to here), and seeing the positive effects of 'globalization' as 'opportunities' and the negative effects as 'challenges' (implying that problems are not insuperable). But economic change is also represented in terms of an 'anti-globalization' discourse which represents globalization, again in a lay language, as meaning 'more for the rich, and less for the poor'. One thing to note is the articulation of this discourse with what one might call the partly 'psychologized' representation of 'views' of globalization in 'the South' – there is 'concern' that globalization means more for the rich, and less for the poor, just as many 'worry' and 'fear' cultural homogenization. Broadly speaking, neo-liberal representations of globalization are either asserted or attributed in reports of what people say, while oppositional and critical representations are construed in terms of mental processes ('concerns', 'fears', etc.).

Moving to more specific aspects, the *representation of social events*, events are represented abstractly and in a generalized way, though there is some reduction in the level of abstraction when specific events (the establishment of the Group of 20) and cases (Ghana) are referred to. There is a range of *process types*, but the most common in main clauses is relational processes, of both types. There are also a number of mental processes (e.g. 'Cultural homogenization <u>worries</u> many') as I mentioned above, and verbal processes ('Others <u>disagree</u>'). There are material processes, but they are mainly metaphorical (e.g. one might see 'set the global agenda' in paragraph 3 as a relational process, e.g. 'be in control' metaphorically construed as a material process). The frequency of relational processes in main clauses can be linked to the density of nominalization, the metaphorical construal of processes as entities. For instance, 'the establishment of the Group of 20 <u>was</u> a step in the right direction' has a type-2 relational process which classifies one nominalized process ('the establishment of the Group of 20') with respect to another ('a step in the right direction'). Nominalization is linked to an abstract representation of events, and to exclusions of elements of events. Take for instance 'the <u>social challenges</u> facing the southern hemisphere'. A more concrete representation of the series and sets of events which would seem to be alluded to might include different social groups and the relations between them, and perhaps how globalization affects local power relations in 'the South' (only touched upon in very general terms here – 'more for the rich, and less for the poor'). This is an omission which is picked up by the email responses.

The main *social actors* are countries (states) and especially groups of countries, represented as collective social actors with for instance 'views' (rather than, say, geographical locations). They are both classified ('developing countries', 'industrial countries') and named ('Ghana', 'the United States', 'Europe'). We can also take 'the South', 'the southern hemisphere', and 'the developing world' as names. The contentious politics of naming is clear in this case, as I have already indicated – for instance, relatively developed countries like Australia are in the southern hemisphere, and it is arguable whether the countries represented are 'developing'. Where they are classified, representation is generic rather than specific, and the same is true of other groups of social actors represented: 'leaders' (or 'governors'), 'protestors', 'the rich' and 'the poor'. Generic representations contribute to the hegemonic universalization of a particular representation. There is also a rather ill-defined category of social actor, perhaps 'the people of the South' though it is never named as such (the closest is 'many in the developing world'), which appears in a quantified way – 'many', 'some', 'others'.

In terms of the *representation of 'space–times'*, one might see the text as in the rather paradoxical position of relating an inclusive and universal global space–time with a regional ('southern') space–time, which is both by definition included within the former, yet also outside it. There is a movement between statements and claims which are spatio-temporally specified, with respect to 'the South', and statements and claims which are not, which have a 'global' scope. This connects with what I said earlier about an implicit protagonist–antagonist relation: the movement from the claims of the antagonist to the claims of the protagonist is simultaneously a movement from the regional space–time of 'the South' to global space–time. So for instance the claim that 'economies that are more transparent tend to have lesser income inequalities' (at the end of paragraph 4) has a global scope.

The question of *style* is complicated by an ambivalence about authorship which I have already alluded to. We can see this in terms of Goffman's (1981) distinction between 'principal', 'author' and 'animator' which I briefly introduced in chapter 1. In particular, what is the relationship between the author of this text, in the sense of the person (or persons – it may be collectively authored) who are responsible for the wording of the text, and principals, those whose positions are represented? Is the author merely reporting the positions of those principals from 'the South' who contributed to the debate, which is apparently the case, or is there also an authorial voice in the sense that the author is speaking on behalf of and as a part of another unidentified principal, maybe the (leadership of the) World Economic Forum itself? If it is the latter, we might say that there is a mixture of styles: the author as reporter, and the author as protagonist.

In terms of *modality*, there is a combination of epistemic and deontic modalities, with the former predominant. Most epistemic modalities are unmodalized assertions (e.g. 'Globalization is now a loaded term', 'Others disagree with this notion') making strong commitments to truth – whether the truth of what was said or thought in the debate, or the truth of what is the case in the world. There is one low commitment modalized statement ('the integration . . . <u>may</u> not be as easy . . .'), and one high-commitment modalized statement which is ambivalent between epistemic ('not possible') and deontic ('not permissible') modality ('The United States and Europe <u>can</u> no longer set the global agenda on their own'). There are also two strong predictions with the auxiliary verb 'will' ('leaders <u>will</u> make things easier by striving for good governance'). There are several high-commitment modalized deontic modalities (e.g. 'the fundamental structures of a market economy . . . <u>must</u> first be in place') which seem to be associated with the voice of the protagonist.

I have already discussed *evaluation* in terms of value assumptions, and suggested that the text is positioned within a neo-liberal value system. With respect to styles and identification, this is a matter of the author's commitment to neo-liberal values, though given the ambivalence of authorship it is not clear whether these are the reported commitments of the principals who contributed to the debate or the commitments of the 'authorial voice', or both. We might say that all involved are by implication positioned within this value system, which is of course contentious.

Let me repeat that this analysis is not exhaustive. As I argued in chapter 1, we should assume that no analysis of a text can tell us all that might be said about it. In critical realist terms, we should distinguish the 'actual' from the 'empirical', and not assume the real nature and properties of events and texts are exhausted by what we happen to see in them from a particular perspective at a particular point in time. But what this analysis has hopefully shown is how different analytical categories and perspectives can be productively combined to enhance our capacity to see things in texts. For instance, I have argued that a central issue in the case of this text is whether it is merely a report on a debate, or an refutation on the part of a 'protagonist' of the 'views' of an 'antagonist'. A number of the analytical categories bear upon this question: the ambivalence is evident in the identification of genre, in the analysis of orientations to difference, in the attribution of voices, in the identification of types of exchange, in the distribution of mental process types, in the identification of styles, in the commitments associated with modality and evaluation.

Manifesto for critical discourse analysis

As I pointed out in chapter 1, this book has been concerned with just a small part of what I see as a larger project – critical discourse analysis (henceforth CDA) as a form of critical social research. Critical social research begins from questions such as these: how do existing societies provide people with the possibilities and resources for rich and fulfilling lives, how on the other hand do they deny people these possibilities and resources? What is it about existing societies that produces poverty, deprivation, misery, and insecurity in people's lives? What possibilities are there for social change which would reduce these problems and enhance the quality of the lives of human beings? The aim of critical social research is better understanding of how societies work and produce both beneficial and detrimental effects, and of how the detrimental effects can be mitigated if not eliminated.

Critical social research designs and changes its research programme to try to respond to the great issues and problems of the day. Much of this research is now focused upon 'new capitalism' – contemporary transformations of capitalism, 'globalization', neo-liberalism, and so forth – because a better understanding of these changes and their effects, and of possibilities to inflect them in particular directions, or resist them and develop alternatives, is widely seen as crucial to improving the human condition. There are winners and there are losers in these social transformations. Amongst the losers: an increasing gap between rich and poor, less security for most people, less democracy, and major environmental damage. There is now a growing perception, not only on the political left but across broad sections of opinion in many countries throughout the world, that if markets are not constrained, the results will be disastrous. I briefly discussed Language in new capitalism as a research programme for CDA in chapter 1. I am going to centre this 'manifesto' on that research programme, though I should emphasize that the claims for CDA as a resource in social research are not at all limited to its contribution to research on new capitalism, and can be made in broader terms (as in Fairclough 1992, for instance). And I call it a 'manifesto' because I begin from the political case for this research.

But why a focus on language and discourse in critical research on new capitalism? We might find convincing the argument for critical social research concentrating its efforts on the transformations of capitalism and their ramifications, but we still need to make the case for a significant focus on language. One argument might be that since these changes are transforming many aspects of social life, then they are necessarily transforming language as one element of social life which is dialectically interconnected with others. But that is not the strongest argument. The more significant point is that the language element has in certain key respects become more salient, more important than it used to be, and in fact a crucial aspect of the social transformations which are going on – one cannot make sense of them without thinking about language.

One doesn't need to be a discourse analyst to think this. Many social researchers with different disciplinary backgrounds have said the same thing. For instance, the distinguished French sociologist Pierre Bourdieu in the last years of his life wrote a number of pieces on neo-liberalism, mainly for non-specialist readerships, in which he stressed the importance of neo-liberal discourse in the political project of neo-liberalism – a project, as he saw it, whose primary aim is removing obstacles (be they welfare states, militant trade unions, or whatever) to the transformations of New Capitalism. Bourdieu and Wacquant (2001) for instance point to a 'new planetary vulgate', which they characterize as a vocabulary ('globalization', 'flexibility', 'governance', 'employability', 'exclusion' and so forth), which 'is endowed with the performative power to bring into being the very realities it claims to describe'. The neo-liberal political project of removing obstacles to the new economic order is on this account to a substantial degree led or driven by discourse. One might see an enhanced role for discourse in initiating social change as implied in characterizations of contemporary economies as 'knowledge economies', or contemporary societies as 'knowledge' or information societies'. The greater salience of 'knowledge' or 'information' in economic and social processes and changes amounts in practical terms to the greater salience of language and discourse – this is the form in which 'knowledge' is produced, distributed, and consumed. (I take this up again below.)

As well as indicating the significance of language in these socio-economic transformations, Bourdieu and Wacquant's (2001) paper shows that social research needs the contribution of discourse analysts. It is not enough to characterize the 'new planetary vulgate' as a list of words, a vocabulary, as they do. We need to analyse texts and interactions to show how some of the effects which Bourdieu and Wacquant identify are brought off. These include: making the socio-economic transformations of new capitalism and the policies of governments to facilitate them seem inevitable; representing desires as facts, representing the imaginaries of interested policies as the way the world actually is. I have addressed some of these issues in the chapters of this book. Bourdieu and Wacquant's account of the effectivity of neo-liberal discourse exceeds the capacity of their sociological research methods. This is at the same time an appreciation of their work and a critique, in the spirit of dialogically working with it: CDA can enhance it, just as engaging with Bourdieu's sociological theory and research can enhance CDA. It is a matter of, on the one hand, recognizing that it is often social theorists who produce the most interesting critical insights about language as an element of social life, yet, on the other hand, challenging them and helping them to engage with language in a far more concrete and detailed way than they generally do. Without detailed analysis, one cannot really *show* that language is doing the work one may theoretically ascribe to it. To put the point contentiously, it is time social theorists and researchers delivered on their promissory notes about the important of language and discourse in contemporary social life.

So what sort of approach to language can best meet the needs of critical social research? I shall now briefly show how CDA (more specifically, that particular version of CDA which I have developed – see Fairclough and Wodak 1997 for a comparison of different versions) can make this contribution. Some of what I shall say has arisen already in the book, but the aim now is to give a more comprehensive outline of CDA.

Theoretical issues

Critical Discourse Analysis is based upon a view of semiosis as an irreducible element of all material social processes (Williams 1977). We can see social life as interconnected networks of social practices of diverse sorts (economic, political, cultural, family etc.). The reason for centring the concept of 'social practice' is that it allows an oscillation between the perspective of social structure and the perspective of social action and agency – both necessary perspectives in social research and analysis (see chapter 2, and Chouliaraki and Fairclough 1999). By 'social practice' I mean a relatively stabilized form of social activity (examples would be classroom teaching, television news, family meals, medical consultations). Every practice is an articulation of diverse social elements within a relatively stable configuration, always including discourse. Let us say that every practice includes the following elements:

Activities

Subjects, and their social relations

Instruments

Objects

Time and place

Forms of consciousness

Values

Discourse

These elements are dialectically related (Harvey 1996a). That is to say, they are different elements but not discrete, fully separate, elements. There is a sense in which each 'internalizes' the others without being reducible to them. So, social relations, social identities, cultural values and consciousness, amongst others, are in part discoursal, but that does not mean that we theorize and research social relations, for example, in the same way that we theorize and research language. They have distinct properties, and researching them gives rise to distinct disciplines. Nevertheless, it is possible and desirable to work across disciplines in a 'transdisciplinary' way – see Fairclough (2000a).

CDA is analysis of the dialectical relationships between discourse (including language but also other forms of semiosis, e.g. body language or visual images) and other elements of social practices. Its particular concern is with the radical changes that are taking place in contemporary social life: with how discourse figures within processes of change, and with shifts in the relationship between discourse and more broadly semiosis and other social elements within networks of practices. We cannot take the role of discourse in social practices for granted, it has to be established through analysis. And discourse may be more or less important and salient in one practice or set of practices than in another, and may change in importance over time.

Discourse figures in broadly three ways in social practices. First, it figures as a part of the social activity within a practice. For instance, part of doing a job (for instance, being a shop assistant) is using language in a particular way; so too is part of governing a country. Second, discourse figures in representations. Social actors within any practice produce representations of other practices, as well as ('reflexive') representations of their own practice, in the course of their activity within the practice. They 'recontextualize' other practices (Bernstein 1990, Chouliaraki and Fairclough 1999) – that is, they incorporate them into their own practice, and different social actors will represent them differently according to how they are positioned within the practice. Representation is a process of social construction of practices, including reflexive self-construction – representations enter and shape social processes and practices. Third, discourse figures in ways of being, in the constitution of identities – for instance the identity of a political leader such as Tony Blair in the UK is partly a discoursally constituted way of being.

Discourse as part of social activity constitutes genres. Genres are diverse ways of acting, of producing social life, in the semiotic mode. Examples are: everyday conversation, meetings in various types of organization, political and other forms of interview, and book reviews. Discourse in the representation and self-representation of social practices constitutes discourses (note the difference between 'discourse' as an abstract noun, and 'discourse(s)' as a count noun). Discourses are diverse representations of social life which are inherently positioned – differently positioned social actors 'see' and represent social life in different ways, different discourses. For instance, the lives of poor and disadvantaged people are represented through different discourses in the social practices of government, politics, medicine, and social science, *and* through different discourses within each of these practices corresponding to different positions of social actors. Finally, discourse as part of ways of being constitutes styles – for instance the styles of business managers, or political leaders.

Social practices networked in a particular way constitute a social order – for instance, the emergent neo-liberal global order referred to above, or at a more local level, the social order of (the 'field' of) education in a particular society at a particular time. The discourse/semiotic aspect of a social order is what we can call an 'order of discourse'. It is the way in which diverse genres and discourses and styles are networked together. An order of discourse is a social structuring of semiotic difference – a particular social ordering of relationships amongst different ways of making meaning, i.e. different discourses and genres and styles. One aspect of this ordering is dominance: some ways of making meaning are dominant or mainstream in a particular order of discourse, others are marginal, or oppositional, or 'alternative'. For instance, there may be a dominant way to conduct a doctor–

patient consultation in Britain, but there are also various other ways, which may be adopted or developed to a greater or lesser extent in opposition to the dominant way. The dominant way probably still maintains social distance between doctors and patients, and the authority of the doctor over the way interaction proceeds; but there are others ways which are more 'democratic', in which doctors play down their authority. The political concept of 'hegemony' can usefully be used in analysing orders of discourse (Butler *et al.* 2000, Fairclough 1992, Laclau and Mouffe 1985). A particular social structuring of semiotic difference may become hegemonic, become part of the legitimizing common sense which sustains relations of domination, but hegemony will always be contested to a greater or lesser extent, in hegemonic struggle. An order of discourse is not a closed or rigid system, but rather an open system, which is put at risk by what happens in actual interactions.

I said above that the relationship between discourse and other elements of social practices is a dialectical relationship – discourse internalizes and is internalized by other elements without the different elements being reducible to each other. They are different, but not discrete. If we think of the dialectics of discourse in historical terms, in terms of processes of social change, the question that arises is the ways in which, and the conditions under which processes of internalisation take place. Take the concept of a 'knowledge economy' and 'knowledge society'. This suggests a qualitative change in economies and societies such that economic and social processes are knowledge-driven – change comes about, at an increasingly rapid pace, through the generation, circulation, and operationalization of knowledges in economic and social processes. Of course knowledge (science, technology) have long been significant factors in economic and social change, but what is being pointed to is a dramatic increase in their significance. The relevance of these ideas here is that 'knowledge-driven' amounts to 'discourse-driven': knowledges are generated and circulate as discourses, and the process through which discourses become operationalized in economies and societies is precisely the dialectics of discourse.

Discourses include representations of how things are and have been, as well as imaginaries – representations of how things might or could or should be. The knowledges of the knowledge-economy and knowledge-society are imaginaries in this sense – projections of possible states of affairs, 'possible worlds'. In terms of the concept of social practice, they imagine possible social practices and networks of social practices – possible syntheses of activities, subjects, social relations, instruments, objects, space–times (Harvey 1996a), values, forms of consciousness. These imaginaries may be enacted as actual (networks of) practices – imagined activities, subjects, social relations etc. can become real activities, subjects, social relations, etc. Such enactments include materialisations of discourses – economic discourses become materialized for instance in the instruments of economic production, including the 'hardware' (plant, machinery, etc.) and the 'software' (management systems, etc.). Such enactments are also in part themselves discoursal/semiotic: discourses become enacted as genres. Consider, for example, new management discourses which imagine management systems based upon 'teamwork', relatively non-hiearchical, networked, ways of managing organizations. They become enacted discoursally as new genres, for instance genres for team meetings. Such specifically discoursal enactments are embedded within their enactment as new ways of acting and interacting in production processes, and possibly material enactments in new spaces (e.g. seminar rooms) for team activities.

Discourses as imaginaries may also come to be inculcated as new ways of being, new identities. It is a commonplace that new economic and social formations depend upon new subjects – for instance, 'Taylorism' as a production and management system depended upon changes in the ways of being, the identities, of workers (Gramsci 1971). The process of 'changing the subject' can be thought of in terms of the inculcation of new discourses – Taylorism would be an example. Inculcation is a matter of, in the current jargon, people coming to 'own' discourses, to position themselves inside them, to act and think and talk and see themselves in terms of new discourses. Inculcation is a complex process, and probably less secure than enactment. A stage towards inculcation is rhetorical deployment: people may learn new discourses and use them for certain purposes while at the same time self-consciously keeping a distance from them. One of the mysteries of the dialectics of discourse is the process in which what begins as self-conscious rhetorical deployment becomes 'ownership' – how people become unconsciously positioned within a discourse. Inculcation also has its material aspects: discourses are dialectically inculcated not only in styles, ways of using language, they are also materialized in bodies, postures, gestures, ways of moving, and so forth.

The dialectical process does not end with enactment and inculcation. Social life is reflexive. That is, people not only act and interact within networks of social practices, they also interpret and represent to themselves and each other what they do, and these interpretations and representations shape and reshape what they do. Moreover, if we are thinking specifically of economic practices in contemporary societies, people's activities are constantly being interpreted and represented by others, including various categories of experts (e.g. management consultants) and academic social scientists (including discourse analysts). What this amounts to is that ways of (inter)acting and ways of being (including the discourse aspects, genres and styles) are represented in discourses, which may contribute to the production of new imaginaries, which may in turn be enacted and inculcated. So it goes on, a dialectic which entails movements across diverse social elements, including movements between the material and the non-material, and movements within discourse between discourses, genres and styles.

There is nothing inevitable about the dialectics of discourse as I have described it. A new discourse may come into an institution or organization without being enacted or inculcated. It may be enacted, yet never be fully inculcated. Examples abound. For instance, managerial discourses have been quite extensively enacted within British universities (for instance as procedures of staff appraisal, including a new genre of 'appraisal interview'), yet arguably the extent of inculcation is very limited – most academics do not 'own' these management discourses. We have to consider the conditions of possibility for, and the constraints upon, the dialectics of discourse in particular cases. This has a bearing on theories of 'social construc- tionism' (Sayer 2000). It is a commonplace in contemporary social science that social entities (institutions, organizations, social agents, etc.) are or have been constituted through social processes, and a common understanding of these processes highlights the effectivity of discourses, as I have done above: social entities are in some sense effects of discourses. Where social constructionism becomes problematic is where it disregards the relative solidity and permanence of social entities, and their resistance to change. Even powerful discourses such as the new discourses of manage- ment may meet levels of resistance which result in them being neither enacted nor inculcated to any degree. In using a dialectical theory of discourse in social research, one needs to take account, case by case, of the circumstances which condition whether and to what degree social entities are resistant to new discourses.

Method

The following gives a schematic picture of how CDA works as a form of language critique (see Chouliaraki and Fairclough 1999 for a fuller discussion). It is a version of the 'explanatory critique' developed by Bhaskar (1986).

---

1   Focus upon a social problem which has a semiotic aspect. Beginning with a social problem rather than the more conventional 'research question' accords with the critical intent of this approach – to produce knowledge which can lead to emancipatory change.

2   Identify obstacles to it being tackled, through analysis of

     a)   the network of practices within which it is located

     b)   the relationship of semiosis to other elements within the particular practice(s) concerned

     c)   the discourse (the semiosis) itself

         (i)   structural analysis: the order of discourse

         (ii)   textual/interactional analysis – both interdiscursive analysis, and linguistic (and semiotic) analysis

The objective here is to understand how the problem arises and how it is rooted in the way social life is organized, by focusing on the obstacles to its resolution – on what makes it more or less intractable.

---

3   Consider whether the social order (network of practices) in a sense 'needs' the problem. The point here is to ask whether those who benefit most from the way social life is now organized have an interest in the problem not being resolved.

4   Identify possible ways past the obstacles. This stage in the framework is a crucial complement to stage 2 – it looks for hitherto unrealized possibilities for change in the way social life is currently organized.

5   Reflect critically on the analysis (1 – 4). This is not strictly part of Bhaskar's explanatory critique. But it is an important addition, requiring the analyst to reflect of where s/he is coming from, how s/he herself/himself is socially positioned.

The main focus of this book is on stage 2c of this schema, and especially on linguistic analysis of texts, though I have also referred to interdiscursive analysis (in terms of hybridity in genres, in discourses, and in styles), and to aspects of orders of discourse (e.g. in discussing genre chains).

This schema gives some sense of CDA as 'method'. More detailed treatments can be found in Fairclough (2001c, 2001d, as well as 1992, 1995a, 1995b). But the critical method summed up here is not overall specific to CDA, it is of general relevance in critical social research, it is just formulated here in a way which foregrounds CDA specifically, and its method of analysis in steps 2(b) and (c). Even then, however, CDA does not in itself provide all the analytical categories and procedures which are entailed: many of the analytical categories I have used in this book come from Systemic Functional Linguistics as I explained in chapter 1, and other methods of language analysis such as those developed in conversation analysis or linguistic pragmatics could be subsumed within CDA to a greater extent than I have indicated here. So CDA is in that sense a method which can appropriate other methods. These also include the methods of corpus linguistics, as I explained in chapter 1.

But it goes further than this. It follows from my concern with CDA as a resource for critical social research that it is best used in combination with theoretical and analytical resources in various areas of social science. For instance, there is a strong case in many types of research for using CDA within the frame of a critical ethnography (Chouliaraki 1995, Pujolar 1997, Rogers forthcoming), if one's primary concern is to reach a deeper understanding of how people live within the new capitalist order (e.g. teenagers in Barcelona, in the case of Pujolar's research), and how discourse figures as an element in their ways of living. One possibility which such a combination of resources opens up is researching the understanding and interpretation of texts (see chapter 1). And CDA can be effectively articulated with political economic and sociological analysis of various types (Chiapello and Fairclough 2002, Fairclough *et al.* 2002). In fact there are now a great many researchers in a great many disciplines who are trying to combine CDA with other theoretical and analytical resources. So while CDA does in a sense constitute a method of analysis, the methods employed in any specific piece of research which draws upon CDA are likely to be a combination of those of CDA and others.

Whether CDA itself is a suitable part of the combination of methods used in a research project can only be decided in the light of the progressive construction of the 'object of research' during the course of the research process. The construction of the object is inevitably a theoretically-informed process – it involves decisions about how to theorize one's area of concern. And as Bourdieu puts it, 'It is only as a function of a definite construction of the object that such a sampling method, such a technique of data collection and analysis, etc., becomes imperative' (Bourdieu and Wacquant 1992: 225).

Summary

In this concluding chapter, we have firstly brought together the various analytical perspectives and categories looked at in the book in the form of a set of questions one can ask of a text, and we have seen how different categories and perspectives can be productively brought together in textual analysis to shed light upon social research issues. Our second concern has been to provide a framing of textual analysis within the broader process of critical discourse analysis, and this has been done in the form of a short 'manifesto' for critical discourse analysis as a resource in social scientific research.

Glossaries

The glossaries include terms used in textual analysis and social research which are used in the book, and the main theorists I have drawn upon. In the case of key social research categories (e.g. 'public sphere'), I have synthesized what has been said in the book. The numbers after glossary entries refer to chapters where the terms are used. Each entry is accompanied by references for further reading. Where an entry refers to other entries, the latter are italicized.

Glossary of key terms

Aestheticization of public identities (10)

The 'aestheticization' of fields such as politics or business is the shift away from these fields being seen as operating according to purely rational principles, and the tendency for both social agents within them and analysts of them to attend more to their aesthetic aspects. The aestheticization of public identities is the more-or-less self-conscious construction of public identities (e.g. the identities of politicians, leading businessmen) to create particular 'images'. Text analysis can contribute to researching this process (and more general processes of 'aestheticizing' social life, including everyday life) by analysing aesthetic (including 'rhetorical') aspects of texts and values in texts. (Chouliaraki and Fairclough 1999, Featherstone 1991, Harvey 1990, Linstead and Höpfl 2000, Lury 1996)

Assumptions (3)

The implicit meanings of texts. Where I use the general term 'assumption', a number of other terms are used in the literature of *pragmatics* and *semantics* (presupposition, entailment, implicature). Three types of assumptions are distinguished in the book: existential, propositional, and value assumptions (about what exists, what is the case, what is desirable or undesirable). (Blakemore 1992, Grice 1981, Levinson 1983, Mey 1993, Verschueren 1999)

'Characters' of new capitalism (10)

The 'characters' of a particular social order are its most distinctive social types (e.g. 'the Manager' in new capitalism). Text analysis can contribute to researching the identities of such 'characters' by for instance showing through analysis of modality and evaluation what they commit themselves to as true or necessary or desirable. 'Characters' can be seen as personal investments of social roles (see *social identity and personality*) – we can show through analysis for instance not only what makes Tony Blair a politician, but how he distinctively invests that role. (McIntyre 1984)

Classification (7)

Classification is in Bourdieu's terms a relationship between 'vision' and 'di-vision': preconstructed and taken-for-granted ways of dividing up parts of the world continuously generate particular 'visions' of the world, ways of seeing it, and acting upon it. Different discourses embody different classifications, so we can research the deployment as well as the challenging and contesting and mixing of classificatory schemes by analysing how discourses are drawn upon and articulated together in texts, and realized in representations, meanings and forms. (Bourdieu 1984, 1991, Bourdieu and Wacquant 1992, Durkheim and Mauss 1963)

Clause (8)

A clause is a simple sentence, as opposed to a complex sentence which combines a number of clauses (e.g. 'she was late' is a clause, 'she was late because the train broke down' is a complex sentence which includes the clause 'she was late'). Clauses have three main types of element: processes (usually realized as verbs), participants (subjects, objects, etc.), circumstances (commonly realized as adverbs). (Eggins 1994, Halliday 1994, Quirk *et al.* 1995)

Collocation (2)

Collocations are more or less regular or habitual patterns of co-occurrence between words – a matter of 'the company a word keeps' as Firth put it. For example, 'poor old' (as in 'poor old man') is a more habitual and predictable combination than 'poor young'. Collocational studies have been considerably advanced by the development of corpus linguistics, allowing co-occurrence patterns to be identified in very large corpora of texts. (Firth 1957, Sinclair 1991, Stubbs 1996)

Communicative and strategic action (4,6)

Communicative action is action oriented to understanding and exchange of meanings (e.g. much conversation), strategic action is action oriented to producing effects (e.g. advertising texts, whose purpose is to sell goods). The distinction is Habermas's, and an important part of his theory of modernization: modern systems (the state, the market) are specialized for strategic action, but there is a tendency for them to 'colonize' non-systemic areas of social life (the 'lifeworld') and for strategic action to displace or appropriate communicative action. These processes are partly textual. For instance in many contemporary texts, what appears to be communicative action can be seen as covertly strategic action. (Fairclough 1992, Habermas 1984, Outhwaite 1996)

Dialectics (2)

Dialectics is a way of thinking and arguing, a method of analysis. It cannot satisfactorily be reduced to a clear-cut analytical procedure, but it can be seen as enacting certain ontological and epistemological principles or assumptions. Some of the most important ones are that processes, flows and relations have primacy over elements, things, structures, etc., the latter being produced as relative 'permanences' out of the former; that 'things' are internally heterogeneous and contradictory because of the diverse processes which produce them; and that change arises out of the contradictions within 'things', structures, and systems.
(Harvey 1996a, Levins and Lewontin 1985, Ollman 1993)

Dialogicality (3)

In Bakhtin's view of language, which is taken up within critical discourse analysis, all texts (written as well as spoken) are dialogical, i.e. they set up in one way or other relations between different 'voices'. But all texts are not equally dialogical. Dialogicality is a measure of the extent to which there are dialogical relations between the voice of the author and other voices, the extent to which these voices are represented and responded to, or conversely excluded or suppressed. This aspect of texts can be approached through distinguishing various orientations to difference (see the entry for *social difference*). (Bakhtin 1981, 1986a, 1986b, Fairclough 1992, Holquist 1981, Gardiner 1992)

Discourse and discourses (2, 7)

'Discourse' is used across the social sciences in a variety of ways, often under the influence of Foucault. 'Discourse' is used in a general sense for language (as well as, for instance, visual images) as an element of social life which is dialectically related to other elements. 'Discourse' is also used more specifically: different discourses are different ways of representing aspects of the world. Discourse analysis in this book is taken to entail detailed linguistic analysis of texts, which is not the case for much discourse analysis in the Foucault tradition. (Chouliaraki and Fairclough 1999, Foucault 1984, Laclau and Mouffe 1985, Van Dijk 1997, Wetherell *et al.* 2001a, 2001b)

Disembedding (4)

Disembedding is a socio-historical process in which elements which develop in one area of social life become detached from that particular context and become available to 'flow' into others. This process is a significant feature of *globalization*. Genres (e.g. various types of interview) may become disembedded, becoming a type of social technology which can be used in different fields and at different scales of social life. (Giddens 1991)

Equivalence and difference (5)

Social processes of *classification* can be seen as involving two simultaneous 'logics': a logic of difference which creates differences, and a logic of equivalence which subverts differences and creates new equivalences. This process can be seen as going on in texts: meaning-making involves putting words and expressions into new relations of equivalence and difference. (Fairclough 2000a, Laclau and Mouffe 1985)

Evaluation (2, 10)

The aspect of text meaning that has to do with values. It includes both explicit evaluative statements (e.g. 'that's a beautiful shirt') and value *assumptions*. Values in text are mainly assumed rather than explicit. Questions of value have tended to be relatively neglected in text analysis, but addressing them allows text analysis to contribute to such value issues in social research as *legitimation*. (Graham 2002, Hunston and Thompson 2000, Lemke 1998, Van Leeuwen and Wodak 1999, White 2001, forthcoming)

Exchange types (6)

An 'exchange' is in the simplest case two conversational turns by different speakers, though the concept can be extended to written language. Two main types of exchange are distinguished: knowledge exchanges, involving exchange of information (e.g. 'Is this a parrot?' 'Yes it is'), and activity exchanges, which are oriented to action (e.g. 'Give me a drink' 'Here you are'). The two types of exchange involve different *speech functions*. (Martin 1992)

Generic structure (3)

The overall structure or organization of a text, which depends upon the main genre upon which the text draws. For instance, news reports are generally structured as: headline + lead paragraph + 'satellite' paragraphs (which elaborate the headline and lead with details of the story). Some texts, especially institutional texts with clear purposes, have well-defined generic structure, others do not. (Halliday and Hasan 1989, Hasan 1996, Martin 1992, Swales 1990)

Genres (2, 4)

A genre is a way of acting in its discourse aspect – for instance, there are various genres of interview such as job interview. Genres can be identified at different levels of abstraction: highly abstract 'pre-genres' such as Narrative or Report, which generalize over many different forms of narrative and report at a more concrete level, disembedded genres (see the entry for *disembedding*), and situated genres which are tied to particular networks of social practices (e.g. genres of political interview in contemporary American of British television). (Bakhtin 1986a, Bazerman 1988, Chouliaraki and Fairclough 1999, Fairclough 2000b, Martin 1992, Swales 1990)

Genre chains (2)

Different genres which are regularly linked together, involving systematic trans-formations from genre to genre (e.g. official documents, associated press releases or press conferences, reports in the press or on television). Genre chains are an important factor in the enhanced capacity for 'action at a distance' which has been taken as a feature of 'globalization'. Change in genre chains is a significant part of social change. (Fairclough 2000a, Graham 2001b, Iedema 1999)

Genre mixing (2)

A text is not simply 'in' a genre. Texts often mix or hybridize different genres (e.g. 'chat' on television tends to be a mixture of conversation, interview, and entertain-ment). Genre mixing is an aspect of the *interdiscursivity* of texts, and analysing allows us to locate texts within processes of social change and to identify the potentially creative and innovative work of social agents in *texturing*. (Bakhtin 1986a, Chouliaraki and Fairclough 1999, Fairclough 1992, 1995a, 1995b, 2000a)

Globalization (2, 4)

The contemporary tendency for economic, political and social processes and relations to operate on an increasingly global scale. The concept is contentious, which is why 'globalization' is put in quotation marks in the book. 'Globalization' is arguably not a specifically contemporary process, but a long-term one, and many parts of the world are marginalized in the 'global' economy. Contemporary changes are perhaps better seen as a new twist in the process of 're-scaling' relations between global, regional, national and local. This re-scaling both affects discourse and depends upon changes in discourse – see the entry on *genre chains*. (Bauman 1998, Castells 1996–8, Giddens 1991, Harvey 1996b, Held *et al.* 1999, Jessop forthcoming b)

Governance (2, 8)

Activity within an institution or organization directed at managing or regulating social practices. The growing popularity of the discourse of 'governance' ('corporate governance', 'global governance', etc.) represents the search for an alternative to the chaos of markets and the hierarchical top-down imposition by states. Greater emphasis is placed upon networks and upon dialogue and deliberation. But the actual governance of contemporary societies can be seen as mixing the three forms: market, hierarchy and network. There are specific genres of governance specialized for *recontextualizing* elements of one social practice within another and transforming these elements in particular ways (e.g. official reports). Changes in governance depend upon changes in genres and *genre chains*. (Jessop 1998, forthcoming a)

Grammatical metaphor (8)

An extension of the usual word-based concept of metaphor to grammar. For instance, processes can be represented either non-metaphorically or metaphorically – if a company fires some of its employees, this may be represented as 'The company fired them' (non-metaphorical) or 'They lost their jobs' (metaphorical). See also the entry on *nominalization*. While the distinction is a useful one, it does problematically imply that one can compare such representations with what actually happened. (Fowler *et al.* 1979, Halliday 1994, Hodge and Kress 1993, Martin 1992)

Grammatical mood (6)

The grammatical distinction between declarative sentences (e.g. 'The window is open'), interrogative sentences (e.g. 'Is the window open?' 'Why is the window open?') and imperative sentences (e.g. 'Open the window.') (Eggins 1994, Halliday 1994, Martin 1992, Quirk *et al.* 1995)

Hegemony (3)

A particular way (associated with Gramsci) of conceptualizing power and the struggle for power in capitalist societies, which emphasizes how power depends on consent or acquiescence rather than just force, and the importance of ideology. Discourse, including the dominance and naturalization of particular representations (e.g. of 'global' economic change) is a significant aspect of hegemony, and struggle over discourse of hegemonic struggle. (Forgacs 1988, Gramsci 1971, Laclau and Mouffe 1985)

Hybridity and postmodernity (2)

Accounts of contemporary social life as 'postmodern' stress the blurring and breakdown of the boundaries characteristic of 'modern' societies, and the pervasive hybridity (mixing of practices, forms, etc.) which ensues. An analysis of *interdiscursive* hybridity in texts provides a resource for researching such processes in detail. (Harvey 1990, Jameson 1991)

Ideology (1, 3, 4)

Ideologies are representations of aspects of the world which contribute to establishing and maintaining relations of power, domination and exploitation. They may be enacted in ways of interacting (and therefore in *genres*) and inculcated in ways of being or identities (and therefore in *styles*). Analysis of texts (including perhaps especially *assumptions* in texts) is an important aspect of ideological analysis and critique, provided it is framed within a broader social analysis of events and social practices. (Eagleton 1991, Larrain 1979, Thompson 1984)

Interdiscursivity (2)

Analysis of the interdiscursivity of a text is analysis of the particular mix of genres, of discourses, and of styles upon which it draws, and of how different genres, discourses or styles are articulated (or 'worked') together in the text. This level of analysis mediates between linguistic analysis of a text and various forms of social analysis of social events and practices. (Chouliaraki and Fairclough 1999, Fairclough 1992)

Intertextuality and reported speech (3)

The intertextuality of a text is the presence within it of elements of other texts (and therefore potentially other voices than the author's own) which may be related to (dialogued with, assumed, rejected, etc.) in various ways (see *dialogicality*). The most common and pervasive form of intertextuality is *reported speech* (including reported writing and thought), though there are others (including irony). Reported speech may or may not be attributed to specific voices, and speech (writing, thought) can be reported in various forms, including direct (reproduction of actual words used) and indirect report (summary). (Bakhtin 1981, Fairclough 1995b, Kristeva 1986a, b, Leech and Short 1981)

Legitimation (5)

Any social order requires legitimation – a widespread acknowledgement of the legitimacy of explanations and justifications for how things are and how things are done. Much of the work of legitimation is textual, though texts vary considerably in how explicit or implicit legitimation is. Textual analysis can identify and research different strategies of legitimation – by reference to authority or utility, through narrative, and so forth. (Berger and Luckman 1966, Habermas 1976, Van Leeuwen and Wodak 1999, Weber 1964)

Mediation (2)

Much action and interaction in contemporary societies is 'mediated', which means that it makes use of copying technologies which disseminate communication and preclude real interaction between 'sender' and 'receiver'. These technologies include print, photography, broadcasting, and the Internet. How we live in contemporary societies is heavily dependent upon mediated texts, which are also crucial in processes of *governance*. (Luhmann 2000, McLuhan 1964, Silverstone 1999, Thompson 1995)

Modality (10)

The modality of a clause or sentence is the relationship it sets up between author and representations – what authors commit themselves to in terms of truth or necessity. Two main types of modality are distinguished, epistemic modality (modality of probabilities), and deontic modality (modality of necessity and obligation). In the case of Statements, explicitly modalized forms (marked by modal verbs such as 'may' or other markers) can be seen as intermediate between categorical Assertion and Denial, and they register varying degrees of commitment to truth or necessity. (Halliday 1994, Hodge and Kress 1988, Palmer 1986, Verschueren 1999.)

New capitalism (1, 2)

Capitalism has the remarkable capacity to sustain itself through major transformations, and 'new capitalism' is the term used for the transformed form of capitalism currently emerging. Referring to new capitalism rather than '*globalization*' amounts to the claim that the re-scaling of relations between global, regional, national and local is fundamentally a matter of the transformation of capitalism. (Boyer and Hollingsworth 1997, Brenner 1998, Crouch and Streek 1997, Jessop 2000)

Nominalization (8)

Nominalization is a type of *grammatical metaphor* which represents processes as entities by transforming clauses (including verbs) into a type of noun. For instance, 'employees produce steel' is a non-metaphorical representation of a process, whereas 'steel production' is a metaphorical, nominalized representation. As this example shows, nominalization often entails excluding social agents in the representation of events (in this case, those who produce). It is a resource for generalizing and abstracting which is indispensible in, for instance, science, but can also obfuscate agency and responsibility. (Fowler *et al.* 1979, Halliday 1994, Lemke 1995)

Order of discourse (2)

An order of discourse is a particular combination or configuration of *genres*, *discourses* and *styles* which constitutes the discoursal aspect of a network of social practices. As such, orders of discourse have a relative stability and durability – though they do of course change. The term derives from Michel Foucault, but is used in critical discourse analysis in a rather different way. We can see orders of discourse in general terms as the social structuring of linguistic variation or difference – there are always many different possibilities in language, but choice amongst them is socially structured. (Chouliaraki and Fairclough 1999, Fairclough 1992, 1995b, Foucault 1984)

Paratactic, hypotactic and embedded relations (5)

These are grammatical distinctions between ways in which clauses can be combined in sentences. Paratactically related clauses are of equal grammatical status, neither being subordinate or superordinate to the other (e.g. 'The car has broken down and the house has been burgled', where the two clauses are conjoined by 'and'). Hypotactically related clauses are in a main (or superordinate)–subordinate relation (e.g. 'I was sad because she left me', where 'because she left me' is subordinate to 'I was sad' – notice that it is possible to reorder the clauses so that the former precedes the latter). In the case of embedding, a clause functions as an element of another clause (its subject for example) or as an element of a phrase (e.g. 'who came to dinner' is a modifier in the phrase 'the man who came to dinner'). (Eggins 1994, Halliday 1994, Martin 1992, Quirk *et al.* 1995)

Pragmatics (3)

Linguistic pragmatics is the study of 'language in relation to its users' (Mey). Its concern is with meaning, but the making of meaning in communication, rather than meaning as relations within language systems in abstraction from actual communication, which is often seen as the concern of *semantics*. Linguistic pragmatics has in particular developed perspectives on language which originated in linguistic philosophy, including speech acts, presuppositions, and implicatures (see *assumptions*). (Austin 1962, Blakemore 1992, Levinson 1983, Mey 1993, Verschueren 1999)

Process types (8)

Types of processes semantically and grammatically available in English for representing events. The following process types are distinguished: material, mental, verbal, relational (two sub-types), and existential. Events can be represented non-metaphorically or metaphorically in terms of process types – see *grammatical metaphor*. (Fowler *et al.* 1979, Halliday 1994, Martin 1992, Van Leeuwen 1995)

Promotional culture (6)

A view of contemporary cultural phenomena as virtually always serving promotional functions in addition to whatever other functions they may have, as simultaneously representing, advocating and anticipating whatever is referred to. The notion of 'consumer culture' is similar. This co-presence of promotion with other functions can fruitfully be examined in detail through textual analysis, for example in policy texts. (Featherstone 1991, Graham 2002, Lury 1996, Wernick 1991)

Public sphere (3, 4, 10)

The domain of social life in which people can engage as citizens is deliberating about and acting upon issues of social and political concern, aiming to influence policy formation. Much of the literature on the public sphere emphasizes its problematic character in contemporary societies, structural constraints (e.g. linked to the position of mass media) on people acting in this way as citizens. From a discourse perspective, problems associated with the public space include problems with forms of dialogue – do what are presented as 'dialogue', 'deliberation', 'consultation', 'participation' and so forth actually have the features they would need to have in order to be effective in the public sphere? (Arendt 1958, Calhoun 1992, Fairclough 1999, Habermas 1989, 1996)

Recontextualization *(2, 8)*

Recontextualization is a relationship between different (networks of) social practices – a matter of how elements of one social practice are appropriated by, relocated in the context of, another. Originally a sociological concept (Bernstein 1990), it can be operationalized in discourse analysis in a *transdisciplinary* way through categories such as *genre chain*, which allow us to show in more detail how the discourse of one social practice is recontextualized in another. (Bernstein 1990, Chouliaraki and Fairclough 1999)

Semantics *(2, 5, 7)*

Semantics is a branch of linguistics which studies meaning in languages. It is conventionally distinguished from grammar, which studies formal aspects of languages. A further distinction is between semantics and *pragmatics*: semantics is often seen as dealing with meaning (e.g. the meaning of words) in abstraction from specific contexts of use, pragmatics as dealing with the meaning of actual texts in actual social contexts. Semantic relations include semantic relations between clauses (reason, consequence, purpose, conditional, temporal, additive, elaborative, contrastive/concessive) and semantic relations between words (synonymy, hyponymy, antonymy). (Allan 2001, Lyons 1977, Verschueren 1999)

Social actors *(8)*

There are a number choices available in the representation of social actors (participants in social processes). An initial question is whether they are included or excluded in representations of events. If they are included, it may be as nouns or as pronouns; in one grammatical role as opposed to another (e.g. Actor or Affected), and more broadly in an 'activated' or 'passivated' role. They may be represented personally or impersonally (e.g. referring to employees as 'human resources'), named (given personal names) or classified (in terms of a class or category, e.g. 'teachers'), referred to specifically or generically (e.g. 'teachers', meaning teachers in general). Which social actors get represented in which ways is a matter of social significance – for instance, if 'the poor' are consistently passivated (represented as subject to the action of others), the implication is that they are incapable of agency. (Halliday 1994, Van Leeuwen 1996)

Social difference *(3)*

Texts vary in their orientation to social difference – from being dialogical exploration of difference, to polemical accentuation of difference, to attempts to overcome difference, to bracketing difference in order to focus on commonality, to suppressing difference. Particular texts may combine these scenarios. It is the nature of its orientation to difference that determines the relative *dialogicality* of a text. (Benhabib 1996, Holquist 1981, Kress 1985)

Social events, practices and structures (2)

Social structures define what is possible, social events constitute what is actual, and the relationship between potential and actual is mediated by social practices. Language (more broadly, semiosis) is an element of the social at each of these levels – languages are a type of social structure, texts are elements of social events, and orders of discourse are elements of (networks of) social practices. One consequence is that rather than starting from texts, one starts from social events (and chains and networks of events), and analyses texts as elements of social events. (Bhaskar 1986, Fairclough *et al.* 2002, Sayer 2000)

Social identity and personality (9, 10)

Social identity and personality (or personal identity) are two analytically distinct aspect of people's identity. Part of one's social identity is a matter of the social circumstances into which one is born and early socialization – aspects of gender identity, for instance. Part of it is acquired later in life – socialization into particular 'social roles' such as politician or teacher, for instance. But there is a dialectical relationship between social identity and personality: the full social development of one's identity, one's capacity to truly act as a social agent intervening in and potentially changing social life, depends upon 'social roles' being personally invested and inflected, a fusion between social identity and personality. It is possible to contribute to research on identity through textual analysis focused upon a textual dialectic between social and personal identity, which takes styles as 'ways of being' or identities in their language (as opposed to bodily, somatic) aspect. (Archer 2000, Giddens 1991, Harré 1983, Ivanič 1998, Taylor 1985)

Social practices

See *social events, practices and structures*.

Social structures

See *social events, practices and structures*.

Societal informalization (4, 10) and conversationalization (4)

Societal informalization is a tendency in especially post-Second World War social life in the most developed liberal societies for relations of power and authority to become more implicit, and for interaction where such relations obtain to become more informal (for instance managers, politicians and even the British royal family increasingly come across as just 'ordinary people' in their interactions with employees and the public). This process can be effectively researched textually by focusing on the 'conversationalization' of public discourse – the tendency towards a simulation of conversation in public interactions and texts. (Fairclough 1992, 1995a, Misztal 2000, Seligman 1997)

'Space–times' (8)

The term 'space–time' is used to register the view that it is difficult or even impossible to treat space and time as different qualities. Space and time are not just naturally given. Space–times are social constructs, different social orders construct space–times differently, and constructions of space–time are dialectically interconnected with other social elements in the construction of a social order as networks of *social practices*. Moreover, a social order constructs relations between different space–times (e.g. between the local and the global in contemporary society), and these relations are a focus of contestation and struggle. These relations are assumed in a banal way, and sometimes contested, in our ordinary activities and texts. Text analysis can contribute to researching them. Bakhtin's concept of 'chronotopes' is also of relevance here. (Bakhtin 1981, Bourdieu 1977, Giddens 1991, Harvey 1996a)

Speech functions (6)

Each of the two *exchange types* distinguished in the book is associated with two major speech functions: knowledge exchanges with Statements and Questions, activity exchanges with Offers and Demands. These are distinctions on a high level of generality which one can see as open to considerable refinement in terms of 'speech act' theory. (Austin 1962, Martin 1992, Sbisá 1995, Searle 1969)

Structure and agency (2, 8)

An emphasis on structure in social (including linguistic and textual) research foregrounds the ways in which pre-given structures and systems limit, shape and determine events and actions. An emphasis on agency foregrounds the ways in which situated agents produce events, actions, texts, etc. in potentially creative and innovative ways. The position taken in this book is that neither emphasis is satisfactory on its own, that both structures and agency have 'causal powers', that events (including texts) need to be seen as the outcome of a tension between structures and agency, and that the relationship between the two is *dialectical*. (Archer 1995, 2000, Bhaskar 1989, Bourdieu and Wacquant 1992, Giddens 1984)

Styles (2)

See *social and personal identity*.

Transdisciplinary (1)

Transdisciplinary research is a form of interdisciplinary or 'post-disciplinary' research. Its specific perspective is that the meeting and dialogue between different disciplines in researching particular issues should be approached in the spirit of developing the theoretical categories, methods of analysis, research agendas, etc. of the one through working with the 'logic' of the other. So, for example, one can see a category such as *genre* in discourse analysis as open to being developed theoretically and methodologically through dialogue with other disciplines and theories (e.g. with Bernstein's sociological theory as suggested in Chouliaraki 1999). (Chouliaraki and Fairclough 1999, Dubiel 1985, Fairclough 2000a)

Types of meaning (action, representation, identification) (2)

Three primary types of meaning can be distinguished for purposes of textual analysis: meanings which a text has as a part of the action in social events (actional), meanings which appertain to the representation of the world in texts (representational), and meanings which appertain to the textual construction of people's identities (identificatory). These three types or aspects of meaning are always co-present in texts. The distinction between them is analogous to the distinction between the major or 'macro' functions of language in Systemic Functional Linguistics. (Halliday 1994, Lemke 1995, Martin 1992)

Universal and particular (3, 8)

The relationship between universal and particular in politics is the relationship between that which appertains to human beings as such and that which appertains to particular groups. There is a crisis of the universal in contemporary politics – for instance, can the general aspiration towards human emancipation have any meaning or become a real political project (as in the socialist tradition)? Nevertheless, the terrain of the universal remains a much contested one – struggles for *hegemony* can be seen as struggles to legitimize claims for the universality of perspectives, interests, projects, etc. which are particular in their origins. This can be seen and researched as a partly textual process in which representations, identities, etc. are textually constructed as universal (e.g. the attempted construction of contemporary economic and social change in terms of a universal 'globalization'). (Butler *et al.* 2000, Laclau 1996)

Glossary of key theorists

Bakhtin, Mikhail

Russian theorist and analyst of literature, culture and language of the mid-twentieth century who (with colleagues such as Volosinov) developed a dialogical view of language (see *dialogicality*) which has recently been influential in the development of alternatives to mainstream formalist Linguistics. Recent focusing of *intertextuality* can be attributed to Bakhtin's influence, as well as much recent thinking about *genre*. Bakhtin's concept of 'chronotopes' is also valuable for analysis of *space-times*. (Bakhtin 1981, 1986a, 1986b, Chouliaraki and Fairclough 1999, Holquist 1981, Volosinov 1973)

Bhaskar, Roy

Philosopher of science and social science who is the main figure in 'critical realism', which I have drawn upon especially in Part 1. (Bhaskar 1979, 1986, 1989)

Bernstein, Basil

British sociologist of education whose work on 'pedagogical discourse' and associated issues of *classification*, framing and *recontextualization* are of particular relevance here. (Bernstein 1990, Chouliaraki and Fairclough 1999)

Bourdieu, Pierre

French sociologist and theorist of the structuring of complex modern societies in terms of social 'fields' and their shifting interconnection, which can be related to the focus here on social practices and their shifting networks, and the 'habitus' (acquired and embodied dispositions to act in certain ways) of socially diverse agents. I have drawn upon his perspective on *classification* and the relationship between *structure and agency*. Bourdieu's recent political intervention on and analysis of neo-liberalism includes an emphasis on the discourse of neo-liberalism. (Bourdieu 1991, Bourdieu and Wacquant 1992, 2001, Chouliaraki and Fairclough 1999)

Foucault, Michel

French philosopher whose theoretical and historical work on discourse has had a huge influence across the social sciences. The categories of *interdiscursivity* and *order of discourse* can be traced back to Foucault, though they are used rather differently within my version of critical discourse analysis. (Fairclough 1992, Foucault 1972, 1984)

Giddens, Anthony

British sociologist who has written extensively on 'globalization' and the social transformations of new capitalism (without using that term). I have drawn on several aspects of this work (see *disembedding, globalization, social identity and personality, space–times, structure and agency*). (Chouliaraki and Fairclough 1999, Giddens 1991)

Habermas, Jürgen

German critical theorist in the Frankfurt School tradition, whose main relevance here comes from the centrality he gives to communication (hence language) in his version of critical theory, his account of modernization in these terms, and his work on the *public sphere*. I have drawn on his distinction between *communicative and strategic action*, and his work on *legitimation*. (Chouliaraki and Fairclough 1999, Habermas 1976, 1984, 1989)

Halliday, Michael

British linguist in the 'functionalist' tradition of J.R. Firth who has been the main figure in the development of Systemic Functional Linguistics as an alternative to the formalism (associated especially with Noam Chomsky) of mainstream Linguistics. Halliday's Linguistics has long been in dialogue with *Bernstein*'s sociological theory, and is in many ways a fruitful resource for social and critical analysis of language and discourse. Halliday is the main source in Linguistics I have drawn upon in this book. (Halliday 1978, 1994, Halliday and Hasan 1976, 1989, Martin 1992)

Harvey, David

British geographer and social theorist whose work on the transformations of new capitalism and on the dialectics of discourse are of particular value here, with respect to *globalization, space–times, aestheticization of public identities, hybridity and postmodernity*). (Chouliaraki and Fairclough 1999, Harvey 1990, 1996a, 1996b)

Jessop, Bob

British sociologist and political economist whose work on the transformations in *new capitalism* and *globalization*, especially with respect to *governance*, is particularly relevant here. (Jessop 1998, 2000, forthcoming a, forthcoming b)

Laclau, Ernesto

Argentinian political theorist working in Britain best known for reworking (with Chantal Mouffe) Gramsci's Marxism and theory of *hegemony* in *discourse* analytical terms. I have suggested in the book that his theorization of the logics of *equivalence and difference* and of the relationship between *universal and particular* could be operationalized in textual analysis. (Butler *et al.* 2000, Chouliaraki and Fairclough 1999, Laclau 1996, Laclau and Mouffe 1985)

Appendix of texts

Transcription conventions   Pauses are shown with dots (short pauses) and dashes (longer pauses). Voiced pauses ('ums and ers') are shown as 'e:' and 'e:m'. Where speakers overlap each other, turns are laid out in order to show the point in one speaker's turn where another speaker begins. Where some words on the tape are unclear, this is indicated in brackets as '(unclear)'.

EXAMPLE 1

The example is taken from T.J. Watson *In Search of Management: Culture, Chaos and Control in Managerial Work*, Routledge 1994, pages 207–8, an ethnographic study of managers and management. The example is an extract from one of the research interviews.

'The culture in successful businesses is different from in failing businesses. It would be the same with a country or a city. You can see this when you go to Liverpool. I don't go there very often, but when I do I come back feeling really depressed. I could really weep when I look at it now; the way it has been destroyed. It has been destroyed by its own stupidity. I remember as a kid the docks, eighteen miles long. It is now dead. It is all a political problem; these areas have been starved over the years. It has been happening since the eighteenth century, so that these people have been downtrodden to the point where they expect to be downtrodden. They are totally suspicious of any change. They are totally suspicious of anybody trying to help them. They immediately look for the rip-off. They have also been educated to believe that it is actually clever to get "one over on them". So they are all at it. And the demarcation lines that the unions have been allowed to impose in those areas, because of this, makes it totally inflexible to the point where it is destructive. I know it. I can see it.'

'And how does this relate to what is happening here?'

'Well, I was going to say, how do you change this sort of negative culture? We have done a lot here. But my greatest fear is that they are going to destroy all the good work that we put onto this site if they keep pushing and pushing and pushing the bottom end like they are doing. I believe that people will react in such a way shortly that they will destroy everything.'

'Bottom end?'

'Of the workforce; pushing them by getting rid, I mean. How the hell can you preach this flexibility, this personal and business development at the same time as you are getting rid? As someone said to me yesterday, an operator, "Why am I in here now doing the best I can getting this product out when tomorrow morning you can give me a brown envelope?" I had no answer.'

'But the good work you refer to?'

'Take IR. There has been a coordinated plan to take the power from the unions and give it back to the managers and give it back to the workforce as well. That was going fairly well. But these continuing rounds of redundancies will give the opportunity to say "We told you so; we knew that was the ground plan all along." The union people can say, "You should have listened to us all the time."'

'And the other changes?'

'Developing Organizational Capability, winning culture, Business Improvement Plan, empowering, and all that: I am totally committed to all of this principle. These changes are the way forward. But what the company is doing is going contrary to what all this is about. This is dangerous – raising expectations and then smashing them. I believe the senior management has a moral responsibility to its workforce and to employ. The firm is an integral part of the society we live in.'

'Which means?'

'All business has got to keep faith with all of those it deals with if it is going to deserve to survive.'

EXAMPLE 2: BÉKÉSCSABA

This text is taken from the 'Property Focus' section of the *Budapest Sun*, 22–8 March 2001. The *Budapest Sun* is an English language newspaper produced in Hungary.

Festival town flourishes

LOCAL FLAVOR: Above left, the town's sports hall and, above right, Sausage Festival participants stuff ground meat into casing.

In the south-east of Hungary lies the pleasant little town of Békéscaba. Officially it became a county seat in 1950, but even before then was the most significant town in its region. It is now the focal point of Békés County, which has a population of 410,000.

Békéscaba's several squares are connected to each other and surrounded by schools and churches. The main square is Szent István tér, where the mayor's office is located, which forms the old town center.

The Town Hall, designed by Miklós Ybl, is

'Békéscsaba is an excellent choice for locating businesses that want to penetrate the market in this part of the world.'
János Pap, City Mayor

close to the upmarket Hotel Fiume and a theater built in 1879. There are also some traditional folk houses in Békéscaba that are considered architecturally of note. One of these is the so-called 'fairy house' which is home to a Slovakian club. The town was rebuilt by Slovakian settlers and their descendants still study in Slovakian-speaking schools. The town will soon house the General Consulate of the Slovakian Republic.

Flood plain

Békéscaba lies in a flood plain in the center of the Körös River Valley, which is excellent agricultural land.

'Traditional events are held in the town every year, for example: An international ethnographical conference; a biannual graphic arts exhibition; an international puppet show; American music days and a cultural market where visitors can become familiar with the art of Eastern Europe,' said János Pap, the Mayor of Békéscaba. 'These programs make Békéscaba a festival-town.'

Pap said the intellectual life of the town and its art and traditions were very important. 'There is a printing house that was established before the 20th century, called Tevan Printing House,' he said. 'The tradition still goes on and we have a printing college.'

Textile industry and trade are traditional in Békéscaba. There are special schools which train people for these jobs.

The town is 200km south-east of Budapest and is easily accessible from the capital by road and train within three hours. The M5 motorway and the number 44 main road link it to the country's main road network.

János Sztankó, Managing Director of the local entrepreneurs' center Békéscabai Vállalkozói Centrum kft, said the town first produced information for investors on a regular basis in 1993. 'First we had just a booklet, but now we have all the information on CD ROM in English as well as Hungarian,' said Sztankó.

Pap said Békéscaba was situated on the crossroads of the trans-European traffic network, serving as the nation's south-eastern gateway to central and eastern Europe. 'Because of its geographical position, Békéscaba is an excellent choice in this region for investment and for locating businesses that want to penetrate the market in this part of the world,' he added.

Sztankó said several foreign multinational, predominantly from France, Italy, Germany and Austria, had already chosen the town as a

PLAY TIME: The town's biggest playhouse, the Jókai Színház

regional base for their businesses.

'The town's agri-food industry, including vegetables, fruit, poultry and pork products, are exported worldwide,' he said. 'Other major industries include printing, bricks and tiles, clothing, knitwear, machinery and milling,' he said. 'The services, commerce, finance and transportation also play an important role in our economic life.'

Currently there are 13 different banks operating in Békéscaba.

'About 39% of the town's active earners work in industry, while about 9% labor in the agriculture and forestry sectors. The remainder find jobs in the commerce and service industries,' said Sztankó.

'A capable workforce, improving infrastructure and flexible labor is readily available. In addition, the local education system offers qualified, multi-lingual professionals.' Sztankó said the average gross monthly salary in the town exceeds $260.

The Békés County Enterprise Agency, the Hungarian Investment and Development Agency and the Chamber of Commerce and Industry of Békés County are all based in the town. The municipality consciously promotes economic development and investment, offering incentives from site locations to tax breaks.

Békéscaba is also the region's educational and training center, with 14 secondary schools. The town's higher education institutions train teachers, economists and mid-level managers. As part of a World Bank project, a regional retraining center was established in the town, based on European standards, to offer such things as vocational training, language courses and consultancy at all levels.

Pap said, 'Existing companies reinvesting their money are already realizing that the regional retraining center project supports their future developments.

'Now we are planning a new commercial and business center on a greenfield site of 21,000 sqm in the town. It will offer sites for both office and factory constructions.'

Sztankó said that over the past few years many new homes have been constructed in the town. Specially-designed apartment blocks and pretty family houses have regularly been among the

Beyond **Budapest**

Békéscsaba

Mayor: János Pap (SZDSZ)
Address: 5600, Békéscsaba, Szent István tér 7
Tel: (06-66) 523-801
Fax: (06-66) 523-804
Population: 65,000
Area: 19.3 sqkm
Average residential property price: Ft80,000–100,000 per sqm
Land price: Ft1,500–18,000 per sqm

National Architectural Prize's winning designs. 'Most of the buildings are family houses that can be recognized by their unique local style,' he added. 'Here prices are lower than the national average.' Pap said that because of its location, Békéscaba, with its many tiny shops and long pedestrian streets, was also the shopping hub of the region, attracting crowds of shopping

tourists from Romania.

'We hope that current commercial developments in the downtown area will bring lots of new retailers into the town,' he said. the open-air market, which offers a wide range of products from vegetables to hand-made items, is packed with visitors every Wednesday and Saturday.

Békéscaba's soccer team is among the nation's top clubs. Next to the football stadium the town also has an indoor sports hall, a swimming pool and tennis courts.

The main hospital in the town was recently upgraded and it is now equipped to international standards, making it the largest such complex in Békés County.

A large green area with rivers, forests and fields, creates a pleasant environment around Békéscaba. 'Many Westerners come to our thermal spas, or to go fishing and hunting,' said Pap.

The town's transport service is well-equipped. Next to the railway station is a modern bus station.

EXAMPLE 3

This example is different from others in that it is made up of extracts from two interactions and a written text which are linked together in an 'intertextual chain' (see page xxx). The example is taken from an academic paper in the area of discourse analysis whose focus is a project planning the renovation of a mental hospital in Australia. (R. Iedema 'Formalizing organizational meaning', *Discourse and Society* **10**(1) 1999: 49–65. The extracts are from pages 59–61.) Here is Iedema's description of the project: 'his [task] involved the hiring of an independent architect-planner. This person was in charge of writing up a report, recording the successful interweaving of government guidelines, physical and technical constraints, user expectations, and bureaucratic procedure, as these were (re)presented by the various stakeholders: Department of Health and Area Health Service officials, a project manager, an engineer-supplier, users (mental hospital staff), and the architect-planner.' The report includes a 'translation' if the agreement reached between stakeholders into two-dimensional drawings, the basis for detailed architectural plans, and eventually the built construction itself. The example includes (a) extract from an interview with the architect-planner, (b) extracts from a meeting of stakeholders, and (c) an extract from the written report.

Extract from interview with architect-planner

It says there's supposed to be three alternatives looked at, all these things, now if someone insists on us going through the full exercise of looking at quite distinct options, I'm sure [DC; head of the architectural firm for whom the architect-planner works as a consultant] would not in the slightest be interested in seeing two other options because he's picked the one he likes, so the question is whether we can create fictitious options that can be knocked down, that often happens, you've got the one you like and two that are not quite as good for various reasons, and then you say, 'well these are three options' . . .

Extracts from a meeting

Extract (1)

Project manager: Can I just, sorry, just to stop you there, eh the criteria, the selection I guess eh seem to be reasonable as one would expect, is there anything else that anybody can comment on as to the other criteria which people think ought to be included in this document, eh they're pretty generalized criteria, I guess I wouldn't expect this thing to say very much different to that, but if there are specific criteria which occur to people which seem to be important on the process of design it's important that we flush everything out by this stage

Architect-planner: Ehm can't think of anything

Area Health Service official: I think [name of Project Manager] one of the major criteria
in getting the preferred design is the eh . . . it looks like an open site but it's so
I guess you've got capital minimization through the re-use of existing spaces and
eh you've got the lowest cost for construction solution . . .

Architect-planner: So OK that we'll add to that

Extract (2)

Architect-planner: Yeah and then eh we tried to look, one of the other advantages of
course of the east–west wing is that you get north–south sun control, ehm, and
eh that's a bit of a compromize on a diagonal if you like, what that does for us
though is it minimizes the amount of excavation by being on a diagonal you see
it runs along a contour, which therefore trades a little bit, it's not ideal, in the
sense that if it was directly east–west you in fact have better sun control, but I
think we were happy that is why the solution that came out was staggered to
try and maintain both the sun the sun control north–south as well as working
up the contour

Extract (3)

Project manager: Could could I just summarize this in my usual naïve way, ehm,
essentially what you're saying is that option D is preferred because it's the most
compact and therefore on any eh measurement it should be the least
cost option, that's also added to by the fact that there is no substantial sort of
building-up or elevation we are ehm biting into the existing hillside, we're saying
that the compactness means you have central staff control with vision virtually
to all units which gets over some of the problems associated with having the two
new units at either end of the building in all the other options, ehm you're saying
however that in this option you'd need two separate accesses basically, one
maintaining the existing function with the hospital, but also providing an access
which comes round to the eastern side of the site

Extract from the report

All of the options examined contained some good points and some bad points but
none were able to meet the majority of the criteria. This means that another option
had to be created to gain the best of all options. The solution was to place the new
accommodation wings on the same side of the building so that the closest functional
adjacency could be achieved. It would be placed on the eastern side of the present
building and by having the non-secure rooms at a diagonal to the present building

would effectively work with the [geographical] contours. To achieve the benefits of the options which had the new wing running east–west, the rooms in option D were staggered so that each room aligned north–south to reduce heat gain. In this way a solution which met most of the criteria was achieved.

EXAMPLE 4

This is a paragraph from a policy paper which was prepared for the European Council by the Competitiveness Advisory Group, which consists of representatives of the employers and trade unions as well as some politicians and officials. The example is taken from a paper by Ruth Wodak ('From conflict to consensus? The co-construction of a policy paper, in P. Muntigl *et al.*, European Union Discourses on Un/Employment, John Benjamins, 2000. The example is taken from page 101). I have retained Wodak's numbering of sentences.

1   But (globalization) is also a demanding process, and often a painful one.
2   Economic progress has always been accompanied by destruction of obsolete activities and creation of new ones.
3   The pace has become swifter and the game has taken on planetary dimensions.
4   It imposes deep and rapid adjustments on all countries – including European countries, where industrial civilization was born.
5   Social cohesion is threatened by a widespread sense of unease, inequality and polarization.
6   There is a risk of a disjunct between the hopes and aspirations of people and the demands of a global economy.
7   And yet social cohesion is not only a worthwhile social and political goal; it is also a source of efficiency and adaptability in a knowledge-based economy that increasingly depends on human quality and the ability to work as a team.
8   It is more than ever the duty of governments, trade-unions and employers to work together

  •   to describe the stakes and refute a number of mistakes;
  •   to stress that our countries should have high ambitions and they can be realized; and
  •   to implement the necessary reforms consistently and without delay.

9   Failure to move quickly and decisively will result in loss of resources, both human and capital, which will leave for more promising parts of the world if Europe provides less attractive opportunities.

EXAMPLE 5

This is an extract from the speech given by Tony Blair, the British Prime Minister, at the Labour Party Conference, Saturday 13 October 2001. The extract is taken from the transcript of the speech on the 10 Downing Street website.

So what do we do?

Don't overreact some say. We aren't.

We haven't lashed out. No missiles on the first night just for effect.

Don't kill innocent people. We are not the ones who waged war on the innocent. We seek the guilty.

Look for a diplomatic solution. There is no diplomacy with Bin Laden or the Taliban regime.

State an ultimatum and get their response. We stated the ultimatum; they haven't responded.

Understand the causes of terror. Yes, we should try, but let there be no moral ambiguity about this: nothing could ever justify the events of 11 September, and it is to turn justice on its head to pretend it could.

The action we take will be proportionate; targeted; we will do all we humanly can to avoid civilian casualties. But understand what we are dealing with. Listen to the calls of those passengers on the planes. Think of the children on them, told they were going to die.

Think of the cruelty beyond our comprehension as amongst the screams and the anguish of the innocent, those hijackers drove at full throttle planes laden with fuel into buildings where tens of thousands worked.

They have no moral inhibition on the slaughter of the innocent. If they could have murdered not 7,000 but 70,000 does anyone doubt they would have done so and rejoiced in it?

There is no compromise possible with such people, no meeting of minds, no point of understanding with such terror.

Just a choice: defeat it or be defeated by it. And defeat it we must.

Any action taken will be against the terrorist network of Bin Laden.

As for the Taliban, they can surrender the terrorists; or face the consequences and again in any action the aim will be to eliminate their military hardware, cut off their finances, disrupt their supplies, target their troops, not civilians. We will put a trap around the regime.

I say to the Taliban: surrender the terrorists; or surrender power. It's your choice. . . .

The values we believe in should shine through what we do in Afghanistan.

To the Afghan people we make this commitment. The conflict will not be the end. We will not walk away, as the outside world has done so many times before.

If the Taliban regime changes, we will work with you to make sure its successor is one that is broad-based, that unites all ethnic groups, and that offers some way out of the miserable poverty that is your present existence.

And, more than ever now, with every bit as much thought and planning, we will assemble a humanitarian coalition alongside the military coalition so that inside and outside Afghanistan, the refugees, four-and-a-half million on the move even before 11 September, are given shelter, food and help during the winter months.

The world community must show as much its capacity for compassion as for force.

The critics will say: but how can the world be a community? Nations act in their own self-interest. Of course they do. But what is the lesson of the financial markets, climate change, international terrorism, nuclear proliferation or world trade? It is that our self-interest and our mutual interests are today inextricably woven together.

This is the politics of globalization.

I realize why people protest against globalization.

We watch aspects of it with trepidation. We feel powerless, as if we were now pushed to and fro by forces far beyond our control.

But there's a risk that political leaders, faced with street demonstrations, pander to the argument rather than answer it. The demonstrators are right to say there's injustice, poverty, environmental degradation.

But globalization is a fact and, by and large, it is driven by people.

Not just in finance, but in communication, in technology, increasingly in culture, in recreation. In the world of the Internet, information technology and TV, there will be globalization. And in trade, the problem is not there's too much of it; on the contrary there's too little of it.

The issue is not how to stop globalization.

The issue is how we use the power of community to combine it with justice. If globalization works only for the benefit of the few, then it will fail and will deserve to fail. But if we follow the principles that have served us so well at home – that power, wealth and opportunity must be in the hands of the many, not the few – if we make that our guiding light for the global economy, then it will be a force for good and an international movement that we should take pride in leading.

Because the alternative to globalization is isolation.

EXAMPLE 6

This is a report from a radio news broadcast (*Today*, BBC Radio 4, 30 September 1993) on the extradition of two Libyans accused of responsibility for the Lockerbie bombing in 1988, when an aircraft exploded near the town of Lockerbie in Scotland killing all those on board.

'Headlines': *Newsreader:* Libya has now told the United Nations that it is willing to see the two men accused of the Lockerbie bombing stand trial in Scotland, but it cannot meet the deadline to hand them over.

Newsreader: Libya has told the United Nations that it's willing to let the two men accused of the Lockerbie bombing come to Scotland to stand trial. The position was spelt out in New York last night by the Foreign Minister, OM, when he emerged from a meeting with the Secretary-General, Dr Boutros-Ghali.

OM: The answers we have received from the UK and the US though the Secretary-General are very acceptable to us and we see them as a positive e: answer and enough guarantees to secure a fair . trial for these two suspects once they submit themselves to e: such jurisdiction.

Newsreader: Libyan officials at the UN, faced by the threat of more sanctions, said they wanted more time to sort out the details of the handover. Relatives of the 270 people who died on Flight 103 in December 1988 are treating the statement with caution. From the UN, our correspondent John Nian.

Correspondent: Western diplomats still believe Libya is playing for time. However on the face of it Libya does appear to be inching closer to handing over the two suspects. If this initiative is only a delaying tactic, its aim would be to persuade the waverers on the Security Council not to vote for the new sanctions, in what is likely to be a close vote. However the UN Secretary-General is reported to have been taking a tough line with Libya, demanding that it specify exactly when the two suspects would be handed over. The Libyan Foreign Minister has promised a reply on that point later today, but he's asked for more time to arrange the handover. Meanwhile the West has maintained the pressure on Libya. The Foreign Secretary Douglas Hurd, and the American Secretary of State Warren Christopher, have both reiterated the threat of sanctions. Western diplomats say that unless the two suspects are handed over immediately, a new resolution will be tabled tomorrow.

EXAMPLE 7

This example is taken from the website of the World Economic Forum during its annual meeting in Davos, Switzerland, in January 2001. The example is rather complex since it contains three different elements. First, a summary of one of the sessions at Davos. Second, selected quotations from the session. Third, edited comments sent to the website on the theme of the session by people from various countries. To reduce the length of the example, I have included only one quotation and one email comment.

Thursday, 25 January 2001

How Can Globalization Deliver the Goods: The View from the South

Globalization is now a loaded term in many parts of the world. It is often associated more closely with the social challenges facing the southern hemisphere rather than with economic opportunities. What are the critical issues that need to be addressed in order for globalization to meet the expectations of the southern hemisphere?

Globalization is often more closely associated with the social challenges facing the southern hemisphere than with the economic opportunities. The future success of globalization requires that developing countries be fully involved in the management of the global economy and that their voices be heard.

Recent demonstrations have made it clear that the priorities and agendas of the developing world must be heard. The United States and Europe can no longer set the global agenda on their own. But the integration of environmental and labour standards into the framework of global governance may not be as easy as the protestors thought. Many in the developing world see these issues as potential excuses for trade barriers.

In terms of global governance, the establishment of the Group of 20 was a step in the right direction. In the Group of 20, unlike the Group of 7, both industrial and developing countries have a say in economic coordination. But, economics are not the only concern. Cultural homogenization worries many. There is fear that over-powering globalization will force the extinction of national cultures and traditions, especially in the southern hemisphere. Others disagree with this notion, saying societies have been changing for all eternity. Globalization increases choice and liberty, while national group identity does the opposite. In a world with close contact between differing cultural identities and ethnic practices, governors must be careful not to steer diversity down the destructive paths of the past. There is also concern that globalization means more for the rich, and less for the poor. But it must be made clear that the benefits of overall growth should reach all, and that economies that are more transparent tend to have lesser income inequalities.

Nonetheless, it is true that some countries are falling behind. Ghana, for example, has strictly followed structural adjustment programmes for 15 years, yet still struggles to attract investment and grow. It is common to blame globalization, but some say such growth won't come by solely focusing on macroeconomic variables. Rather, the fundamental structures of a market economy, freely moving prices and guaranteed contracts and property, must first be in place.

While addressing these concerns, and helping globalization meet the expectations of the southern hemisphere, leaders will make things easier by striving for good governance. More transparency, more accountability, and more participation by all involved will help make the process seem more humane.

Quote from the session

'World trade liberalization has to be a two-way street. We are tired of hearing "we want to sell to you, but you can't sell to us".'

Marcus Vinicius Pratini de Moraes, Minister of Agriculture
and Food Supply of Brazil

Email comment

There is not only a problem of equal distribution North–South, but also within many developing countries (Brazil, S. Africa, Indonesia . . .). Whilst we develop programmes to empower local farmers and informal entrepreneurs, the rich of these countries choose their new private jet. No fair distribution is possible without political change.

Jo, Antwerp, Belgium

EXAMPLE 8

This extracts are from a two-hour long TV 'debate' on the future of the monarchy (broadcast on Independent Television, Channel 3, in January 1997) which was simultaneously a 'referendum' by telephone on the question 'Do you want a monarchy?' ('debate' and 'referendum' are the producer's self-descriptions). The format is relatively rapid shifts between the following elements:

openings and closings from the 'anchor' in the studio
filmed reports by 'columnists'
studio panel of 'experts', etc. 'crossing swords'
studio reporter: results of a public opinion poll about the monarchy
polls of opinions of studio audience (presented by 'anchor')
reporter soliciting studio audience members' opinions
commercial breaks

The following sample includes extracts from the studio panel of 'experts', and the reporter soliciting audience opinions.

Extract I

Roger Cook: Stephen Haseler as chairman of the Republican Movement e: do you as James Whittaker suggests e: are you about to lead the storming the ramparts
Stephen Haseler: no we're not going to storm anything but we – we're increasingly em attracting more and more people to our cause and republicanism is now on

the agenda of British politics really for the first time since the nineteenth century this show is an is an example of that and republicanism can only grow but contrary to James Whittaker who has spent most of his life prying into the royals poking around them and now wants to defend them contrary to him I don't think that the issue is simply the scandals of the royal family e: there have been enough of those we have an insensitive Prince and so on that's not the real issue the real issue I think is that the British public are increasingly wanting to choose their next head of state (unclear)

Roger Cook: that they may well do and that they may get a chance to indicate this evening – Frederick Forsyth is the monarchy . in terminal decline

Frederick Forsyth: no I don't think it is e:m it's going through an extremely troubled period that actually has happened oh twenty thirty forty fifty times . in the course of em the the monarchic history of this country which goes back nearly a thousand years e: it's been troubled e:m these past few years but I think that one has to get one thing quite certain if we are talking about . the royal family OK I don't know what we are talking about on this programme by the way but I'd like you to adjudicate are we talking about the royal family because if we are OK . there are thirty five members of them all descended from three dukes

Roger Cook: we're

talking about the monarchy

Frederick Forsyth: right or are we talking about the monarchy if we're talking about the monarchy and the monarch then let's do that let's talk about a magnificent Queen who has been forty four years a monarch and put no foot wrong . you sir are not British . you are not (unclear) Mr Haseler . (SH: this country) because every family every family with thirty five members in it in this country has got a couple . (SH: th-) that they really would prefer not to have

Stephen Haseler: this country is not no no

Roger Cook: the Queen the Queen can't reign for ever we have to look forward . and that's where that's where the problems lie surely

Frederick Forsyth: no no no let's be let's be realistic the Queen

SH: we – we're facing Frederick we're facing Charles the Third the real reason

RC: hold on hold on

FF: you're not facing (unclear) – you're not facing anything

SH: the real reason why this programme's on and why republicanism is growing is because we're facing the prospect of Charles the Third now I admit when the Queen

FF: when when

SH: I'll tell you I'll tell you when the Queen when the Queen when the Queen

FF: you haven't the faintest idea

SH: came to the throne she came with a united country when Charles the Third takes over he is going to divide this country and that is why people are now thinking about this issue and they want to choose their next head of state they don't want

FF: no

SH: him imposed on them

Extract 2

John Stapleton: OK let's find out some views behind those votes from our audience here and on the day when the Queen has been to Sandringham where better to start than th- with our friends from East Anglia you said yes you did think that these scandals have e damaged the country's reputation why do you take that view

Audience I: well I think like any scandal presidents of the United States these scandals have damaged and reflected badly on our country what we're doing here and what Mr S- people like Mr Starkie are doing is turning it our monarchy into some kind of royal soap opera trivializing it we've got the Duchess of York being referred to as Fergie and we're not really addressing the issues the royal family is not a soap opera and I think we ought to raise the level of debate and that's the real problem here we've lowered it to real guttersnipe gutter street level

John Stapleton: OK . gentleman over here gentleman over here in our Manchester camp you said e: no these scandals haven't damaged the country's reputation why do you take that view

Audience 2:   for the simple reason (unclear) for centuries the ordinary working class out there couldn't care less what royalty do they've got more to think about trying to make ends meet find a job than worry about what the royal family's doing

John Stapleton: OK let me let me introduce you all to someone who I suspect we could describe as Britain's most ardent royal family you'll know what I mean when you look around Margaret Tyler's rather remarkable house

FILM INSERT, *Margaret Tyler voice-over:*   well I have actually got the Queen and the Duke on my balcony waving to the neighbours of course and sometimes you can find me sitting on the throne I have to say I suppose you could call me Queen Margaret of North Wembley I just collect everything about the royal family and I really love them Charles and Diane are my very favourite couple and I absolutely loved their wedding day and I do think that one day they might just get back together again

JS: well . well Queen of North Wembley there was a mixture of cheers and jeers there do you really mean that

MT: I would like it to happen very much

JS: I think you might be the only person in the audience who would Alan Ahurst down here former Conservative MP is your place a shrine to the royal family

AA: no it isn't the Qu- the Queen is the head of the Church of England she's the richest woman in the world she's the head of a rotten class-ridden corrupt political and social establishment which is directly responsible for this nation's dreadful decline I have no problem with that lady's royal knick-knacks but I am just saddened that she should want to glorify people who are basically parasites and hypocrites

JS: isn't it a rather . if you don't mind me saying so isn't it a rather odd posture for a former Tory MP

AA: no I've seen the light this is the truth she is a symbol of everything that is rotten about this country and the sooner we get rid of her the better

JS: OK just . just a . cheers jeers and boos just a taste of our audience's views lots more later on

EXAMPLE 9

Extract from Rosabeth Moss Kanter *Evolve!* Harvard Business School Press 2001, pages 169–70.

Companies that are successful on the web operate differently from their laggard counterparts. On my global e-culture survey, those reporting that they are much better than their competitors in the use of the Internet tend to have flexible, empowering, collaborative organizations. The 'best' are more likely than the 'worst' to indicate, at statistically significant levels, that

- Departments collaborate (instead of sticking to themselves).
- Conflict is seen as creative (instead of disruptive).
- People can do anything not explicitly prohibited (instead of doing only what is explicitly permitted).
- Decisions are made by the people with the most knowledge (instead of the ones with the highest rank).

Pacesetters and laggards describe no differences in how hard they work (in response to a question about whether work was confined to traditional hours or spilled over into personal time), but they are very different in how collaboratively they work.

Working in e-culture mode requires organizations to be communities of purpose. Recall the elements of community sketched in chapter 1. A community makes people feel like members, not just employees – members with privileges but also responsibilities beyond the immediate job, extending to colleagues in other areas. Community means having things in common, a range of shared understandings transcending specific fields. Shared understandings permit relatively seamless processes, interchangeability among people, smooth formation of teams that know how to work together even if they have never previously met, and rapid transmission of information. In this chapter we will see how the principles of community apply inside organizations and workplaces, sometimes facilitated by technology but also independent of it. And I will examine the challenges that have to be overcome to create organizational communities.

The greater integration that is integral to e-culture is different from the centralization of earlier eras. Integration must be accompanied by flexibility and empowerment in order to achieve fast response, creativity, and innovation through improvization. Web success involves operating more like a community than a bureaucracy. It is a subtle but important distinction. Bureaucracy implies rigid job descriptions, command-and-control hierarchies, and hoarding of information, which is doled out top-down on a need-to-know basis. Community implies a willingness to abide by standardized procedures governing the whole organization, yes, but also voluntary collaboration that is much richer and less programmed. Communities can be mapped in formal ways, but they also have an emotional meaning, a feeling of connection. Communities have both a structure and a soul.

EXAMPLE 10

The following is an extract is from a meeting of mainly supervisors in an Australian subsidiary of a large multinational car manufacturer discussing meetings they have recently convened in accordance with 'quality' practices required by the multinational. Participants are: Sally – the facilitator, a workplace literacy teacher employed by the company under a government scheme; Ben – Warping Shed Supervisor; Grace – Weaving Shed Supervisor; Peter – Production Coordinator; James – a Warper; Mary – Mending Room Supervisor. The meeting was recorded for research purposes by Lesley Farrell, and I am grateful to her for permission to use this extract.

Ben: we thought you know maybe maybe I should be the facilitator for Grace's group or something where I'm away from the people a bit and um

Sally: yeah

Ben: just have a background in what's going on but just sort of keep them on the right track and let them they've got to really then rely on each other instead of relying on the supervisor to do the work

Grace: well I think kind of in the groups that are gonna come along that's what's gonna have to happen. I mean I know the the first ones that start off I think we have to go down this path to try to direct people onto the path and therefore we kind of will be in charge of the meeting but then we have to get people to start their own teams and us sort of just being a facilitator rather than

James: the team leader

[. . .] yeah

Grace: I mean it's hard to get started I think that's where people are having trouble and that's why they're kind of looking to you Ben and you know things like that

Peter: I'm not the only one I'm having trouble maintaining the thing

[. . .] yeah

Peter: I just can't maintain it at the moment you know a couple of days you know a couple of days crook there and you know just the amount of work that builds up it just goes to the back of the queue sort of thing it's shocking

James: so what you really want is the um you've got a a group you start a group and you want one of those people to sort of come out and facilitate the group

Peter: just to maintain the group you know like just to keep it just keep the work flowing

Ben: what I'm trying to get across

Peter: cause

Ben: is I'm too close to those people because I

[. . .] yeah

Ben: already go outside of the group and then I'm their supervisor outside on the on the floor where maybe if I was facilitating another group where I'm not I'm not above them you know I'm not their supervisor or whatever um I can go back to my job they can go back to theirs and they still um you know it's this their more their team than

Sally: yours

EXAMPLE 11

Extracts from the Introduction to *The Learning Age*, a consultation paper produced by the UK Department of Education and Employment, The Stationery Office,1998, pages 9–10. (The paper sets out a government strategy for 'lifelong learning', and invites responses from individuals and organizations.)

The Learning Age

I We are in a new age – the age of information and global competition. Familiar certainties and old ways of doing things are disappearing. The types of jobs we do have changed as have the industries in which we work and the skills they need.

At the same time, new opportunities are opening up as we see the potential of new technologies to change our lives for the better. We have no choice but to prepare for this new age in which the key to success will be the continuous education and development of the human mind and imagination.

2 Over a generation we have seen a fundamental change in the balance between skilled and unskilled jobs in the industrialized world. Since the 1960s, employment in manufacturing has fallen from one in three of the workforce to under one in five. This has been mirrored by a huge rise of jobs in services which now account for over two-thirds of all workers; more people today work in film and televsion than in car-manufacturing. There are three million self-employed and 6.5 million part-time workers, and women make up nearly half the workforce compared with less than a third 50 years ago.

3 The Industrial Revolution was built on capital investment in plant and machinery, skills and hard physical labour. British inventors pushed forward the frontiers of technology and then manufacturers turned their inventions into wealth. We built the world's first calculator, jet engine, computer and television. Our history shows what we are capable of, but we must now apply the same qualities of skill and invention to a fresh challenge.

4 The information and knowledge-based revolution of the twenty-first century will be built on a very different foundation – investment in the intellect and creativity of people. The microchip and fibre optic cable are today what electricity and the steam engine were to the nineteenth century. The United Kingdom is also pioneering this new age, combining ingenuity, enterprise, design and marketing skills. We are world leaders in information and communication technologies and bio-technology.

5 To continue to compete, we must equip ourselves to cope with the enormous economic and social change we face, to make sense of the rapid transformation of the world, and to encourage imagination and innovation. We will succeed by transforming inventions into new wealth, just as we did a hundred years ago. But unlike then, everyone must have the opportunity to innovate and to gain reward – not just in research laboratories, but on the production line, in design studios, in retail outlets, and in providing services.

6 The most productive investment will be linked to the best educated and best trained workforces, and the most effective way of getting and keeping a job will be to have the skills needed by employers.

7 Our greatest single challenge is to equip ourselves for this new age with new and better skills, with knowledge and with understanding.

EXAMPLE 12

(R. Sennett, *The Corrosion of Character*, W.W. Norton 1998, pages 122–9.)

Lippmann has often been on my mind in attending to a group of middle-aged programmers I've come to know, men who were recently downsized at an American IBM office. Before they lost their jobs, they – rather complacently – subscribed to the belief in the long-term unfolding of their professional careers. As high-tech programmers, they were meant to be the masters of the new science. After they were let go, they had to try out different interpretations of the events which wrecked their lives; they could summon no self-evident, instant narrative which would make sense of their failure. . . .

The River Winds Café, not far from my neighbours' old offices, is a cheery hamburger joint, formerly tenanted during daylight hours only by women out shopping or sullen adolescents wasting time after school. It is here that I've heard these white-shirted, dark-tied men, who nurse cups of coffee while sitting attentively as if at a business meeting, sort out their histories. One knot of five to seven men sticks together; they were mainframe programmers and systems analysts in the old IBM. The most talkative among them were Jason, a systems analyst who had been with the company nearly twenty years, and Paul, a younger programmer whom Jason had fired in the first downsizing wave. . . .

At the River Winds Café, the engineers' attempt to make sense of what had happened fell roughly into three stages. When I entered the discussions, the men felt themselves passive victims of the corporation. But by the time the discussions came to a conclusion, the dismissed employees had switched focus to their own behaviour.

When the pain of dismissal was still raw, discussion revolved around IBM's 'betrayals,' as if the company had tricked them. The programmers dredged up corporate events or behaviour in the past that seemed to portend the changes which subsequently came to pass. These acts of recall included such bits of evidence as a particular engineer's being denied use of the golf-course for a full eighteen rounds, or unexplained trips by a head programmer to unnamed destinations. At this stage the men wanted evidence of premeditation on the part of their superiors, evidence which would then justify their own sense of outrage. Being tricked or betrayed means a disaster is hardly one's own fault. . . .

But in the River Winds Café these first reactions didn't hold. The programmers found that as an explanation, *premeditated* betrayal wouldn't wash logically. . . .

So in a second stage of interpretation they focused on finding external forces to blame. At the River Winds Café, the 'global economy' now appeared the source of all their misfortunes, particularly in its use of foreign workers. IBM had begin 'outsourcing' some of its programming work, paying people in India a fraction of the wages paid to the Americans. The cheap wages paid to these foreign professionals were cited as a reason the company had made the Americans redundant. . . .

Yet again, though, this shared interpretation would not hold. The turning point in rejecting the perfidy of outsiders came when the employees first began to discuss their own careers, particularly their professional values. . . . As they focused on the profession, the programmers began to speak about what they personally could and should have done earlier in their own careers in order to prevent their present plight. In this third stage, the discourse of career had finally appeared . . . matters of personal will and choice, professional standards, narratives of work, all emerged – save that the theme of this career discourse was failure rather than mastery.

These discussions were indeed premised on the act that IBM had stayed committed to mainframe computers at a time when growth in the industry occurred in the personal-computer sector; most of the programmers were mainframe men. The IBM men began to blame themselves for having been too company-dependent . . .

EXAMPLE 13

I have taken the following example from a book written by two long-standing members of the Labour Party, Ken Coates (who is a Member of the European Parliament) and Michael Barratt Brown (they are now operating within the Independent Labour Network). (M. Barratt Brown and K. Coates, *The Blair Revelation*, Spokesman Books 1996, pages 172–4, 177–8.)

They are writing here about New Labour's view of what they call 'capitalist globalization' ('the new global economy' in New Labour terms):

Capital has always been global, moving internationally from bases in the developed industrial countries. What has changed is not that capital is more mobile . . . but that the national bases are less important as markets and production centres. In other words, the big transnational companies are not only bigger but more free-standing . . . the European Union, far from offering a lead and a challenge to the nation-states of Europe, reinforces their status as clients of the transnational companies. Indeed, this clientism applies not only to companies based in Europe. . . . While it is true that a national capitalism is no longer possible in a globalized economy, it is not true that national governments – and by extension the European Union – are totally lacking in powers to employ against the arbitrary actions of transnational capital. There is much that governments can do in bargaining – in making or withholding tax concessions for example. . . . But such bargaining has to have an international dimension or the transnational companies can simply continue to divide and conquer . . . New Labour appears to have abandoned what remained of Labour's internationalist traditions.

... Yet the ICFTU, the European TUC and the Geneva trade groups all offer potential allies for strengthening the response of British labour to international capital.

(pages 172–4)

...

Some NGOs ... have developed in their international relations what professor Diane Elson, the Manchester economist, has called 'the economy of trust'. Most commercial organizations spend much time and energy on controlling, monitoring, checking and counter-checking their business transactions. In a highly competitive market they simply do not trust their suppliers or customers not to take advantage of them. There is an alternative – to build up a relationship of trust ... one of the lessons learnt by some NGOs working the Third World, where for long there was a relationship of domination and exploitation [was that] nothing less than total openness and respect could build up a new relationship ... if all the words in New Labour's pronouncements about partnership and social markets, cooperation and not confrontation were to be taken seriously, the economy of trust would surely have a special appeal. Instead we find that 'the enterprise of the market and the rigour of competition' are always put before 'partnership and cooperation'.

(pages 177–8)

EXAMPLE 14

Materials and notes collected by the author from a staff appraisal training session, Lancaster University 2000 (bulleted material is the overheads used by the trainer, other material is my notes on the event).

The purposes of staff appraisal:

- To provide every employee with the opportunity to evaluate their work and to receive constructive and informed feedback on their performance
- To clarify a department's goals and objectives and to agree personal objectives related to those goals
- To support individual development to meet the needs of current and future roles, within available resources

'Key features' of staff appraisal:

- All staff should receive feedback and have the opportunity to discuss their progress and development as part of an annual cycle of events

- All staff should negotiate clear and measurable objectives for the review period
- All staff should receive written confirmation of feedback and of the agreed objectives for the following review period
- Appraisal should be managed by someone trained to lead the process
- All staff should be properly prepared for appraisal via training or briefing
- Appraisal should become a logical and effective part of the University's quality assurance/enhancement process

The trainer added that 'the process should be mostly owned by the appraisee'.

The main stages in appraisal are:

- Preparation
- Discussion
- Recording
- Dissemination

'Two principles' govern selection of appraisers:

- the choice of appraiser shall be made by the appraisee
- appraisers shall be experienced members of staff with knowledge of the work of the appraisee

Preparation involves the appraisee sending the appraiser an up-to-date CV (academic staff) or job description (assistant staff), plus other relevant material such as feedback from colleagues or students, and a list of topics for discussion (a 'reflective document, showing how you see things or how you feel', the trainer added). The content of this documentation 'should be up to the appraisee', the trainer commented. A meeting is then arranged, and 'both parties agree the agenda before starting discussion' – the trainer commented that it 'shouldn't include something the appraisee isn't happy about'. The 'general focus' of appraisal discussion should be 'teaching, research and publication, administration, other professional activities' (academic staff), and 'headings in job description' (assistant staff).

A three-stage appraisal discussion:

- Review appraisee's current situation and the issues arising from it
- Develop 'preferred-scenario' possibilities and how these might be translated into viable goals (the trainer clarified these preferences as the appraisee's)
- Determine how to get to the 'preferred scenario' – develop a plan of action

Skills used by the appraiser include:

- Listening (specified as 'active')
- Questioning
- Summarizing
- Reflecting back (specified as echoing back the appraisee's own words to him/her)
- Challenging (justified because 'they might be underselling themselves')

Appraisers should give 'constructive feedback' (glossed by the trainer as 'helping individuals get a clearer view of themselves and how they are seen by others').

- Start with the positive
- Be specific
- Offer alternatives
- Refer to behaviour that can be changed
- Own the feedback
- Leave the appraisee with a choice

The appraisal report is 'a summary written up by the appraiser and agreed with the appraisee' covering:

- The areas discussed
- Conclusions arrived at as a result of discussion
- Agreements made
- Goals identified
- Any development required by the appraisee

The report 'is confidential to the appraisee, the appraiser and the Head of Department'.

EXAMPLE 15

Extracts from a meeting organized somewhere in England to discuss farm trials of genetically-modified (GM) foods taking place in the area (this is based upon a real case which has been anonymized, which was an agreed condition of recording it). These trials are designed to test whether GM crops have more adverse environmental effects than non-genetically-modified equivalents. There were several speakers who were given the floor in the first part of the meeting, and in the second part of the meeting members of the audience were invited to put questions to the speakers.

Extract 1

From the government official's opening speech, in which he is talking about 'the consultation process' and the European Union Directive which controls it:

> One of the issues which occurs very frequently at public meetings such as this is the issue of consultation and I'd like to spend just a little bit of time explaining the constraint under which the consultation process currently has to operate. We have a Directive at the moment which dates back to 1990 and under that Directive there is very limited scope for consultation about individual sites where GM crops might be grown. Their legislation requires that the applications submitted to the Government have to be judged on their merits and once a consent has been granted it can only be revoked on valid scientific grounds. There is always scope for new scientific evidence to be considered.
>
> The process of informing people about prospective FSE sites is that there is information advertised in local newspapers. We publish a news release every time there is to be a new sowing round and we identify in our news release the particular sites to six-figure grid references. We also write to all parish councils like this one to say where the sites are and to provide as much relevant background information as we can. And we always say that we are willing to come and address meetings like this to explain what the programme is all about.

Extract 2

From the opening by the representative of a GM seed company:

> Why would the farmer be interested in this technology? Okay, well I've already talked about yield and I'll come back to that yet again in a second. But what's great about this is you can use a particular sort of herbicide called Liberty. Now normally with oilseed rape what you do as a farmer is you go in and you put a thin layer of herbicide onto the soil, okay. This is what they call a pre-emergence herbicide. And what happens is that as the weeds come through they come into contact with the herbicide and they die. Okay? . . .
>
> Liberty is different, no point spraying it on the soil, it's just about inactivated on contact. What that means is you have to spray it onto the weeds. There is no point spraying it onto the soil and letting the weeds come through it. The weeds just carry on growing. OK? If that's the case what we're looking at now is rather than a 'just in case' it's an 'if we actually need it'. So the farmer will come along, look and see those weeds in that crop and say 'ok, do I need to spray?' and 'if so how much do I need to spray?' So there are weeds in that field and he'll make that decision. So we're moving away from the idea of 'oh well I'll spray it just in case anything comes through' to 'if we need to we'll use it'. And that's a very exciting thing for a farmer.

Extract 3

From a contribution from the floor which the speaker prefaces by saying he has a 'three-part question':

> First of all much use is being of the word consultation. To the gentleman from DEFRA I'd like to say we had a referendum in our village last year which said that we didn't want GM trials in our village. We had another survey carried out this year, the majority of people said that we didn't want it in our village. It's falling on deaf ears, stony ground. Our views are not taken into account although you from Government say yes, it's a dialogue with the deaf I feel. Basically, no consultation, no notice taken of us.

Extract 4

An exchange initiated by a question from a male member of the audience, MI:

> MI: There are two or three problems or concerns really. One really is the lack of time the parish has been given with respect of when we know. We don't know when the site is to be. We only know when the site is to be drilled. The County Council has put a motion through that we would ask DEFRA to let us know when the site is agreed, and then we could have a meeting like this if you like before it all gets out of hand. The other thing is there's a massive increase in nose problems through spores that are in the air now. Years ago we used to have hay fever problems at hay time, now we seem to get them – Is there any difference between the spores of genetically modified crops and the conventional crop. I think those are two major concerns that locally are causing problems. I don't know whether there's an answer to both but there certainly is an answer in time delay and there may be an answer to the other.
>
> M2: Could I just make a point as well? I mean the first part of that, this year the first we knew about these crops was in the newspaper.
>
> MI: Exactly.
>
> M2: And when we did draw some information off the Internet, it was the day they'd stated for sowing. So that's when the Parish Council knew –
>
> MI: The County Council has asked the Government to – if we can know – when the site is decided upon then we need the information. And I think that will give us a reasonable length of time to evaluate whether it is or isn't going to be a problem.
>
> *Government Official:* Can I [unclear word]. Well, I think that I said that our practice is to write to all Parish Councils when a trial site is proposed and we did that –
>
> MI: No, that isn't what happened –

Government Official: Could I just say what we do? [Extended account of the notification procedure omitted.] So we do our very best to make sure that the people know.

M1: At what point do you know which site you are going to use?

References

Allan, K. (2001) *Natural Language Semantics*, Oxford: Blackwell.

Allan, S. (1999) *News Culture*, Buckingham: Open University Press.

Althusser, L. and Balibar, E. (1970) *Reading Capital,* London: New Left Books.

Archer, M. (1995) *Realist Social Theory: the Morphogenetic Approach*, Cambridge: Cambridge University Press.

Archer, M. (2000) *Being Human: the Problem of Agency*, Cambridge: Cambridge University Press.

Arendt, H. (1958) *The Human Condition*, Chicago: University of Chicago Press.

Austin, J.L. (1962) *How to Do Things with Words*, Oxford: Oxford University Press.

Bakhtin, M. (1981) *The Dialogical Imagination*, Austin: University of Texas Press.

Bakhtin, M. (1986a) 'The problem of speech genres', in *Speech Genres and Other Late Essays*, Austin: University of Texas Press, 60–102.

Bakhtin, M. (1986b) 'The problem of the text in Linguistics, Philology and the Human Sciences: an experiment in philosophical analysis', in *Speech Genres and Other Late Essays*, Austin: University of Texas Press, 103–131.

Bal, M. (1997) *Narratology: Introduction to the Theory of Narrative*, Toronto: University of Toronto Press.

Bauman, Z. (1998) *Globalization*, Cambridge: Polity Press.

Bazerman, C (1988) *Shaping Written Knowledge: the Genre and Activity of the Experimental Article in Science*, Madison, Wis.: University of Wisconsin Press.

Benhabib, S. (1996) *Democracy and Difference*, Princeton: Princeton University Press.

Berger, P. and Luckmann, T. (1966) *The Social Construction of Reality*, Harmondsworth: Penguin.

Bernstein, B. (1990) *The Structuring of Pedagogic Discourse*, London: Routledge.

Bhaskar, R. (1979) *A Realist Theory of Science*, 2nd edition, Brighton: Harvester.

Bhaskar, R. (1986) *Scientific Realism and Human Emancipation*, London: Verso.

Bhaskar, R. (1989) *Reclaiming Reality*, London: Verso.

Bjerke, F. (2000) *Discursive Governance Structures*, Working Paper, Institute of Social Sciences and Business Economics, Roskilde University, Denmark.

Blakemore, D. (1992) *Understanding Utterances: an Introduction to Pragmatics*, Oxford: Blackwell.

Boltanski, L. and Chiapello, E. (1999) *Le Nouvel Esprit du Capitalisme*, Paris: Gallimard.

Bourdieu, P. (1977) *Outline of a Theory of Practice*, Cambridge: Cambridge University Press.

Bourdieu, P. (1984) *Distinction: a Social Critique of the Judgement of Taste*, London: Routledge.

Bourdieu, P. (1991) *Language and Symbolic Power*, Cambridge: Polity Press.

Bourdieu, P. (1998) *On Television*, New York: New Press.

Bourdieu, P. and Wacquant, L. (1992) *An Invitation to Reflexive Sociology*, Cambridge: Polity Press.

Bourdieu, B. and Wacquant, L. (2001) 'New-Liberal Speak: notes on the new planetary vulgate', *Radical Philosophy* **105**: 2–5.

Boyer, R. and Hollingsworth, J.R. (eds) (1997) *Contemporary Capitalism: the Embeddedness of Capitalist Institutions*, Cambridge: Cambridge University Press.

Brenner, R. (1998) 'The economics of global turbulence', *New Left Review* **229** (special edition).

Brown, R. and Gilman, A. (1960) 'The pronouns of power and solidarity', in P. Giglioli (ed.) *Language and Social Context*, Harmondsworth: Penguin.

Butler, J. (1998) 'Merely cultural', *New Left Review* **227**, 33–44.

Butler, J., Laclau, E. and Žižek, S. (2000) *Contingency, Hegemony, Universality*, London: Verso.

Calhoun, C. (1992) *Habermas and the Public Sphere*, Cambridge, Mass.: MIT Press.

Callinicos, A. (1995) *Theories and Narratives: Reflections on the Philosophy of History*, Durham, N.C.: Duke University Press.

Cameron, D. (2000) *Good to Talk? Living and Working in a Communication Culture*, London: Sage.

Cameron, D. (2001) *Working with Spoken Text*, London: Sage.

Carter, R., Goddard, A., Reah, D., Sanger, K. and Bowring, M. *Working with Texts*, London: Routledge.

Castells, M. (1996–8) *The Information Age*, 3 volumes, Cambridge: Blackwell.

Chiapello, E. and Fairclough, N. (2002) 'Understanding the new management ideology: a transdisciplinary contribution from Critical Discourse Analysis and the New Sociology of Capitalism', *Discourse and Society* **13**(2): 185–208.

Chouliaraki, L. (1995) 'Regulation in "progressivist" pedagogic discourse: individualized teacher–pupil talk', *Discourse and Society* **9**(1): 5–32.

Chouliaraki, L. (1999) 'Media discourse and national identity: death and myth in a news broadcast', in R. Wodak and C. Ludwig (eds) *Challenges in a Changing World: Issues in Critical Discourse Analysis*, Vienna: Passagen Verlag.

Chouliaraki, L. and Fairclough, N. (1999) *Discourse in Late Modernity*, Edinburgh: Edinburgh University Press.

Connerton, P. (1989) *How Societies Remember*, Cambridge: Cambridge University Press.

Crouch, C. and Streek, W. (1997) *Political Economy of Modern Capitalism*, London: Sage.

Dant, T. (1991) *Knowledge, Ideology and Discourse: a Sociological Perspective*, London: Routledge.

De Beaugrande, R. (1997) *New Foundations for a Science of Text and Discourse*, Norwood, N.J.: Ablex.

De Beaugrande, R. and Dressler, W. (1981) *Introduction to Text Linguistics*, London: Longman.

Donadio, P. (2002) 'Modal variations and ideological change', LAUD Symposium, Landau.

Dubiel, H. (1985) *Theory and Politics: Studies in the Development of Critical Theory*, Cambridge, Mass.: MIT Press.

Durkheim, E. and Mauss, M. (1963/1903) *Primitive Classification*, Chicago: University of Chicago Press.

Eagleton, T. (1991) *Ideology*, London: Verso.

Eggins, S. (1994) *An Introduction to Systemic Functional Linguistics*, London: Pinter.

Eggins, S. and Martin, J. (1997) 'Genres and registers of discourse', in T. van Dijk (ed.) *Discourse as Structure and Process*, London: Sage.

Fairclough, N. (1988) 'Discourse representation in media discourse', *Sociolinguistics* **17**: 125–39.

Fairclough, N. (1992) *Discourse and Social Change*, Cambridge: Polity Press.

Fairclough, N. (1993) 'Critical discourse analysis and the marketisation of public discourse: the universities', *Discourse and Society* **4**: 133–68.

Fairclough, N. (1995a) *Critical Discourse Analysis*, London: Longman.

Fairclough, N. (1995b) *Media Discourse*, London: Edward Arnold.

Fairclough, N. (1999) 'Democracy and the public sphere in critical research on discourse', in R. Wodak and C. Ludwig (eds) *Challenges in a Changing World: Issues in Critical Discourse Analysis*, Vienna: Passagen Verlag.

Fairclough, N. (2000a) 'Discourse, social theory and social research: the case of welfare reform', *Journal of Sociolinguistics* **4**: 163–95.

Fairclough, N. (2000b) *New Labour, New Language?*, London: Routledge.

Fairclough, N. (2000c) 'Represenciones del cambio en discurso neoliberal', *Cuadernos de Relaciones Laborales* **16**: 13–36.

Fairclough, N. (2001a) 'The dialectics of discourse', *Textus* **14**: 231–42.

Fairclough, N. (2001b) *Language and Power*, 2nd edition, London: Longman.

Fairclough, N. (2001c) 'The discourse of New Labour: critical discourse analysis', in M. Wetherell *et al.* (eds) *Discourse as Data*, London: Sage and the Open University.

Fairclough, N. (2001d) 'Critical discourse analysis as a method in social scientific research', in R. Wodak and M. Meyer (eds) *Methods of Critical Discourse Analysis*, London: Sage.

Fairclough, N. and Wodak, R. (1997) 'Critical discourse analysis', in T. van Dijk (ed.) *Discourse as Social Interaction*, London: Sage.

Fairclough, N. Jessop, R. and Sayer, A. (2002) 'Critical realism and Semiosis', *Journal of Critical Realism* **5**(1): 2–10.

Fairclough, N., Pardoe, S. and Szerszynski, B. (forthcoming) 'Critical discourse analysis and citizenship', in A. Bora and H. Hausendorf (eds) *Constructing Citizenship*, Amsterdam: John Benjamins.

Featherstone, M. (1991) *Consumer Culture and Postmodernism*, London: Sage.

Firth, J.R. (1957) *Papers in Linguistics*, London: Oxford University Press.

Fiske, J. (1987) *Television Culture*, London: Routledge.

Forgacs, D. (1988) *A Gramsci Reader*, London: Lawrence & Wishart.

Foucault, M. (1972) *The Archaeology of Knowledge*, New York: Pantheon.

Foucault, M. (1984) 'The order of discourse', in M. Shapiro (ed) *The Language of Politics*, Oxford: Blackwell.

Foucault, M. (1994) 'What is enlightenment?', in P. Rabinow (ed.) *Michel Foucault: Essential Works vol 1 (Ethics)*, Harmondsworth: Penguin, pages 303–19.

Fowler R., Hodge, B., Kress, G. and Trew, T. (1979) *Language and Control*, London: Routledge.

Fraser, N. (1998) 'Heterosexism, misrecognition and capitalism: a reply to Judith Butler', *New Left Review* **228**: 140–9.

Gardiner, M. (1992) *The Dialogics of Critique: M.M. Bakhtin and the Theory of Ideology*, London: Routledge.

Gee, J. (1999) *An Introduction to Discourse Analysis*, London: Routledge.

Giddens, A. (1984) *The Constitution of Society*, Cambridge: Polity Press.

Giddens, A. (1991) *Modernity and Self Identity*, Cambridge: Polity Press.

Giddens, A. (1993) *New Rules of Sociological Method*, 2nd edition, Cambridge: Polity Press.

Gieve, S. (2000) *Discourse Learning and 'Being Critical'* PhD thesis, Lancaster University.

Goatly, A. (1997) *The Language of Metaphors*, London: Routledge.

Goffman, E. (1981) *Forms of Talk*, Oxford: Blackwell.

Graham, P. (2001a) 'Space: irrealis objects in technology policy and their role in a new political economy', *Discourse and Society* **12**(6): 761–88.

Graham, P. (2001b) 'Contradictions and institutional convergences: genre as method', *Journal of Future Studies* **5**(4): 1–30.

Graham, P. (2002) 'Predication and propogation: a method for analyzing evaluative meanings in technology policy', *Text* **33**: 227–68.

Gramsci, A. (1971) *Selections from the Prison Notrebooks*, London: Lawrence & Wishart.

Grice, H.P. (1975) 'Logic and conversation', in P. Cole and J. Morgan (eds) *Syntax and Semantics 3: Speech Acts*, New York: Academic Press.

Grice, H. (1981) 'Presupposition and conversational implicature', in P. Cole (ed.) *Radical Pragmatics*, New York: Academic Press.

Habermas, J. (1976) *Legitimation Crisis*, London: Heinemann.

Habermas, J. (1984) *Theory of Communicative Action*, Vol. 1, London: Heinemann.

Habermas, J. (1989) *The Structural Transformational of the Public Sphere*, Cambridge: Polity Press.

Habermas, J. (1996) *Between Facts and Norms*, Cambridge: Polity Press.

Halliday, M. (1978) 'The sociosemantic nature of discourse', in *Language as Social Semiotic*, London: Edward Arnold.

Halliday, M. (1994) *An Introduction to Functional Grammar*, 2nd edition, London: Edward Arnold.

Halliday, M. and Hasan, T. (1976) *Cohesion in English*, London: Longman.

Halliday, M. and Hasan, R. (1989) *Language, Context and Text: Aspects of Language in a Social-Semiotic Perspective*, Oxford: Oxford University Press.

Halliday, M. and Martin, J. (1993) *Writing Science: Literacy and Discursive Power*, London: Falmer.

Harré, R. (1983) *Personal Being*, Oxford: Blackwell.

Harvey, D. (1990) *The Condition of Postmodernity*, Oxford: Blackwell.

Harvey, D. (1996a) *Justice, Nature and the Geography of Difference*, Oxford: Blackwell.

Harvey, D. (1996b) 'Globalization in question', *Rethinking Marxism* **8**(4): 1–17.

Hasan, R. (1996) *Ways of Saying: Ways of Meaning*, London: Cassell.

Hawisher, G. and Selfe, C. (eds) (2000) *Global Literacies and the World-Wide Web*, London: Routledge.

Held, D., McGrew, A., Goldblatt, D. and Perraton, J. (1999) *Global Transformations: Politics, Economics and Culture*, Cambridge: Polity Press.

Hodge, B. and Kress, G. (1988) *Social Semiotics*, Cambridge: Polity Press.

Hodge, B. and Kress, G. (1993) *Language as Ideology*, 2nd edition, London: Routledge.

Hoey, M. (1983) *On the Surface of Discourse*, London: George, Allen & Unwin.

Hoey, M. (2001) *Textual Interaction*, London: Routledge.

Holquist, M. (1981) *Dialogism: Bakhtin and his Works*, London: Routledge.

Hunston, S. and Thompson, G. (2000) *Evaluation in Text*, Oxford: Oxford University Press.

Iedema, R. (1999) 'Formalising organisational meaning', *Discourse and Society* 10(1): 49–65.

Ivanič, R. (1998) *Writing and Identity*, Amsterdam: John Benjamins.

Jameson, F. (1991) *Postmodernism, Or, The Cultural Logic of Late Capitalism*, London: Verso.

Jessop, B. (1998) 'The rise of governance and the risks of failure: the case of economic development', *International Social Science Journal* **155**: 29–45.

Jessop B. (2000) 'The crisis of the national spatio-temporal fix and the ecological dominance of globalising capitalism', *International Journal of Urban and Regional Research* **24**(2): 323–60.

Jessop B. (forthcoming a) 'The social embeddedness of the economy and its implications for global governance', in F. Adaman and P. Devine (eds) *The Socially Embedded Economy*, Montreal: Black Rose Books.

Jessop, B. (forthcoming b) 'On the spatio-temporal logics in capital's globalization and their manifold implications for state power'.

Kress, G. (1985) *Linguistic Processes in Sociocultural Practice*, Geelong, Victoria: Deakin University Press.

Kress, G. and Van Leeuwen, T. (2001) *Multimodal Discourse*, London: Arnold.

Kristeva, J. (1986a) 'Word, dialogue and novel', in T. Moi (ed.) *The Kristeva Reader*, Oxford: Blackwell, pages 34–61.

Kristeva, J. (1986b) 'The system and the speaking subject', in T. Moi (ed.) *The Kristeva Reader*, Oxford: Blackwell, pages 24–33.

Laclau, E. (1996) *Emancipation(s)*, London: Verso.

Laclau, E. and Mouffe, C. (1985) *Hegemony and Socialist Strategy*, London: Verso.

Lakoff, G. and Johnson, M. (1980) *Metaphors We Live By*, Chicago: University of Chicago Press.

Larrain, J. (1979) *The Concept of Ideology*, London: Hutchinson.

Leech, G.N. and Short , M. (1981) *Style in Fiction*, London: Longman.

Lehtonen, M. (2000) *The Cultural Analysis of Texts*, London: Sage.

Lemke, J. (1988) 'Text structure and text semantics', in R. Veltman and E. Steiner (eds) *Pragmatics, Discourse and Text: Systemic Approaches*, London: Pinter.

Lemke, J. (1995) *Textual Politics*, London: Taylor & Francis.

Lemke, J. (1998) 'Resources for attitudinal meaning: evaluative orientations in text semantics', *Functions of Language* **5**(1): 33–56.

Levins, R. and Lewontin, R. (1985) *The Dialectical Biologist*, Cambridge, Mass.: MIT Press.

Levinson, S. (1983) *Pragmatics*, Cambridge: Cambridge University Press.

Linstead, S. and Höpfl, H. (2000) *The Aesthetics of Organization*, London: Sage.

Livingstone, S. and Lunt, P. (1994) *Talk on Television: Audience Participation and Public Debate*, London: Routledge.

Luhmann, N. (2000) *The Reality of the Mass Media*, Cambridge: Polity Press.

Lury, C. (1996) *Consumer Culture*, Cambridge: Polity Press.

Lyons, J. (1977) *Semantics*, 2 vols, Cambridge: Cambridge University Press.

Macdonell, D. (1986) *Theories of Discourse: an Introduction*, Oxford: Basil Blackwell.

McEnery, T. and Wilson, A. (2001) *Corpus Linguistics*, Edinburgh, Edinburgh University Press.

McIntyre, A. (1984) *After Virtue*, Notre Dame, Indiana: University of Notre Dame Press.

McLuhan, M. (1964) *Understanding Media*, New York: McGraw Hill.

Martin, J. (1992) *English Text*, Amsterdam: John Benjamins.

Martin, J. (2000) 'Beyond exchange: APPRAISAL system in English', in S. Hunston and G. Thompson (eds) *Evaluation in Text*, Oxford: Oxford University Press, pages 142–75.

Merleau-Ponty, M. (1964) *Signs*, Evanston, Ill.: Northwestern University Press.

Mey, J. (1993) *Pragmatics: an Introduction*, Oxford: Blackwell.

Mills, S. (1997) *Discourse*, London: Routledge.

Misztal, B. (2000) *Informality: Social Theory and Contemporary Practice*, London: Routledge.

Mitchell, T.F. (1957) 'The language of buying and selling in Cyrenaica: a situational statement', *Hesperis* **26**: 31–71.

Morris, P. (1986) *The Baby Book*, London: Newbourne.

Morrow, R with D. Brown (1994) *Critical Theory and Methodology*, London: Sage.

Muntigl, P., Weiss, G. and Wodak, R. (2000) *European Union Discourses on Un/employment*, Amsterdam: John Benjamins.

Myers, G. (1999) *Ad Worlds: Brands, Media, Audiences*, London: Arnold.

Ochs, E. (1997) 'Narrative', in T. van Dijk (ed.) *Discourse as Social Structure and Process*, London: Sage.

Ollman, B. (1993) *Dialectical Investigations*, New York: Routledge.

Outhwaite, W. (ed.) (1996) *The Habermas Reader*, Cambridge: Polity Press.

Palmer, F. (1986) *Mood and Modality*, Cambridge: Cambridge University Press.

Pujolar, J. (1997) *De Que Vas Tio? I Llengua en la Cultura Juvenil*, Barcelona: Editorial Empuries.

Quirk, R., Greenbaum, S., Leech, G.N. and Svartvik, J. (1972) *A Grammar of Contemporary English*, London: Longman.

Quirk, R., Greenbaum, S., Leech, G.N. and Svartvik, J. (1995) *A Comprehensive Grammar of the English Language*, London: Longman.

Rogers, R. (ed.) (forthcoming) *New Directions in Critical Discourse Analysis: the Role of Language Learning in Social Transformation*, New York: Erlbaum.

Sayer, A. (2000) *Realism and Social Science*, London: Sage.

Sbis, M. (1995) 'Speech act theory', in J. Verschueren, J-O. Östman, J. Blommaert and C. Bulcaen (eds) *Handbook of Pragmatics*, Amsterdam: John Benjamins, pages 28–36.

Scannell, P. (1991) 'Introduction: the relevance of talk', in P. Scannell (ed.) *Broadcast Talk*, London: Sage.

Schegloff, E. (1997) 'Whose text? Whose context?', *Discourse & Society* **8**(2): 165–87.

Searle, J. (1969) *Speech Acts: an Essay in the Philosophy of Language*, Cambridge: Cambridge University Press.

Seligman, A. (1997) *The Problem of Trust*, Princeton: Princeton University Press.

Sennett, R. (1974) *The Fall of Public Man*, New York: W.W. Norton & Co.

Sennett. R. (1998) *The Corrosion of Character: Personal Consequences of Work in the New Capitalism*, New York: W.W. Norton & Co.

Silverstone, R. (1999) *Why Study the Media?* London: Sage.

Sinclair, J. McH. (1991) *Corpus, Concordance, Collocation*, Oxford: Oxford University Press.

Stillar, G. (1998) *Analyzing Everyday Texts*, London: Sage.

Stubbs, M. (1996) *Text and Corpus Analysis*, Oxford: Blackwell.

Swales, J. (1990) *Genre Analysis*, Cambridge: Cambridge University Press.

Talbot, M. (1996) *Gender and Language*, Cambridge: Polity Press.

Taylor, C. (1985) *Human Agency and Language*, Cambridge: Cambridge University Press.

Thibault, P. (1991) *Social Semiotics as Praxis*, Minneapolis: University of Minessota Press.

Thompson, J. (1984) *Studies in the Theory of Ideology*, Cambridge: Polity Press.

Thompson, J. (1995) *The Media and Modernity*, Cambridge: Polity Press.

Titscher, S., Meyer, M., Wodak, R. and Vetter, E. (2000) *Methods of Text and Discourse Analysis*, London: Sage.

Toolan, M. (1998) *Narrative*, London: Routledge.

Toulmin, S. (1958) *The Uses of Argument*, Cambridge: Cambridge University Press.

Touraine, A. (1997) *What is Democracy?*, Boulder, Col.: Westview Press.

Van Dijk, T. (ed.) (1997) *Discourse Studies: a Multidisciplinary Introduction* (Vol. 1: *Discourse as Structure and Process*; Vol. 2: *Discourse as Social Interaction*), London: Sage.

Van Dijk, T. (1998) *Ideology: a Multidisciplinary Approach*, London: Sage.

Van Eemeren, F., Grootendorst, R., Jackson, S. and Jacons, S. (1997) 'Argumentation', in T. van Dijk (ed.) *Discourse as Structure and Process*, London: Sage.

Van Leeuwen, T. (undated) 'The grammar of legitimation', Working Paper, London College of Printing.

Van Leeuwen, T. (1993) 'Genre and field in critical discourse analysis', *Discourse & Society* 4(2): 193–223.

Van Leeuwen, T. (1995) 'Representing social action', *Discourse and Society* 6(1): 81–106.

Van Leeuwen, T. (1996) 'The representation of social actors', in C. R. Caldas-Coulthard and M. Coulthard (eds) *Texts and Practices*, London: Routledge.

Van Leeuwen, T. and Wodak, R. (1999) 'Legitimizing immigration control: a discourse-historical analysis', *Discourse Studies* 1(1): 83–118.

Verschueren, J. (1999) *Understanding Pragmatics*, London: Arnold.

Volosinov, V.I. (1973) *Marxism and the Philosophy of Language*, Cambridge, Mass.: Harvard University Press.

Weber, M. (1964) *The Theory of Social and Economic Organization*, New York: The Free Press.

Wernick, A. (1991) *Promotional Culture*, London: Sage.

Wertsch, J. (1991) *Voices of the Mind*, Hemel Hempstead: Harvester Wheatsheaf.

Wetherell, M. (1998) 'Positioning and interpretative repertoires: CA and post-structuralism in dialogue', *Discourse and Society* 9(3): 387–412.

Wetherell, M., Taylor, S. and Yates, S.J. (2001a) *Discourse as Data*, London: Sage and the Open University.

Wetherell, M., Taylor, S. and Yates, S.J. (2001b) *Discourse Theory and Practice*, London: Sage and the Open University.

White, P. (2001) An introductory tour through appraisal theory, Appraisal Website (www.grammatics.com/appraisal)

White, P. (forthcoming) 'Attitude and arguability: appraisal and the linguistics of solidarity', *Text*.

Williams, R. (1977) *Marxism and Literature*, Oxford: Oxford University Press.

Winter, E. (1982) *Towards a Contextual Grammar of English*, London: George Allen & Unwin.

Wodak, R. (2000) 'From conflict to consensus? The co-construction of a policy paper', in P. Muntigl, G. Weiss and R. Wodak (eds) *European Union Discourses on Un/Employment*, Amsterdam: John Benjamins.

Wynne, B. (2001) 'Creating public alienation: expert cultures of risk and ethics on GMOs', *Science as Culture* **10**(4): 445–81.

Index